Joshua Reynolds

Sir Joshua Reynold's Discourses

Joshua Reynolds

Sir Joshua Reynold's Discourses

ISBN/EAN: 9783337733483

Printed in Europe, USA, Canada, Australia, Japan

Cover: Foto ©ninafisch / pixelio.de

More available books at **www.hansebooks.com**

Sir Joshua Reynolds's

DISCOURSES

EDITED WITH NOTES AND AN HISTORICAL AND
BIOGRAPHICAL INTRODUCTION

BY

EDWARD GILPIN JOHNSON

With Illustrations

CHICAGO
A. C. McCLURG AND COMPANY
1891

TABLE OF CONTENTS.

INTRODUCTION. 13

DISCOURSE I.

THE ADVANTAGES PROCEEDING FROM THE INSTITUTION OF A ROYAL ACADEMY. — HINTS OFFERED TO THE CONSIDERATION OF THE PROFESSORS AND VISITORS. — THAT AN IMPLICIT OBEDIENCE TO THE RULES OF ART BE EXACTED FROM THE YOUNG STUDENTS — THAT A PREMATURE DISPOSITION TO A MASTERLY DEXTERITY BE REPRESSED. — THAT DILIGENCE BE CONSTANTLY RECOMMENDED, AND (THAT IT MAY BE EFFECTUAL) DIRECTED TO ITS PROPER OBJECT. 53

DISCOURSE II.

THE COURSE AND ORDER OF STUDY. — THE DIFFERENT STAGES OF ART. — MUCH COPYING DISCOUNTENANCED. — THE ARTIST AT ALL TIMES AND IN ALL PLACES SHOULD BE EMPLOYED IN LAYING UP MATERIALS FOR THE EXERCISE OF HIS ART. 63

DISCOURSE III.

THE GREAT LEADING PRINCIPLES OF THE GRAND STYLE. — OF BEAUTY. — THE GENUINE HABITS OF NATURE TO BE DISTINGUISHED FROM THOSE OF FASHION. 81

DISCOURSE IV.

GENERAL IDEAS, THE PRESIDING PRINCIPLE WHICH REGULATES EVERY PART OF ART; INVENTION, EXPRESSION, COLORING, AND DRAPERY. — TWO DISTINCT STYLES OF HISTORY-PAINTING: THE GRAND, AND THE ORNAMENTAL. — THE SCHOOLS IN WHICH EACH IS TO BE FOUND. — THE COMPOSITE STYLE. — THE STYLE FORMED ON LOCAL CUSTOMS AND HABITS, OR A PARTIAL VIEW OF NATURE. 99

DISCOURSE V.

CIRCUMSPECTION REQUIRED IN ENDEAVORING TO UNITE CONTRARY EXCELLENCES. — THE EXPRESSION OF A MIXED PASSION NOT TO BE ATTEMPTED. — EXAMPLES OF THOSE WHO EXCELLED IN THE GREAT STYLE. — RAPHAEL, MICHAEL ANGELO, THOSE TWO EXTRAORDINARY MEN COMPARED WITH EACH OTHER. — THE CHARACTERISTICAL STYLE. — SALVATOR ROSA MENTIONED AS AN EXAMPLE OF THAT STYLE; AND OPPOSED TO CARLO MARATTI. — SKETCH OF THE CHARACTERS OF POUSSIN AND RUBENS. — THESE TWO PAINTERS ENTIRELY DISSIMILAR, BUT CONSISTENT WITH THEMSELVES. — THIS CONSISTENCY REQUIRED IN ALL PARTS OF THE ART. . . 123

DISCOURSE VI.

IMITATION. — GENIUS BEGINS WHERE RULES END. — INVENTION: ACQUIRED BY BEING CONVERSANT WITH THE INVENTIONS OF OTHERS. — THE TRUE METHOD OF IMITATING. — BORROWING, HOW FAR ALLOWABLE. — SOMETHING TO BE GATHERED FROM EVERY SCHOOL. 143

DISCOURSE VII.

THE REALITY OF A STANDARD OF TASTE, AS WELL AS OF CORPORAL BEAUTY. — BESIDES THIS IMMEDIATE TRUTH, THERE ARE SECONDARY TRUTHS, WHICH ARE VARIABLE; BOTH REQUIRING THE ATTENTION OF THE ARTIST, IN PROPORTION TO THEIR STABILITY OR THEIR INFLUENCE. 171

DISCOURSE VIII.

THE PRINCIPLES OF ART, WHETHER POETRY OR PAINTING, HAVE THEIR FOUNDATION IN THE MIND; SUCH AS NOVELTY, VARIETY, AND CONTRAST; THESE IN THEIR EXCESS BECOME DEFECTS. — SIMPLICITY, ITS EXCESS DISAGREEABLE. — RULES NOT TO BE ALWAYS OBSERVED IN THEIR LITERAL SENSE: SUFFICIENT TO PRESERVE THE SPIRIT OF THE LAW. — OBSERVATIONS ON THE PRIZE PICTURES. 207

DISCOURSE IX.

ON THE REMOVAL OF THE ROYAL ACADEMY TO SOMERSET PLACE. — THE ADVANTAGES TO SOCIETY FROM CULTIVATING INTELLECTUAL PLEASURE. 237

DISCOURSE X.

SCULPTURE: — HAS BUT ONE STYLE. — ITS OBJECTS, FORM, AND CHARACTER. — INEFFECTUAL ATTEMPTS OF THE MODERN SCULPTORS TO IMPROVE THE ART. — ILL EFFECTS OF MODERN DRESS IN SCULPTURE. 241

DISCOURSE XI.

GENIUS, — CONSISTS PRINCIPALLY IN THE COMPREHENSION OF A WHOLE; IN TAKING GENERAL IDEAS ONLY. 259

DISCOURSE XII.

PARTICULAR METHODS OF STUDY OF LITTLE CONSEQUENCE.— LITTLE OF THE ART CAN BE TAUGHT. — LOVE OF METHOD OFTEN A LOVE OF IDLENESS. — PITTORI IMPROVVISATORI APT TO BE CARELESS AND INCORRECT; SELDOM ORIGINAL AND STRIKING. — THIS PROCEEDS FROM THEIR NOT STUDYING THE WORKS OF OTHER MASTERS. 279

DISCOURSE XIII.

ART NOT MERELY IMITATION, BUT UNDER THE DIRECTION OF THE IMAGINATION. — IN WHAT MANNER POETRY, PAINTING, ACTING, GARDENING, AND ARCHITECTURE, DEPART FROM NATURE. 305

DISCOURSE XIV.

CHARACTER OF GAINSBOROUGH. — HIS EXCELLENCES AND DEFECTS. 327

DISCOURSE XV.

THE PRESIDENT TAKES LEAVE OF THE ACADEMY. — A REVIEW OF THE DISCOURSES. — THE STUDY OF THE WORKS OF MICHAEL ANGELO RECOMMENDED. 349

LIST OF ILLUSTRATIONS.

SIR JOSHUA REYNOLDS, P.R.A.	*Frontispiece*
MISS NELLY O'BRIEN	*To face page* 13
SCHOOLBOYS (JOHN BELLENDEN AND HENRY GAWLER)	17
SIR W. HAMILTON	33
LADY CHARLES SPENCER	39
MRS. SIDDONS AS THE TRAGIC MUSE	53
THE AGE OF INNOCENCE	63
MISS KITTY FISHER AS CLEOPATRA	81
LADY SOPHIA ST. ASAPH AND CHILD	99
MRS. MERRICK	123
MRS. LUCY HARDINGE	143
LADY LOUISA MANNERS (COUNTESS DYSART)	171
MRS. ROBINSON	207
SIR JOSEPH BANKS	237
ST. AGNES	241
MRS. ANN HOPE	259
MASTER JACOB BOUVERIE (AFTERWARDS EARL OF RADNOR, 1776)	279
MRS. BILLINGTON AS ST. CECILIA	305
MISS NELLY O'BRIEN	327
JOHN, EARL OF UPPER OSSORY	349

TO THE KING.

THE regular progress of cultivated life is from necessaries to accommodations, from accommodations to ornaments. By your illustrious predecessors were established Marts for manufactures, and Colleges for science; but for the arts of elegance, those arts by which manufactures are embellished, and science is refined, to found an Academy was reserved for your Majesty.

Had such patronage been without effect, there had been reason to believe that Nature had, by some insurmountable impediment, obstructed our proficiency; but the annual improvement of the Exhibitions which Your Majesty has been pleased to encourage shows that only encouragement had been wanting.

To give advice to those who are contending for royal liberality has been for some years the duty of my station in the Academy; and these Discourses hope for Your Majesty's acceptance, as well-intended endeavors to incite that emulation which your notice has kindled, and direct those studies which your bounty has rewarded.

May it please Your Majesty,
Your Majesty's
Most dutiful servant
And most faithful subject,

[1778.]   JOSHUA REYNOLDS.

TO THE MEMBERS

OF

THE ROYAL ACADEMY.

GENTLEMEN,

That you have ordered the publication of this discourse is not only very flattering to me, as it implies your approbation of the method of study which I have recommended, but likewise, as this method receives from that act such an additional weight and authority as demands from the students that deference and respect which can be due only to the united sense of so considerable a BODY of ARTISTS.

I am,
With the greatest esteem and respect,
GENTLEMEN,
Your most humble,
And obedient Servant,

JOSHUA REYNOLDS.

Miss Nelly O'Brien.

INTRODUCTION.

ALTHOUGH SIR JOSHUA REYNOLDS contributed more perhaps than any other one man to the elevation and reputation of the art of his country, the title of "founder of the English school," sometimes bestowed upon him, implies a distinction to which he is not justly entitled. The expression is in itself a loose one; doubly so as applied to Reynolds, who, though he left successors — more or less attenuated — in portraiture, as well as in his less frequent flights into ideal and historical painting, formed no school; and essentially so, because there is not, strictly speaking, and in the sense in which we speak of the several Italian schools or of the Dutch or Flemish schools, an English school of painting at all. The term "school" as thus used has a special and technical sense, embracing the common methods of *technique*, the special traditions and processes tending to the production of one general type of picture or fixed national ideal, to which painters of the same age and country have been constrained to submit; and the rise of a school of painting implies a general diffusion of artistic taste, and a close system of training and apprenticeship such as have never prevailed in England. The English painter, after leaving the academy schools, is generally free to follow his personal bent; and no art owes more to individual initiative and less to the cumulative force of consistent principle and tradition than English art. To say, then, that this or that painter is of the English school means little more than that he is an English painter, — not that he is one who in his work carries out certain national conventions and processes, for these have not as yet been developed in England.

Still, while England has not, in the confined sense, evolved a school of painting, while her art is, consequently, richly varied, "full of surprises and unexpected originality," and not, indeed, free from that "mania of eccentricity" remarked by the foreigner, its productions, stamped throughout with the genius of the race, form a connected and considerable whole. Lacking in the academic uniformity which springs from a consistent aim and a fixed ideal, English painting, like English literature, presents through all its contrasts of form a marked national character. "From whatever side one regards it," observes a recent French critic,[1] "the English school always discloses some idiosyncracy peculiar to the ordinary British mind;" and it is hardly necessary to add that the "ordinary British mind" has not an æsthetic bent; that it must be appealed to on other, and, as it holds, higher and more "serious" grounds than that innate feeling for harmony and sensuous beauty characteristic of the Latin races. "The prosaic British mind," said Emerson, "seeks the prose in nature." Purely decorative and sensuous forms of art, the spontaneous outgrowth of the southern temperament, are exotics in England; and no system of hot-house forcing and observance of patent method and recipe have produced there anything but the feeblest reflection of the theological and "historical" painting of the Latin schools.

Seeking for the prevailing tendency of English painters as a body, one may say that it is to impute to their art the special office of language, — to make the picture unduly

---

[1] M. Chesneau, *The English School of Painting.*

subsidiary to the thought expressed or fact described; and it is in the branches which allow this tendency freest play — in pictorial narrative, *genre* and historical-*genre*, and in literary illustration — that English art is notably profuse; while even in portraiture and landscape the aim is rarely a purely æsthetic one, the painter's success depending, says Ruskin, "on his desire to convey a truth, rather than to produce a merely beautiful picture, — that is to say, to get a likeness of a man or of a place." The predominance of the moral element, too, is as noticeable in the national art as in the national literature, — English painters, like English novelists and playwrights, rarely failing in some degree to point the moral while adorning the tale.

Such being the general characteristics, it is not difficult to name the early master whose work bears the closest affinity to the great body of English art. Hogarth, not Reynolds, is the Giotto of the "school," — the first native painter who shook off foreign influences and ideals and held up to the life around him " Nature's unflatt'ring glass." And he is as English in aim as in subject. Hogarth was not sensitive to beauty, in art or nature; and the stray touches of it that one finds in his works — a turn of expression, an attitude, a face here and there — are not of his seeking, still less of his producing; they exist on the canvas because they existed in the model. He ministered to the pleasures of his countrymen only in so far as they could take pleasure in laughing at the national humors and condemning the national vices. Like his literary prototype, he used his art to —

> "strip the ragged follies of the time
> Naked as at their birth . . . and with a whip of steel
> Print wounding lashes on their iron ribs."

"His graphic representations," said Charles Lamb, "are indeed books; they have the teeming, fruitful, suggestive meaning of *words*. Other pictures we look at, — his we read."

How different all this from Reynolds, — a true painter's painter who sought to delight the eye even at the expense of a little gentle flattery, " discreetly touched, just enough to make all men noble, all women lovely." His superb portraits, " Italian music set to English words," are anthologies of the beauties of his sitters and of the lighter graces of the old masters. In aim and accomplishment he is the least English, as the moralizing bluntly truthful Hogarth is the most English, of painters; and his artistic charm is an essence distilled from flowers gathered in fields where the founder of British painting never trod. Reynolds's incense is ever burning at the shrines of the great Italians whose names adorn his Discourses. " Even when painting the most graceful lady, the most English — in other words the brightest and freshest — of boys, he never becomes so lost in his model as to forget the old masters." [1]

Reynolds's art, rich as it was in the results of personal observation of nature, was a forced but magnificent hot-house growth, exotic and necessarily ephemeral; that of Hogarth was a hardy native plant, which sprang from the soil and throve and multiplied in a fit environment; and the homely truth, the fondness for everyday life, the turn for humor, satire, and narrative that prevail in English art to-day were first manifest in " The Harlot's Progress."

In fixing the rise of English painting proper with Hogarth, it is not, of course, meant that before him the art was unknown in England, or that no Englishman had practised it. English art begins under him, as every national art begins, with reflecting the life and temper of the times; yet he learned the rudiments of his profession from an Englishman and a Londoner. The monastery was the cradle of the arts

---

[1] M. Chesneau, *The English School of Painting.*

Schoolboys.
(John Bellenden and Henry Gawler).

in England; and the real first fruits of the artistic instincts of the race are to be found in the relics of that school of illuminators who from an early date, possibly the beginning of the seventh century, until the suppression of the monastic houses, were employed in the decoration of breviaries, missals, and other religious books, confining their efforts at first to ornate capitals and painted and gilded letters, then essaying borders of flowers, foliage, etc., and finally venturing upon text illustrations and miniatures,[1] the latter usually portraits of those to whom the work was to be given.

Later and more ambitious attempts may be seen in the Gothic cathedrals and on the walls of the Chapter House at Westminster. These works, done in the thirteenth century, compare not unfavorably with similar contemporary productions of France, Italy, and the Netherlands. With the next century came a complete pause in English pictorial art, not to be broken until the splendid revival under George III. For this long term of sterility it is difficult to account; especially so for the fact that a period which produced Shakspeare (I may cautiously add, and Bacon) and his brilliant following should not have boasted at least a Holbein or a Van Dyck. Mr. Ruskin suggests, among kindred reasons, a lack of mountains; but as the Dutch and Flemings seem to have done very well without them, and as the want was certainly not supplied in the day of Reynolds and Gainsborough, we may ascribe the pause rather to the unfavorable social conditions brought about by the French wars and the Wars of the Roses, to the chilling influence of early Protestantism, and to the influx of a long line of foreign painters, who set the mode and warped

---

[1] "The word 'miniatura' in its original sense had no reference to the size of the work, being derived from the Latin word *minium*, signifying red lead, in which material all the headings, capital letters, etc., of the most ancient MSS. were drawn." — J. L. PROPERT, *History of Miniature Art*.

or repressed the native talent. It is mainly in the lives of these foreigners that the history of English art from Henry III. (1216-1292) down to the second quarter of the eighteenth century is to be read.

The first of them whom we need mention is Jean de Mabuse, a Fleming, who drifted into England rather unaccountably during the reign of Henry VII., a monarch little given to munificence. "He reigned," says Walpole, "as an attorney would have reigned, and would have preferred a conveyancer to Praxiteles."

Of a very different temper was Henry VIII., a liberal, ostentatious prince, whose bounty attracted and sustained several foreign painters of merit, notably the great Holbein, — a man in whom universality of talent did not preclude special excellence. As a portrait painter he is, take him all in all, unsurpassed; while his "Madonna" at Darmstadt is one of the glories of religious art. Henry's high opinion of him is recorded in his rebuke to a courtier who had insulted the painter: "You have not to do with Holbein, but with me; and I tell you that of seven peasants I can make seven lords, but not one Holbein." Holbein's superb portraits are usually models of accuracy, — a quality which on one occasion he rashly disregarded. Henry having determined to take a fourth wife, Anne of Cleves was selected as the candidate for decapitation, and Holbein was despatched by Thomas Cromwell, who favored the match, to paint her portrait. In obedience to the minister he grossly flattered his model; so that Henry, who was completely taken in, upon seeing the original landing at Dover, roared out in disgust, "She is a great Flanders mare!" and wanted to send her back to Germany. Cromwell paid for the deceit with his head, but Holbein escaped unnoticed. Henry's patronage of the arts was due, not so much to his love for or appreciation of them, as to his emulation of Francis I.; and the crudity of his own ideas, as well as the state of the public taste at the time, may be inferred from the directions he left for a monument to his memory. The note directs that "the king shall appear on horseback of the stature of a goodly man, while over him shall appear the image of God the Father, holding the king's soul in his left hand and his right extended in the act of benediction," — a conceit which proves at least the royal faith in the capabilities of art.

Under the reign of Edward VI., a minor prince, and amidst a struggle of religions, the arts were in abeyance, nobody having leisure to patronize, practise, or record them. Holbein was, however, still alive, and he drew several portraits of the young king.

The reign of Mary, though shorter even than that of her brother, is more considerable in the annals of painting. Her favorite painter was Antonio Moro, who had been sent to England by Charles V. Many of his English portraits, painted in the realistic manner of Holbein, and fine examples of color, are extant. Moro was a striking figure at the Spanish court, to which he returned after Mary's death. Though a courtier as well as painter he lacked discretion, even venturing upon familiarities with such a tiger as Philip II. One day while Moro was at work, Philip, who was looking on, rested his arm on the shoulder of the painter, who, to the dismay of surrounding flunkeydom, dipped his brush in carmine and with it smeared the royal hand. The king surveyed the member seriously a while, and in that moment of suspense the fate of Moro balanced on a hair; but caprice, perhaps even pity, turned the scale, and Philip passed the silly jest off with a smile of complacency.

The long and eventful reign of Elizabeth is almost a blank in the history of art, the royal taste for painting extending only to representations of her own dubious charms. Art could flatter; therefore she employed it. It is only fair to the profession, however, to add that there is not a single

portrait of Elizabeth that can be called beautiful, — the
"Virgin Queen" serving, in general, as a mere lay figure
for the display of robes and trinkets — "like an Indian idol,
all hands and necklaces," says the sarcastic Walpole. "A
pale Roman nose, a head of hair loaded with crowns and
powdered with diamonds, a vast ruff, a vaster fardingale,
and a bushel of pearls are the features by which everybody
knows at once the pictures of Queen Elizabeth." Her
chief painters were the Italian Zuccaro, the Flemings De
Heere and Hetel, and the Englishman Isaac Oliver, a miniature painter unrivalled in England, save by his own son
Peter, and later, Cooper, a pupil of Van Dyck. Elizabeth's
appetite for flattery is shown in a curious portrait of her by
De Heere. She is represented as coming out of a palace,
"in maiden meditation, fancy free," with her crown, sceptre,
and globe, and two female attendants. Before her, flying
in dismay from her combined charms, are Juno, Venus, and
Minerva; Juno drops her sceptre, Venus her roses, while
Cupid, abashed, perhaps, before such adamantine virtue,
flings away his bow and arrows and clings to his mother.

Luckily for the arts, James I., a tasteless pedant, was not
disposed to meddle with them, and he may be dismissed
with a quotation from Hayley: —

> "James, both for empire and for arts unfit
> (His sense a quibble, and a pun his wit),
> Whatever works he patronized, debased;
> But haply left the pencil undisgraced."

The accession of Charles I. marks the first era of real
taste in England. Elizabeth was avaricious and pompous,
James I. lavish and mean. Charles I., a scholar, a man of
taste, and a gentleman, knew how and where to bestow,
encouraging men of the first merit only, and these abundantly. Jones was his architect, and Van Dyck his painter;
he royally entertained and employed Rubens, and purchased
the cartoons of Raphael. "The art of reigning was the

only art of which he was ignorant." To the taste and enlightened liberality of Charles I. England owes some of her choicest treasures.

The arts were virtually banished from England with the royal family, and the restoration brought them back — but not taste. Charles II. had, in addition to his turn for gallantry, a turn for the sciences, but none for art. His chief painter was Sir Peter Lely, a Westphalian, an artist of questionable taste but talented, a favorite with the ladies, whom he flattered liberally. He is well represented in the collection of portraits at Hampton Court, where a bevy of Charles's Paphian beauties, their charms half hidden in "a sort of fantastic night-gowns fastened with a single pin," look down in a most un-Puritan way upon the visitor. Lely was not always called upon to flatter. When Cromwell sat to him he said, "Mr. Lely, I desire you would use all your skill to paint my picture truly like me, and not flatter me at all; but remark all these roughnesses, pimples, warts, and everything as you see me, otherwise I will never pay a farthing for it" — a command which was literally obeyed. Lely died in 1680, and was succeeded by Godfrey Kneller, of Lübeck, who reigned supreme in English portraiture until his death in 1723, the year of Sir Joshua Reynolds's birth. Kneller was a painter of varied instruction, of some talent and even originality, but his influence was, on the whole, debasing to the national taste. He preferred portrait painting, for, as he said, "painters of history make the dead live, and do not begin to live themselves till they are dead. I paint the living and they make me live," — a characteristic reason, for, as Walpole states, "where he offered one picture to fame, he sacrificed twenty to lucre." He is even charged with the meanness of selling copies of his pictures for originals.

Many anecdotes are related of Kneller's excessive vanity. He once said to a low fellow whom he overheard cursing himself: "God d—— you! God may d—— the Duke of Marlborough, and perhaps Sir Godfrey Kneller; but do you think he will take the trouble of d——g such a scoundrel as you?" Pope used to say, "Have you heard Sir Godfrey's dream? I thought I had ascended a very high hill to heaven, and saw Saint Peter at the gate with a great crowd behind him. When arrived there Saint Luke [1] immediately descried me, and asked if I were not the famous Sir Godfrey Kneller? We had a long conversation about our beloved art, and I had forgotten all about Saint Peter, who called out to me, 'Sir Godfrey, enter in, and take whatever station you like best.'"[2] Pope was once badly worsted in an encounter with the witty painter. Having laid a wager that there was no flattery so gross but that Kneller would swallow it, he said to him as he was painting, "Sir Godfrey, I believe if God Almighty had had your assistance, the world would have been formed more perfect." "'Fore God, sir," replied Kneller, "I believe so!" and he laid at the same time his hand gently upon the poet's *deformed shoulder*. Kneller lived through the reigns of Charles II., James II., William and Mary, Anne, and George I. who knighted him.

Naturally the presence in England of so many foreign painters of merit was not without its effect in stimulating and awakening the native talent; and there had been all along native artists, some of them "painters to the King," such as were Nicholas Hilliard (1547–1619) and Isaac Oliver (1555–1617), the celebrated miniature painters; George Jamesone (1586–1644), called by Walpole "the

---

[1] The patron saint of painters.

[2] Sir Godfrey, vain as he was, was a modest man compared with his contemporary, Jervas. It is related of this poor dauber that, having copied, and as he thought, surpassed, a picture of Titian, he looked first at one and then at the other, exclaiming with parental complacency, "Poor little Tit! how he would stare!"

Scottish Van Dyck;" William Dobson (1610-1646), called by Charles his "English Tintoret;" Robert Walker, Cromwell's painter; Richard Gibson (1615-1690), the dwarf; and Robert Streater[1] (1624-1680). These men, however, were successful only as clever imitators of the ruling style; they were content to follow, without a thought of emulating, much less of innovating; and it was only when patrons saw that painting was not, in the nature of things, extraneous, that it might be independently practised and improved by their own countrymen, that native art had a chance of free development. In Anne's reign Sir James Thornhill was elected over his competitor, the Italian Ricci, to paint the dome of St. Paul's; and henceforth Englishmen began to hold the field. Sir James Thornhill was Hogarth's father-in-law, and Hogarth was, as we have seen, the Giotto of the "school," the first native painter whose work bears upon it "the strong stamp of the native land."

Endeavoring to state more specifically the genealogies of English painting, we may say that in so far as it treats the incidents and philosophy of social life it flows, through Wilkie, Mulready, Leslie, and the older *genre* painters, direct from Hogarth, — whose art, *minus* its satirical and narrative spirit, was a heritage from the Dutch; English landscape takes its origin from Wilson and Gainsborough, and English portraiture from Reynolds. With Hogarth,

---

[1] Streater was the painter whose decoration of the Oxford theatre inspired the silly panegyric, —

"That future ages must confess they owe
To Streater more than Michael Angelo."

Graham called him "the greatest and most universal painter that England ever had;" and says that his being a good historian contributed not a little to his being a good historical painter; upon which Walpole tartly remarks, "He might as well say that reading the 'Rape of the Lock' would make one a good haircutter."

Reynolds, and Gainsborough we reach the grand period of English art; and we may turn from following its general course to a brief sketch of its chief luminary.

The life of Sir Joshua Reynolds, prince of portrait painters and most affable of men, was free from instances of that instability and unfitness for the ordinary business of life which proverbially mark the children of genius, and were so amusingly shown in his friend Goldsmith. Sir Joshua's success was two-fold; he was the successful man as well as the successful painter, his career throughout supporting his own theory that effects commonly ascribed to innate powers, or "genius," are really due to unremitting, well-directed effort.

He was born, July 16, 1723, at Plympton, Devonshire, where his father, the Reverend Samuel Reynolds (a "Parson Adams" in real life), rector of the Plympton grammar-school, initiated him into those classical studies which, later, contributed to the refinement and grace of his pencil. He early discovered an inclination for his art — to the dissatisfaction of his father who would have made him an apothecary — by diligently copying the prints that fell in his way, notably those in Cats's "Book of Emblems" and Plutarch's "Lives," and by mastering and applying, while in his eighth year, the Jesuit's "Rules of Perspective," and, afterwards, Richardson's "Theory of Painting." Overborne by the advice of friends the senior Reynolds was, in 1740, induced to yield to his son's preference of the palette and brush over the mortar and pestle; and Joshua was sent to London and placed under the tuition of Hudson, a portrait painter of more vogue and pretension than merit. Under this barren source of instruction, however, he rapidly overtook his master, who did not, it seems, like Cimabue in a similar case,

"smile upon the lad
At the first stroke which passed what he could do."

but, on the contrary, soon contrived to make things so unpleasant for the too promising pupil that he remained in the studio but two of the four years for which he was bound, returning in 1743 to Devonshire, and setting up for himself as portrait painter. He settled at Plymouth, where he met with prompt and unexpected success, painting some thirty portraits, and finding patrons whose good offices secured his future success. At this period he derived great benefit from the works and practical hints of William Gandy, of Exeter, a fine colorist whose father had been a pupil of Van Dyck. One of Gandy's maxims, never forgotten by Sir Joshua, was that "a picture ought to have a richness in its texture, as if the colors had been composed of cream or cheese, and the reverse of a hard and husky or dry manner."

While at Plymouth Reynolds saw his early dream of one day visiting the painter's Parnassus, the land of Raphael and Michael Angelo, shape itself into reality. Commodore Keppel, to whom he had been recommended by Lord Edgecombe, his life-long friend and patron, being appointed to the Mediterranean station, invited the young painter to accompany him, and he sailed from Plymouth early in 1749, and on his arrival at Leghorn proceeded to Rome, whence he reported, "I am now at the height of my wishes, in the midst of the greatest works of art that the world has produced."

Reynolds's practice and habit of study during his two years in Rome were regulated by the soundest judgment. Seeking truth, taste, and beauty at the fountain-head, he diligently copied, sketched, and mentally analyzed such portions of the works of Raphael, Michael Angelo, Guido, Titian, Veronese, and many others, as seemed to him to bear most directly upon his chosen branch, rarely copying the whole of a picture, but endeavoring to fix in his mind the peculiar excellence of each; aspiring to the conceptions of the master as well as analyzing his processes, and studying the masterpieces in the Vatican for their subjective effect rather than with the view of carrying them away piecemeal for future recombination, — though, as his notes and his whole theory and practice show, the borrowing and transplanting of the ideas of others was as little abhorrent to his artistic conscience as to Raphael's.

It need not surprise us that Reynolds's first feeling on viewing the wonders of Italian art was one of disappointment, — especially when we reflect that the processes which in our day multiply masterpieces on every hand were unknown in his. Works conceived and wrought out in the spirit of noble simplicity and quiet dignity of the Greek sculptures — the true school of Michael Angelo and Raphael — seemed to him lacking in precisely those qualities, richness of color and striking effects of light and shade, which he had been used to regard as the crowning excellences of painting. The rhapsodies of Richardson had prepared him to be dazzled, like Saul of Tarsus, by a blaze of visual splendor; and, his ideals not reaching beyond the showy effects of the painter's rhetoric, he did not at once perceive the less obvious qualities which place the works of Raphael and Michael Angelo beside those of poets and philosophers. Among his notes Reynolds left the following ingenuous account of his first visit to the Vatican; and certainly no portion of his writings is more instructive and more characteristic of their author: —

"It has frequently happened, as I was informed by the keeper of the Vatican, that many of those whom he had conducted through the various apartments of that edifice, when about to be dismissed, have asked for the works of Raphael, and would not believe that they had already passed through the rooms where they are preserved; so little impression had these performances made on them. One of the first painters in France told me that this circumstance happened to himself;

though he now looks on Raphael with that veneration which he deserves from all painters and lovers of art. I remember very well my own disappointment when I first visited the Vatican; but on confessing my feelings to a brother student, of whose ingenuousness I had a high opinion, he acknowleged that the works of Raphael had the same effect on him; or rather, that they did not produce the effect which he expected. This was a great relief to my mind; and, on inquiring farther of other students, I found that those persons only who from natural imbecility appeared to be incapable of ever relishing these divine performances, made pretensions to instantaneous raptures on first beholding them. In justice to myself, however, I must add that, though disappointed and mortified at not finding myself enraptured with the works of this great master, I did not for a moment conceive or suppose that the name of Raphael and those admirable paintings in particular owed their reputation to the ignorance and prejudice of mankind; on the contrary, my not relishing them as I was conscious I ought to have done was one of the most humiliating things that ever happened to me. I found myself in the midst of works *executed upon principles with which I was unacquainted*. I felt my ignorance, and stood abashed.

"All the indigested notions of painting which I had brought with me from England, where the art was at the lowest ebb — it could not indeed be lower — were to be totally done away with and eradicated from my mind. It was necessary, as it is expressed on a very solemn occasion, that I should become *as a little child*. Notwithstanding my disappointment, I proceeded to copy some of those excellent works. I viewed them again and again; I even affected to feel their merits and to admire them more than I really did. In a short time a new taste and new perceptions began to dawn upon me, and I was convinced that I had originally formed a *false opinion of the perfection of art*, and that this great painter was well entitled to the high rank which he holds in the estimation of the world.

"The truth is that if these works had been really what I expected, they would have contained beauties superficial and alluring, but by no means such as would have entitled them to the great reputation which they have long and so justly obtained.

"Having since that period frequently revolved the subject in my mind, I am now clearly of opinion that a relish for the higher excellences of the art is an acquired taste, which no man ever possessed without long cultivation and great labor and attention. On such occasions as that which I have mentioned we are often ashamed of our apparent dulness, as if it were expected that our minds, like tinder, should instantly catch fire from the divine spark of Raphael's genius. I flatter myself that *now* it would be so, and that I have a just perception of his great powers; but let it be remembered that the excellence of his style is not on the surface, but lies deep, and at the first view is seen but mistily. It is the florid style which strikes at once, and captivates the eye for a time, without ever satisfying the judgment. Nor does painting in this respect differ from other arts. A just poetical taste, and the acquisition of a nice discriminative ear, are equally the work of time. Even the eye, however perfect in itself, is often unable to distinguish between the brilliancy of two diamonds, though the experienced jeweller will be amazed at its blindness, — not considering that there was a time when he himself could not have been able to pronounce which of the two was the most perfect, and that his own power of discrimination was acquired by slow and imperceptible degrees."

As already stated, Sir Joshua, while in Rome, by no means neglected the executive parts of his art, but was at the utmost pains to discover and acquire the various artifices by which the great masters had obtained their effects; and I may say parenthetically that although he seems at times in his discourses disposed to belittle technical skill, no one more thoroughly knew its vital importance or owed more to its effects than himself. That he was, theoretically, so determined a stickler for the intellectual in art may be regarded as the outcome, in a measure, of his debates with the jealous Johnson, who, with characteristic urbanity, pretended to despise his friend's profession as a handicraft. Critics are apt enough to undervalue those accomplishments of which they know least; and had the

doctor himself made a serious practical essay with the
pencil he must have discovered that the "handicraft"
which painting certainly includes implies in itself, when
fully attained, a rare combination of mental and physical
gifts, — gifts in which, by the way, the short-sighted and un-
pliable philosopher was himself eminently deficient. That
Reynolds, though his chief aim at this period was to grasp
the conceptions and imbibe something of the spirit of the
great masters, did not overlook those details which are,
after all, the blood, bone, and sinew of his calling, is shown
in his voluminous notes, a specimen or two of which may be
quoted as illustrative of his methods : —

"The Adonis of Titian in the Colonna palace is dead colored
white, with the muscles marked bold; the second painting he
scumbled a light *color* over it; the lights a mellow flesh color;
the shadows, in the light parts, of a faint purple hue; at least
they were so at first. That purple hue seems to be occasioned
by blackish shadows under, and the color scumbled over them.

"I copied the Titian in the Colonna collection with white,
umber, minio, cinnabar, black; the shadows thin of color,
perhaps little more than the dark ground left.

"In respect to painting the flesh tint, after it has been finished
with very strong colors, such as ultramarine and carmine, pass
white over it, very thin with oil. I believe it will have a wonderful effect.

"Or paint carnation *too red*, and then scumble it over with
white and black.

"Then dead color with white and black only; at second sitting, carnation. (To wit, the Barocci at the palace Albani, and
Correggio in the Pamphili.)[1]

---

[1] In Reynolds's memoranda of December, 1755, we find the following record of the colors which he then made use of, and of the order in
which they were arranged on his palette : —

"For painting the flesh : black, blue-black, white, lake, carmine,
orpiment, yellow ochre, ultramarine, and varnish.

"To lay the palette : first lay carmine and white, in different

"Avoid the chalk, the brick-dust, and the charcoal; and think on a pearl or a ripe peach."[1]

Thus Reynolds, while in Rome, "forged for his own use an armory of weapons, a magazine of rules and well-tried systems." Regarding, as he did, a great work of art, not as the reflection of a fitful, half-fortuitous flash of innate genius or "inspiration," but as the forced fruit of deliberate method and selection, he used his gleanings from the old masters as material to be reduced into fixed and definite principles for his own future guidance.

On leaving Rome he visited other Italian cities, Parma, where he fell under Correggio's influence, Florence, Venice, where he remained six weeks studying the great colorists upon whose works his own style was chiefly founded.[2]

He had now been absent from England about three years, when he began to think of returning. He arrived in London in 1752, and took rooms in St. Martin's Lane, afterwards removing to the large house on Newport Street where he remained until his final removal to Leicester Square.

English art, as a national art, had already begun, as we have seen, under Hogarth; and it remained for the genius of Reynolds to mature and elevate it, — his influence extending more directly, of course, to his peculiar branch. That Sir Joshua, with his leaning toward what he called "the grand style," chose portraiture as his profession was due partly to his consciousness of an ignorance of anatomy which made it impossible for him at any period of his life

degrees; second, lay orpiment and white, ditto; third, lay blue-black and white, ditto.

"The first sitting, for expedition, make a mixture on the palette as near the sitter's complexion as you can."

[1] An agreeable variation from the prosaic Gandy's "cream or cheese."

[2] His style "is precisely that denominated in his lectures the ornamental style." — THOMAS PHILLIPS, R. A., *Rees's Cyclopædia*.

to draw the nude figure accurately, and partly to the fact that portrait painting was in England then the only path to substantial success. His propensity for ideal and historical painting, however, made him ambitious of infusing something of its variety and picturesqueness into his chosen branch, and it was largely to this ambition that his superiority and the novelty of his style were due. At the period of his return the rapacity of Kneller and the affectations of Lely had contributed to reduce portraiture to its lowest ebb. Hogarth had already passed his prime, Wilson and Gainsborough were painting landscape, Hudson and a few others were making likenesses of the wooden, sign-post order. The art of elevating a portrait — by the addition of pleasing and suggestive accessories and by imparting life, character, and action to the figure — from a bald likeness into a true picture, a work charming and interesting irrespective of the name and condition of the sitter, was unknown or forgotten. So far as they had gone, it was the Dutch side, the purely imitative side of their talent, that English painters had developed; and painting was with them the merest mechanical operation, uninformed by taste, a simple transferring of the object before them to the canvas, without reference to an animated or pleasing effect. If the painter chanced to be a man of unusually exuberant fancy, he modified the dress of the sitter, or, perhaps, by adding a sheep, or a dog, or a crook, aspired to the pastoral. But such flights, inspired by Lely, were rare; and the artist was commonly content to hand his patrons down to posterity, fishily staring, in the hats and wigs they usually wore.

The advent of Reynolds, equipped with the weapons and fired with the spirit of a higher school, revealed to his countrymen possibilities in the art hitherto undreamed of by them. His portraits were entirely unlike the vapid performances — mere transcripts of the sitter's outer shell — to which they were accustomed. By placing his figures in the midst of active life, by revealing the individuality in th mind and form of each, and by surrounding them with appropriate circumstances and speaking details, he imparted to his portraits a spirit and attractiveness, an element of general and lasting interest, that seemed to raise them to the dignity of a higher branch of art. " They remind the spectator," said Burke, " of the invention of history, and the amenity of landscape. In painting portraits he appeared not to be raised upon that platform, but to descend to it from a higher sphere."

Naturally, such expansive ideas did not at first hit the taste of the town. The jealousy of competitors — notably of his old master Hudson, who, on seeing one of his pieces, exclaimed, " Reynolds, you don't paint so well now as you did before you went to Italy," — and the prepossession in favor of Kneller and Lely were not easily overcome. Ellis, an eminent painter of the time, on seeing the picture which had displeased Hudson, was equally dissatisfied, or alarmed, and observed, with a prophetic shake of the head, " Oh, Reynolds, this will never answer; why, you don't paint in the least degree in the manner of Kneller ; " and when the young artist began to vindicate his methods, the veteran, finding himself unable to defend his position logically, cried out in a rage, " Shakspeare in poetry, and Kneller in painting, damme ! " and immediately left the room.

But the scale was finally and decisively turned when Reynolds exhibited his portrait of Commodore Keppel, — a work of such truth and spirit, combined with richness of color and picturesque general effect, as to silence disparagement. Alluding to this portrait Malone has observed : " The whole interval between the time of Charles I. and the conclusion of the reign of George II., though distinguished by the performances of Lely, Riley, and Kneller, seemed to be annihilated ; and the only question was whether the new

Sir W. Hamilton.

painter or Van Dyck were the more excellent." Reynolds speedily became the vogue, and his studio was thronged, says Northcote, "with women who wished to be transmitted as angels, and men who wished to appear as heroes and philosophers."

From this time forward Reynolds's life, during a brilliant period of upwards of thirty years, was one of unbroken success. Other painters rose from time to time to share his popularity, — Gainsborough, Romney, Opie, Hoppner, — but not to contest his supremacy. Not to be painted by Reynolds was, for a person of note, almost a breach of duty; and in his canvases we see mirrored the men and women who contributed, in whatever department, to the eminence of the period. Garrick, Siddons, Burke, Johnson, Goldsmith, Sterne, Fox, Boswell, Erskine, Gibbon, — philosophers, statesmen, actors, soldiers, — all are there, not stiffly or affectedly posturing, but snatched, as it were, from the midst of life, the expression and action of the moment caught and held in suspension by the genius of the painter. We read in the German fairy-tale that, when the princess pricked her finger with the spindle, all life and motion in the castle was in an instant checked. Bound by the spell of the bad fairy, the queen sat, stilled for a hundred years, with uplifted finger and parted lips, upon which a syllable still trembled; the maid at her needle remained with bent head, and thread half-drawn; the servant stood with bowl outstretched and foot advanced in the midst of the hall; and the angry cook in the kitchen paused with spit in air and malediction half-uttered, while his victim's fleeting look and attitude of terror were frozen into perpetuity. So with Reynolds's figures; the painter seems to have stolen upon his model unawares, and to have held in check, as if by magic, the passing act and look until he could fix it forever upon his canvas. Forever? No. The saddest defect in his portraits is their evanescence. As with the auroral canvases of Turner, their pristine splendor is passing into tradition. Italian paintings done three, or four, or five centuries ago are in many cases as bright and firm, almost, as when they left the easel; while Reynolds's, after less than a century, are already fading into dimness. "Reynolds filled the halls of England," says Ruskin, "with the ghosts of her noble squires and dames." "But alas!" adds a commentator, "they are now, too many of them, the ghosts of ghosts." [1]

Sir Joshua's "flying colors," so exquisite when newly laid, were partly due, no doubt, to his lack of thorough elementary training, and in part to a fondness for dabbling in experimental mixtures,[2] — a *damnosa haereditas*, perhaps, of his early studies in pharmacy. A firm believer in the "Venetian secret," he spent a great portion of his life in exploring arcana the key to which might endow his canvases with the richness of Titian and the flowery hues of Veronese; and to such a length did he carry experiment that he utterly destroyed several fine paintings of the Venetian school to trace the process of laying on, and to analyze the chemical mixture of the tints. "There is not a man on earth," he used to say, "who has the least notion of coloring; we all of us have it equally to seek for and find out, as at present it is totally lost to the art." That Reynolds did not realize that *permanence* was the one quality lacking in his work to place him beside the world's greatest colorists is one of the most deplorable facts in the history of English painting.

[1] When a collection of them was exhibited at the Grosvenor Gallery, in 1884, "it was seen," said Ruskin, "broadly speaking, that neither the painter knew how to paint, the patron to preserve, nor the cleaner to restore." (*Art of England*.) It is well to qualify this characteristic statement by quoting Sir George Beaumont's conclusion when some one complained that Sir Joshua "made his pictures die before the man" "Never mind," said Sir George, "a faded portrait by Reynolds is better than a fresh one by any one else"

[2] "The wonder is," said Haydon, alluding to this practice, "that the pictures did not crack beneath the brush."

Sir Joshua's career was, as has been stated, one of unbroken success, and it is in the ascending scale of his prices that his rising reputation is most readily traced. His original price for a head was five guineas; in 1755 he raised it to twelve; five years later it was twenty-five, ten years later thirty-five, while in his later years it was fifty. His industry may be judged from the fact that at the time when his price was twenty-five guineas, he told Dr. Johnson that he was making £6,000 a year. He received six sitters a day, and calculated upon finishing a portrait in four hours. Yet his diligence was not the rapacious haste of Kneller. He said to Northcote that whenever a new sitter came for a portrait he began it with a full determination to make it the best of his works, even if the subject were unfavorable; for there was always nature, and this was enough. One of the speediest of painters, Sir Joshua boasted that he had covered more canvas than any preceding artist in the three generations which he portrayed; and within two years after his death Richardson published a list of seven hundred prints from his works. Taylor thinks that his authenticated pictures numbered about 3,000; and Hamilton's Catalogue states that there are 2,000 that can be placed.

Sir Joshua's life was not without external honors. In 1768, when the Royal Academy was founded, he was elected president by acclamation, and was knighted by the king, — an honor that has ever since been bestowed upon the holder of the office. In 1773 he was chosen mayor of his native town, Plympton, — a distinction, he told the king, which gave him more pleasure than any he had ever received, except, he politely added, "that which your Majesty so graciously conferred upon me." The academy dinners were started by him, and his discourses were delivered before the students at the annual prize-giving. In order that means might not be lacking to follow his constantly reiterated advice, "study the old masters," he offered the academy his own collection of pictures at a very low price, but the proposal was unwisely declined. A quarrel with the directors, the one embitterment of his life, was perhaps the outcome of this refusal. The ostensible ground of dispute was the election of the eccentric Anglo-Swiss Fuseli to the professorship of perspective over Reynolds's candidate, Bonomi. During the contest Gibbon wrote him from Lausanne: "I hear you have had a quarrel with your academicians. Fools as they are! for such is the tyranny of character that no one will believe your enemies can be in the right."

In 1789, when he was in his sixty-sixth year, his left eye became suddenly darkened while he was painting a portrait. Within ten weeks its sight was totally gone, and he was thenceforth compelled to practically relinquish his profession, taking up the pencil only occasionally to retouch the many portraits which had been left on his hands. "There is now an end of the pursuit," said he to Sheridan; "the race is over, whether it is won or lost."

His final discourse was delivered December 10, 1790; he was afterwards seized with a liver complaint, and after a long illness, "borne with a mild and cheerful fortitude," he died on February 23, 1792. A magnificent funeral was accorded the dead painter. The pall-bearers were the Dukes of Dorset, Leeds, and Portland; the Marquises of Abercorn and Townshend; the Earls of Carlisle, Inchiquin, and Upper Ossory; and Lords Palmerston and Eliot. Ninety-one carriages followed the hearse, bearing a noble company of peers and knights, scholars and prelates, and the entire body of the Royal Academicians. Burke wrote that "everything turned out fortunately for poor Sir Joshua, from the moment of his birth to the hour I saw him laid in the grave. Never was a funeral of ceremony attended with so much sincere concern by all sorts of people." He was buried in St. Paul's Cathedral, the resting-place of Sir

Christopher Wren and the great Van Dyck, and his eulogy was written by Burke, who characterized him as "one of the most memorable men of his time, and the first Englishman who added the praise of the elegant arts to the other glories of his country."

On Sir Joshua's deficiencies as a painter we need not dwell. For the most of us there is little to be gained and much to be lost in prying into and analyzing things primarily meant for our enjoyment. Beauty analyzed is beauty slain; and it is, after all, wiser to rest satisfied with inhaling the fragrance of the flower of art and enjoying its perfections, than to pull it to pieces, count the petals and stamens, and resolve the perfume into an essence scientifically procurable from wayside weeds.[1]

Reynolds's defects are, for the most part, implied in his perfections. He was too wise to put in practice what at times he impliedly preached, — the attempt at blending "contrary excellences;" and one may as well regret that the crimson of the rose is not added to the whiteness of the lily as to impute to his works a lack of qualities negative to those to which they owe their peculiar charm. The dash and freedom, the light touch and ready artifice, the preference of the momentary grace and prettiness, the transient look and act, give to his portraits a sketchiness or littleness of effect when we compare them with the best of the old masters; yet the defect is the concomitant of the charm; and the world is certainly the richer in that to the finish and consummate workmanship of a Holbein is added the "magnificent sketching" of a Reynolds.

---

[1] There is a fine moral to be drawn from Heine's summary of a too dialectical man: —

"In seinem Streben nach dem Positivum hatte der arme Mann sich alles Herrliche aus dem Leben herausphilosophiert, alle Sonnenstrahlen, allen Glauben und alle Blumen, und es blieb ihm nichts übrig als das kalte, positive Grab."

He is the painter of English gentlemen, and English ladies, and English children, painting these to perfection and painting little else — save charming bits of English landscape to set them in. This is his range; but within that range, how various he is! He is the courtliest, the most graceful of his craft. His portraits stir no profound thoughts, challenge no inquiry. He rarely meddles with the deeper moods and passions, and in his world one finds none of those sombre, solemn-thoughted people of Italian portraiture, faces with an under-glow of smouldering passion or hidden import, like that of Leonardo's "Mona Lisa," — a Sphinx-face with its veiled eyes and enigmatic smile. "The style is the man." From the profusion of nature the painter selects the facts most congenial to his temperament, sequesters them, and fixes them upon the canvas. Sir Joshua was all gentleness and affability, one of the most gracious of recorded characters, in the best sense a courtier; his lines had fallen in pleasant places, and he reflected the world as he saw it, — a trim, well-kept English world of park and woodland and cheerful vista, of smooth-rolling greensward chequered with flickering lights and shadows, peopled with the stateliest of gentlemen, the loveliest of ladies, the most artless of children. The grace of Reynolds has passed into a proverb; and in this quality, within certain limits, he is equal to any of the Italians. As a painter of children he stands pre-eminent, — thanks, perhaps, in part to his models, for no children are so charming as English children, with their unspoiled naturalness and dainty freshness and purity of color. There was something in the kindly nature of the painter keenly responsive to the humors of the little ones, to whom he never failed to endear himself; and, oddly enough, no one has rendered so lovingly and accurately, and in such manifold phases, the special charm of childhood as the childless Reynolds.

His greatness stopped with portraiture. Admirable and

Lady Charles Spencer.

various as he was within his scope, his scope itself was strangely limited, petty, even, when one recalls the magnificent universality of a Raphael, whose genius swept the field of pictorial achievement, taking all art for its province, equally at home amid the flowering arabesques of the Loggie, and the sublime conceptions of the Camera della Segnatura. Reynolds's attempts at ideal and historical compositions are failures, — at the best, pale reflections, sometimes, it must be confessed, mere caricatures. When he touches the tragical and supernatural he is at his worst; as bad, almost, as Fuseli, Barry, West, Haydon, and the rest of the Italianized group, — "moths who burnt their poor wings in the flame of Latin art." Let the reader mentally compare the grotesque goblins, the paltry pantomine terrors of his "Macbeth and the Witches," or the vapid symbolical figures that debase his superb portrait of Mrs. Siddons, with the terrific forms,

"The airy shapes, and beckoning shadows dire,"

that rose at the beck of Michael Angelo, and his feebleness becomes apparent.

To this slight sketch of Reynolds the painter, it remains to add a few words of Reynolds the man. Northcote, his pupil and biographer, has thus described him: —

"In his stature Sir Joshua Reynolds was rather under the middle size, of a florid complexion, roundish blunt features, and a lively aspect, — extremely active, with manners uncommonly polished and agreeable. In conversation his manner was perfectly natural, simple, and unassuming. He most heartily enjoyed his profession, in which he was both famous and illustrious; and I agree with Mr. Malone, who says he appeared to him to be the happiest man he had ever known."

Eminent as he was in his profession, Reynolds is perhaps even better known as a member of the Boswellian coterie, — as a sharer, with Johnson, Goldsmith, Burke, Gibbon, Garrick, and the other Olympians, in the famous symposia at the "Turk's Head." No name appears more frequently in the memoirs of the time, and none is more tenderly treated. He was the founder, with Johnson, of the Literary Club, — the original purpose of which seems to have been to afford the "Great Cham" a fair field and plenty of heads for the exercise of his controversial cudgel. Goldsmith's crown was cracked the most frequently, — except, of course, Boswell's, — and Sir Joshua's the least. "Sir Joshua Reynolds, sir," Johnson once said to Boswell, " is the most invulnerable man I know; the man with whom if you should quarrel, you would find the most difficulty how to abuse." With the disputatious scholars of the day conversation meant a duel *à outrance*. The monologue epoch, the epoch of Coleridge, Macaulay, Carlyle, had not yet dawned, and the giants of talk loved an antagonist who, like Burke, "calls forth all your powers," and "puts his mind fairly to yours." It was pre-eminently the age of dispute, and Lord Ashburton — himself no mean combatant — once said to Reynolds, after a specially stormy sitting, " The last time I dined in your house the company was of such a sort that, by ——! I believe all the rest of the world enjoyed peace for that afternoon." Like the beasts in a menagerie, the quarrelsome literati seem to have been most unruly at feeding-time. At the "Turk's Head," where the Genius of Discord was often active, Sir Joshua's function seems to have been that of moderator or peacemaker in general. No voice was so potent as his to still the angry growls of the dread lexicographer, who even admitted that " when Sir Joshua Reynolds, sir, tells me something, I consider myself as possessing an idea the more." Not that Reynolds did not come in for an occasional tap from the lion's paw. Upon one occasion, when the argument turned upon the use of wine, Johnson, who was rather worsted in the dispute, impatiently exclaimed, " I won't argue any more with you, sir; you are too far gone!" "I should have thought so indeed, sir," mildly replied the painter, "had I made such a speech as you have now," — which was perhaps the most effective rebuke ever received by the bullying Doctor. Such scenes, however, were rare between these illustrious friends, each of whom, in his way, admired and reverenced the other. "Reynolds," says Northcote, "was truly the *dulce decus*, and with whom he maintained an uninterrupted intimacy to the last of his life." Johnson, though no judge of art, respected his friend's genius, sitting to him several times,[1] and denouncing reluctance to sit for one's portrait as "an anfractuosity of the human mind." He even took up the cudgels for Sir Joshua's branch of art as contradistinguished from ideal and historical painting. "Genius," he said, "is chiefly exerted in historical pictures, and the art of the painter of portraits is often lost in the obscurity of his subject. But it is in painting as it is in life; what is greatest is not always best. I should grieve to see *Reynolds* transfer to heroes and to goddesses, to empty splendor and to airy fiction, that art which is now employed in diffusing friendship, in renewing tenderness, in quickening the affections of the absent, and continuing the presence of the dead." It was at Reynolds's house that the Doctor had his famous bout with the Dean of Derry, whom he grossly insulted. Naturally, the Dean lost his temper, which, as became his cloth, he afterwards regretted. He signified his admiration of the placid de-

[1] In the famous portrait in the National Gallery he is shown reading, with the book held close to the eyes after the manner of near-sighted people, — a mode of representation strenuously objected to by the philosopher. "It is not friendly," he said, "to hand down to posterity the imperfections of any man. . . . Let Sir Joshua do his worst, . . . he may paint himself as deaf as he chooses; but I will not be *Blinking Sam*." Upon some one else, however, remarking that the portrait lacked dignity, he growled out, "No, sir! the pencil of Reynolds never wanted dignity or the graces."

meanor of the painter under like trials in the following verses : —

> "Dear Knight of Plympton, teach me how
> To suffer with unclouded brow
> And smile serene as thine,
> The jest uncouth, and truth severe;
> Like thee to turn my deafest ear,
> And calmly drink my wine.
>
> "Thou say'st not only skill is gained
> But genius too may be attained
> By studious invitation;
> Thy temper mild, thy genius fine,
> I'll study till I make them mine
> By constant meditation."

With Goldsmith, Sir Joshua's relations were no less friendly. When the Royal Academy was founded the poet was, at his instance, appointed Professor of Ancient History, an honor which he thus amusingly mentioned in a letter to his brother : —

"The King has lately been pleased to make me Professor of Ancient History in a Royal Academy of Painting which he has just established; but there is no salary annexed, and I took it rather as a compliment to the Institution than any benefit to myself. Honors to one in my situation are something like ruffles to a man that wants a shirt."

Reynolds's portrait of the poet is an excellent example of his faculty of elevating his works by showing the sitters in their finer moods, — for there are moments when the plainest faces light into a sort of beauty, — preserving at the same time strict accuracy of likeness. Leslie called this portrait the most pathetic picture Reynolds ever painted, and he was right. It is not the childish "Goldy" of Boswell, the vagrant flute-player, the whimsical lodger who used to put the candle out by throwing his slipper at it, that the painter shows us; the cap and bells (so often associated with the profoundest pathos) are laid aside;

the cloud of folly, absurdity, caprice, seems to have fallen from him like a mantle; it is the patient, kindly scholar, the genius who left the nations in his debt, that looks out from the canvas.

Goldsmith inscribed "The Deserted Village" to Reynolds in the following touching words: "The only dedication I ever made was to my brother, because I loved him better than most other men. He is since dead. Permit me to inscribe this poem to you." Had Reynolds never limned a canvas these words should have kept his memory green. Goldsmith's last work — left unfinished — was the sportive epitaph which, Taylor thinks, will ever remain the best epitome of Sir Joshua's character. It reads as follows:

> "Here Reynolds is laid; and, to tell you my mind,
> He has not left a wiser or better behind.
> His pencil was striking, resistless, and grand;
> His manners were gentle, complying, and bland;
> Still born to improve us in every part, —
> His pencil our faces, his manners our heart.
> To coxcombs averse, yet most civilly steering,
> When they judged without skill he was still hard of hearing;
> When they talked of their Raphaels, Correggios, and stuff,
> He shifted his trumpet, and only took snuff."

Northcote says that on the day of Goldsmith's death Sir Joshua did not touch the pencil, — "a circumstance the most extraordinary for him, who passed no day without a line."[1]

Reynolds's character may be fitly summed up in the words of Edmund Burke, who said, "I do not know a fault or a weakness of his that he did not convert into something that bordered on a virtue, instead of pushing it to the confines of a vice."

---

[1] Some of Reynolds's friends used to remonstrate with him on his habit of working at his art on Sundays. Johnson's death-bed request to him was, never to paint on Sunday, to read his Bible often, and to forgive him a debt of £30.

Like all original thinkers, Sir Joshua Reynolds has been, to adapt the words of Falstaff, not only wise in himself, but the cause that wisdom is in other men, his discourses having long served as a quarry for subsequent builders, as well as a pretext for laborious comment and confutation. Their composer was too shining a mark to escape detraction; and the genial painter has even been made the victim of a phase of criticism that displays its acumen in beclouding the titles of authors to their own works, — a curious, and not very amiable "anfractuosity of the human mind," as Dr. Johnson might have said, which bred the suspicion that Sir Joshua Reynolds's discourses were the work of Burke, of Johnson, of any one, in fact, rather than of the man who claimed them, and to whom they were credited by the common sense of mankind. Death is thus armed with a new terror for authors; but, happily, in Sir Joshua's case the charge of imposture has been fully disproved.

In addition to their character as a collection of precepts and observations drawn from the experience of a great painter, the discourses embody a definite attempt at a philosophy of art, the first serious essay in the English language in the direction of æsthetic science; and it is, naturally, on their speculative side that they have provoked attack. Sir Joshua has been accused, not entirely without reason, of belittling personal greatness, of denying the existence of genius, or, what amounts to the same thing, of asserting that it may be acquired. The visionary Blake, to whom Reynolds's substitution of reason for rhapsody in æsthetic discussion was both distasteful and unintelligible, was specially bitter on this point. "Reynolds's opinion," he said, "was that genius may be taught, and all pretence to inspiration is a lie or a deceit, to say the least of it. If it is deceit, the whole Bible is madness." The famous Third Discourse Blake vehemently denounced as "particularly interesting to blockheads, as it endeavors to prove that there is no such thing as inspiration, and that any man of plain understanding may, by thieving from others, become a Michael Angelo." Again: "It is evident that Reynolds wished none but fools to be in the arts, and in order to compass this, he calls all others rogues, enthusiasts, or madmen. What has reasoning to do with the art of painting?" Reasoning had certainly very little to do with his own distempered productions, and the calm, philosophical Reynolds had certainly very little sympathy with mystics who ascribe to their own incoherent whimsies a divine origin; but that the strictures quoted are absurdly overstrained, those who read the discourses throughout, and fairly consider them as a whole, need not be told.

Still, there is color of truth in Blake's censures, and the casual reader is not unlikely to fall into his error as to Reynolds's idea of genius, — which, as interpreted by Blake, is certainly a comfortable one for the rank and file of mankind. The meaning of an author may be easily distorted by citing, or mistaken by reading, him in detached passages; and this is especially true of Reynolds, whose discourses were delivered at long intervals, and who, in those portions in which he assumes the dual rôle of speculative thinker and practical teacher, is occasionally led into inconsistencies. Reynolds the painter not infrequently qualifies the *dicta* of Reynolds the theorist; and it is only by reading him as a a whole that his real sense is to be got. At times, in his anxiety for the logical compactness of his scheme, he seems to justify the censures of Blake; while in the next sentence, perhaps, loosed from the meshes of his metaphysical web, he bows to the truth that every truly great art-product is the unique fruit of personal qualities which, it is infinity to one, will never be exactly repeated in an individual. That so sensible a man as Sir Joshua Reynolds really believed in the efficacy of his own system, or of any system whatsoever, to produce artistic figs from intellectual thistles, to transform the incipient daubers to whom he was trying to convey a proper conception of their art into Raphaels or Michael Angelos, is too absurd to be supposed for a moment. Indeed, he cautiously prefaces his famous definition of great art, to be quoted presently, by saying, "It is not easy to define in what this great style consists; nor to describe by words the proper means of acquiring it, *if the mind of the student should be at all capable of such an acquisition*," — a courteous but sufficiently forcible way of stating that in no event is one to expect the blast of a trumpet from a penny whistle. Touching this point, too, it is to be remembered that the lectures were primarily addressed to students, and it was a part of the speaker's duty to lay stress upon the potency of well-directed industry; and I may add that its noble results in his own case may stand as his best justification.

Reynolds's system is the reflection of his own career and character. He was an intellectual rather than an imaginative man, — a man accustomed to observe closely,[1] and to systematize his observations; his own art was largely the result of careful study and selection, a splendid victory of the will; and his mental complexion led him to believe — or, at least, when the brush was out of his hand, to believe that he believed — that "the whole beauty and grandeur of the art" could be reduced to a few set principles, and packed away snugly in a definition. Great art he held to be largely a matter of method and procedure; those who had attained it had obeyed certain rules and carried out certain principles; and to ascertain those rules and principles was the task he proposed to himself, — not that he hoped to formulate a recipe by which average men could produce the effects of genius, as Blake hints. Setting the wayfarer upon the high road is one thing; guaranteeing

[1] "I know no man who has passed through life with more observation than Sir Joshua Reynolds," said Johnson.

his arrival at his destination is quite another. "It needs a divine man to exhibit anything divine."

That Reynolds was far from underrating what was unique and unteachable in the genius of the great masters whose names were so often upon his lips, his writings testify. His profound veneration of Michael Angelo, for example, as expressed at the close of the last discourse, could scarcely have been due to a conception of Michael Angelo as a phenomenally industrious and methodical man. "Yet however unequal," he says, "I feel myself to that attempt, were I to begin the world again, I would tread in the steps of that great master; to kiss the hem of his garment, to catch the slightest of his perfections, would be glory and distinction enough for an ambitious man. I feel a self-congratulation in knowing myself capable of such sensations as he intended to excite.[1] I reflect, not without vanity, that these discourses bear testimony to my admiration of that truly divine man; and I should desire that the last words which I should pronounce in this Academy and from this place might be the name of *Michael Angelo*." These are not words of detraction.

Reynolds's theory as to the nature of great art was largely the fruit of his Italian studies, and may be described as the dawning consciousness in English art-criticism that there is an excellence in painting distinct from that belonging to manual skill; and that the tooth-drawings, fisticuffs, and boorish merrymakings of a Brouwer or a Teniers, exquisitely painted and, in their degree, desirable though they may be, do not fulfil the highest office of art. Greatness of style consisted essentially, he held, in a preference of the general to the particular; of the typical to the individual; in

---

[1] In his Roman notes Sir Joshua naïvely speaks of passing an entire day in the Sistine Chapel, "walking up and down it with great self-importance," glorying in the fact that he was able to comprehend the works of Michael Angelo.

the suppression of all incident and detail in favor of general harmony. Perfect beauty exists in the individual only in so far as the individual conforms to the type. As he expressed it, greatness of style lies "in being able to get above all singular forms, local customs, particularities, and details of every kind;" and the first study of the painter who aims at excellence should be the " long, laborious comparison " which, by "observing what any set of objects of the same kind have in common, has acquired the power of discerning what each wants in particular." The painter so equipped is "enabled to distinguish the accidental deficiencies, excrescences, and deformities of things from their general figures," and thus " makes out an abstract idea of their forms more perfect than any original."

To Reynolds, as we have seen, great art was but the lengthened shadow of the Italian masters; in their works alone were the elements of grandeur to be sought, and his definition of greatness of style is essentially a statement of the tendency of Latin, as distinguished from Saxon art, — its disposition to generalize, to soar into the abstract, to get above, or, at least, to get away from, the plain facts of actual life. One can fancy Reynolds, broadly speaking, to have reasoned the matter out in this way: Italian art is the only great art; Italian art generalizes; therefore, great art generalizes. From the art of a race and an epoch he extracted the spirit, and pronounced it the criterion of excellence for all races and all time. That there could be another phase of greatness, another field in which another type of genius could expatiate, does not seem to have occurred to him, — nor the folly of attempting to ingraft upon his countrymen ideals and aspirations as foreign to their dispositions as are the olive and the vine to their soil.

We need not enter here upon the old discussion of the relative merits of the two styles, the Latin and the Saxon, — one of those time-honored, futile questions in which, as

Sancho Panza sagely observed, "there is a great deal that may be said on both sides," and in respect of which no human being was ever yet brought by force of logic to change his opinion. This much is certain, the world's greatness is not of one race or period, nor is true greatness even a reflected light; "whatever is to be truly great and truly affecting must have on it the strong stamp of the native land."

To accept Reynolds's standard literally would be to exclude from the pale of great art a multitude of works — his own certainly included — justly reckoned among the glories of painting, and to confine the term to a grand but narrow class best exemplified by the works of Michael Angelo and a few incomparable fragments of Greek sculpture. His definition is insufficient rather than wholly false, for it touches a vital characteristic of a great class, and dimly foreshadows the truth as to detail in art, — that high art "gets above," not the details themselves, but the paltry use of them, the treating them as an end rather than a means; for genius is as "the wind which bloweth where it listeth," making free use of even "all singular forms, local customs, particularities, and details of every kind," whenever they may be made to serve its purposes.

It may, perhaps, be argued in support of Reynolds's views that the *greatest examples* of great art have been wrought out upon principles identical with or analogous to those he advances. That there may be, when the hand of the workman is fitted to the task, an added grandeur due to the departure from the individual and the approach to the type, one cannot but feel when comparing certain masterpieces that conform to his rule with kindred representations that do not. Compare, for example, the Venus de Milo, that highly artificial synthesis in marble of womanly perfections, with the coquettishly beautiful Queen of the Tribuna, the Venus de Medicis. There can be no doubt in which of these two cases the sculptor has held to the rule that "nature herself is not to be too closely imitated." In the former work one sees, not portraiture, but the result of a deliberate selective process, the material embodiment of an ideal; it is not the wanton Aphrodite whom Vulcan snared in his net amid the laughter of high Olympus, but a goddess divinely unconscious of the passions over which she presides, — the ideal of Lucretius, "the desired of men and gods, the universal mother, who beneath the circling stars gives increase to the ship-bearing sea, gives increase to the earth the mother of harvests, and favors the conception of every living creature, and their birth into the light of day." The Medicean Venus is simply the model transferred to marble, a beautiful woman — her individuality emphasized by the immodestly modest attitude and modishly dressed hair — posing as Aphrodite; some forgotten Phryne, perhaps, who still

> "loves in stone, and fills
> The air around with beauty."

The spirit that informs Sir Joshua Reynolds's discourses is a noble one. Aim at the highest, — "hitch your wagon to a star," — is the burden of his counsel. He has left an eloquent and convincing plea for mind in the arts; for the strangely controverted truth that the painter's work — leaving for the moment executive merit out of the count — rises in quality with the degree of taste, culture, intellectual power it exhibits. Given two men of like manual dexterity, it is the one whose mind is enriched with the fruits of a liberal culture that will climb the higher. To insist upon intellectual quality as the final test; to adopt the rule that "the art is greatest which includes the greatest ideas,"[1] is not to detract from technical skill, but to presuppose it. In art or in literature the expression of great ideas implies

[1] Ruskin.

grandeur of diction, and a consummate power over materials or words, without which the genius of a Raphael or a Francia, a Milton or a Byron would be inarticulate and null.

On the other hand, a high degree of technical merit may exist in a work which a man like Reynolds would not hesitate to pronounce despicable, and hopelessly outside the pale of the fine arts. To cite a very moderate example: "A few years ago," says Professor Middleton, "a gold medal was won at the Paris *salon* by a naturalist picture, a masterpiece of technical skill. It represented Job as an emaciated old man covered with ulcers, carefully studied in Paris hospitals for skin diseases." As a piece of *technique* this normal fruit of a deplorable canon of artistic criticism may have been as perfect as the "Transfiguration;" we may admit that it was so, and yet blush to institute, even for the sake of illustration, the comparison between them.

Sir Joshua Reynolds set his standards high, — much too high for average human achievement; and, in his exaltation of the Grand Style he would seem to have forgotten that the snow-clad peaks, the glacier regions of solitary grandeur, to which he pointed the gaze and ambition of the student, tower remotely above the real interests and affections of men; that the teeming valleys below the regions of eternal snow are infinitely richer in the elements of human sympathy and enjoyment.

Sublime as he was, and, in his province and degree, incomparably great, there are few of us, I think, who do not turn with heart-felt if shame-faced pleasure from the chilling intellectual sublimity of a Michael Angelo to the gentler graces, the sweet humanity, and familiar charm of a Gainsborough, a Steen, a Wilkie, a REYNOLDS.

E. G. J.

July 16, 1891.

Mrs. Siddons as the Tragic Muse.

SIR JOSHUA REYNOLDS'S DISCOURSES.

DISCOURSE I.

Delivered at the Opening of the Royal Academy, January 2, 1769.

THE ADVANTAGES PROCEEDING FROM THE INSTITUTION OF A ROYAL ACADEMY. — HINTS OFFERED TO THE CONSIDERATION OF THE PROFESSORS AND VISITORS. — THAT AN IMPLICIT OBEDIENCE TO THE RULES OF ART BE EXACTED FROM THE YOUNG STUDENTS. — THAT A PREMATURE DISPOSITION TO A MASTERLY DEXTERITY BE REPRESSED. — THAT DILIGENCE BE CONSTANTLY RECOMMENDED, AND (THAT IT MAY BE EFFECTUAL) DIRECTED TO ITS PROPER OBJECT.

AN academy in which the polite arts may be regularly cultivated is at last opened among us by royal munificence. This must appear an event in the highest degree interesting, not only to the artist, but to the whole nation.

It is, indeed, difficult to give any other reason why an empire like that of Britain should so long have wanted an ornament so suitable to its greatness, than that slow progression of things which naturally makes elegance and refinement the last effect of opulence and power.

An institution like this has often been recommended upon considerations merely mercantile; but an academy founded upon such principles can never effect even its own narrow purposes. If it has an origin no higher, no taste can ever be formed in manufactures; but if the higher arts of design flourish, these inferior ends will be answered of course.

We are happy in having a prince who has conceived the design of such an institution according to its true dignity, and who promotes the arts as the head of a great, a learned, a polite, and a commercial nation; and I can now congratulate you, gentlemen, on the accomplishment of your long and ardent wishes.

The numberless and ineffectual consultations which I have had with many in this assembly to form plans and concert schemes for an academy afford a sufficient proof of the impossibility of succeeding but by the influence of Majesty. But there have, perhaps, been times when even the influence of Majesty would have been ineffectual; and it is pleasing to reflect that we are thus embodied when every circumstance seems to concur from which honor and prosperity can probably arise.

There are at this time a greater number of excellent artists than were ever known before at one period in this nation; there is a general desire among our nobility to be distinguished as lovers and judges of the arts; there is a greater superfluity of wealth among the people to reward the professors; and, above all, we are patronized by a monarch who, knowing the value of science and of elegance, thinks every art worthy of his notice that tends to soften and humanize the mind.

After so much has been done by His Majesty it will be wholly our fault if our progress is not in some degree correspondent to the wisdom and generosity of the institution. Let us show our gratitude in our diligence, that, though our merit may not answer his expectations, yet, at least, our industry may deserve his protection.

But whatever may be our proportion of success, of this we may be sure, that the present institution will at least contribute to advance our knowledge of the arts, and bring us nearer to that ideal excellence which it is the lot of genius always to contemplate, and never to attain.

The principal advantage of an academy is that, besides furnishing able men to direct the student, it will be a repository for the great examples of the art. These are the materials on which genius is to work, and without which the strongest intellect may be fruitlessly or deviously employed. By studying these authentic models that idea of excellence which is the result of the accumulated experience of past ages may be at once acquired; and the tardy and obstructed progress of our predecessors may teach us a shorter and easier way. The student receives at one glance the principles which many artists have spent their whole lives in ascertaining; and, satisfied with their effect, is spared the painful investigation by which they came to be known and fixed. How many men of great natural abilities have been lost to this nation for want of these advantages! They never had an opportunity of seeing those masterly efforts of genius which at once kindle the whole soul and force it into sudden and irresistible approbation.

Raphael, it is true, had not the advantage of studying in an academy; but all Rome, and the works of Michael Angelo in particular, were to him an academy. On the sight of the Capella Sistina, he immediately, from a dry, Gothic, and even insipid manner, which attends to the minute accidental discriminations of particular and individual objects, assumed that grand style of painting which improves partial representation by the general and invariable ideas of nature.

Every seminary of learning may be said to be surrounded with an atmosphere of floating knowledge, where every mind may imbibe somewhat congenial to its own original conceptions. Knowledge thus obtained has always something more popular and useful than that which is forced upon the mind by private precepts or solitary meditation. Besides, it is generally found that a youth more easily receives instruction from the companions of his studies, whose minds are nearly on a level with his own, than from those who are much his superiors; and it is from his equals only that he catches the fire of emulation.

One advantage, I will venture to affirm, we shall have in our Academy which no other nation can boast; we shall have nothing to unlearn. To this praise the present race of artists have a just claim. As far as they have yet proceeded, they are right. With us the exertions of genius will henceforward be directed to their proper objects. It will not be as it has been in other schools, where he that travelled fastest only wandered farthest from the right way.

Impressed as I am, therefore, with such a favorable opinion of my associates in this undertaking, it would ill become me to dictate to any of them. But as these institutions have so often failed in other nations, and as it is natural to think with regret how much might have been done, I must take leave to offer a few hints by which those errors may be rectified, and those defects supplied. These the professors and visitors may reject or adopt as they shall think proper.

I would chiefly recommend that an implicit obedience to the *Rules of Art*, as established by the practice of the great masters, should be exacted from the *young* students, — that those models which have passed through the approbation of ages should be considered by them as perfect and infallible guides; as subjects for their imitation, not their criticism.

I am confident that this is the only efficacious method of making a progress in the arts; and that he who sets out with doubting will find life finished before he becomes master of the rudiments. For it may be laid down as a maxim that he who begins by presuming on his own sense has ended his studies as soon as he has commenced them. Every opportunity, therefore, should be taken to discountenance that false and vulgar opinion, that rules are the fetters of genius; they are fetters only to men of no genius, — as that armor which upon the strong is an ornament and a defence, upon the weak and misshapen becomes a load, and cripples the body which it was made to protect.

How much liberty may be taken to break through those rules, and, as the poet expresses it,

"To snatch a grace beyond the reach of art,"

may be a subsequent consideration, when the pupils become masters themselves. It is then, when their genius has received its utmost improvement, that rules may possibly be dispensed with. But let us not destroy the scaffold until we have raised the building.

The directors ought more particularly to watch over the genius of those students who, being more advanced, are arrived at that critical period of study on the nice management of which their future turn of taste depends. At that age it is natural for them to be more captivated with what is brilliant than with what is solid, and to prefer splendid negligence to painful and humiliating exactness.

A facility in composing, a lively, and what is called a masterly, handling of the chalk or pencil, are, it must be confessed, captivating qualities to young minds, and become, of course, the objects of their ambition. They endeavor to imitate these dazzling excellences which they will find no great labor in attaining. After much time spent in these frivolous pursuits, the difficulty will be to retreat; but it will be then too late; and there is scarce an instance of return to scrupulous labor after the mind has been debauched and deceived by this fallacious mastery.

By this useless industry they are excluded from all power of advancing in real excellence. While boys they are arrived at their utmost perfection; they have taken the shadow for the substance, and make the mechanical felicity the chief excellence of the art, which is only an ornament, and of the merit of which few but painters themselves are judges.

This seems to me to be one of the most dangerous sources of corruption; and I speak of it from experience, not as an error which may possibly happen, but which has actually infected all foreign academies. The directors were probably pleased with this premature dexterity in their pupils, and praised their despatch at the expense of their correctness.

But young men have not only this frivolous ambition of being thought masters of execution inciting them on one hand, but also their natural sloth tempting them on the other. They are terrified at the prospect before them of the toil required to attain exactness. The impetuosity of youth is disgusted at the slow approaches of a regular siege, and desires, from mere impatience of labor, to take the citadel by storm. They wish to find some shorter path to excellence, and hope to obtain the reward of eminence by other means than those which the indispensable rules of art have prescribed. They must, therefore, be told again and again that labor is the only price of solid fame, and that whatever their force of genius may be, there is no easy method of becoming a good painter.

When we read the lives of the most eminent painters every page informs us that no part of their time was spent in dissipation. Even an increase of fame served only to augment their industry. To be convinced with what persevering assiduity they pursued their studies, we need only reflect on their method of proceeding in their most celebrated works. When they conceived a subject, they first made a variety of sketches; then a finished drawing of the whole; after that a more correct drawing of every separate part, — heads, hands, feet, and pieces of drapery; they then painted the picture, and after all, retouched it from the life. The pictures thus wrought with such pains now appear like the effect of enchantment, and as if some mighty genius had struck them off at a blow.

But, while diligence is thus recommended to the students, the visitors will take care that their diligence be effectual; that it be well directed, and employed on the proper object. A student is not always advancing because he is employed; he must apply his strength to that part of the art where the real difficulties lie, — to that part which distinguishes it as a liberal art; and not by mistaken industry lose his time in that which is merely ornamental. The students, instead of vying with each other which shall have the readiest hand, should be taught to contend who shall have the purest and most correct outline; instead of striving which shall produce the brightest tint, or, curiously trifling, shall give the gloss of stuffs so as to appear real, let their ambition be directed to contend which shall dispose his drapery in the most graceful folds, which shall give the most grace and dignity to the human figure.

I must beg leave to submit one thing more to the consideration of the visitors, which appears to me a matter of very great consequence, and the omission of which I think a principal defect in the method of education pursued in all the academies I have ever visited. The error I mean is that the students never draw exactly from the living models which they have before them. It is not, indeed, their intention, nor are they directed to do it. Their drawings resemble the model only in the attitude. They change the form according to their vague and uncertain ideas of beauty, and make a drawing rather of what they think the figure ought to be than of what it appears. I have thought this the obstacle that has stopped the progress of many young men of real genius; and I very much doubt whether a habit of drawing correctly what we see will not give a proportionable power of drawing correctly what we imagine. He who endeavors to copy nicely the figure before him not only acquires a habit of exactness and precision, but is continually advancing in his knowledge of the human figure; and though he seems to superficial observers to make a slower progress, he will be found at last capable of adding (without running into capricious wildness) that grace and beauty which is necessary to be given to his more finished works, and which cannot be got by the moderns, as it was not acquired by the ancients, but by an attentive and well-compared study of the human form.

What I think ought to enforce this method is that it has been the practice (as may be seen by their drawings) of the great masters in the art. I will mention a drawing of Raphael, "The Dispute of the Sacrament," the print of which, by Count Caylus, is in every hand. It appears that he made his sketch from one model; and the habit he had of drawing exactly from the form before him appears by his making all the figures with the same cap, such as his model then happened to wear; so servile a copyist was this great man, even at a time when he was allowed to be at his highest pitch of excellence. I have seen also academy figures by Annibale Caracci, though he was often sufficiently licentious in his finished works, drawn with all the peculiarities of an individual model.

This scrupulous exactness is so contrary to the practice of the academies that it is not without great deference that I beg leave to recommend it to the consideration of the visitors, and submit to them whether the neglect of this method is not one of the reasons why students so often disappoint expectation, and, being more than boys at sixteen, become less than men at thirty.

In short, the method I recommend can only be detrimental where there are but few living forms to copy; for then students, by always drawing from one alone, will by habit be taught to overlook defects and mistake deformity for beauty. But of this there is no danger, since the council has determined to supply the academy with a variety of subjects; and indeed those laws which they have drawn up, and which the secretary will presently read for your confirmation, have in some measure precluded me from saying more upon this occasion. Instead, therefore, of offering my advice, permit me to indulge my wishes, and express my hope, that this institution may answer the expectation of its ROYAL FOUNDER; that the present age may vie in arts with that of LEO the Tenth; and that the dignity of the dying art (to make use of an expression of Pliny) may be revived under the Reign of George III.

The Age of Innocence.

DISCOURSE II.

Delivered to the Students of the Royal Academy, on the Distribution of the Prizes, December 11, 1769.

THE COURSE AND ORDER OF STUDY. — THE DIFFERENT STAGES OF ART. — MUCH COPYING DISCOUNTENANCED. — THE ARTIST AT ALL TIMES AND IN ALL PLACES SHOULD BE EMPLOYED IN LAYING UP MATERIALS FOR THE EXERCISE OF HIS ART.

I CONGRATULATE you on the honor which you have just received. I have the highest opinion of your merits, and could wish to show my sense of them in something which possibly may be more useful to you than barren praise. I could wish to lead you into such a course of study as may render your future progress answerable to your past improvement, and while I applaud you for what has been done, remind you how much yet remains to attain perfection.

I flatter myself that from the long experience I have had, and the unceasing assiduity with which I have pursued those studies in which, like you, I have been engaged, I shall be acquitted of vanity in offering some hints to your consideration. They are, indeed, in a great degree, founded upon my own mistakes in the same pursuit. But the history of errors, properly managed, often shortens the road to truth. And although no method of study that I can offer will of itself conduct to excellence, yet it may preserve industry from being misapplied.

In speaking to you of the theory of the art, I shall only consider it as it has a relation to the *method* of your studies.

Dividing the study of painting into three distinct periods, I shall address you as having passed through the first of them, which is confined to the rudiments; including a facility of drawing any object that presents itself, a tolerable readiness in the management of colors, and an acquaintance with the most simple and obvious rules of composition.

This first degree of proficiency is, in painting, what grammar is in literature, a general preparation for whatever species of the art the student may afterwards choose for his more particular application. The power of drawing, modelling, and using colors is very properly called the language of the art, and in this language the honors you have just received prove you to have made no inconsiderable progress.

When the artist is once enabled to express himself with some degree of correctness, he must then endeavor to collect subjects for expression, — to amass a stock of ideas, to be combined and varied as occasion may require. He is now in the second period of study, in which his business is to learn all that has been known and done before his own time. Having hitherto received instructions from a particular master, he is now to consider the art itself as his master. He must extend his capacity to more sublime and general instructions. Those perfections which lie scattered among various masters are now united in one general idea, which is henceforth to regulate his taste and enlarge his imagination. With a variety of models thus before him he will avoid that narrowness and poverty of conception which attends a bigoted admiration of a single master, and will cease to follow any favorite where he ceases to excel. This period is, however, still a time of subjection and discipline. Though the student will not resign himself blindly to any single authority when he may have the advantage of consulting many, he must still be afraid of trusting his own judgment and of deviating into any track where he cannot find the footsteps of some former master.

The third and last period emancipates the student from subjection to any authority but what he shall himself judge to be supported by reason. Confiding now in his own judgment, he will consider and separate those different principles to which different modes of beauty owe their original. In the former period he sought only to know and combine excellence, wherever it was to be found, into one idea of perfection; in this he learns, what requires the most attentive survey and the most subtle disquisition, to discriminate perfections that are incompatible with each other.

He is from this time to regard himself as holding the same rank with those masters whom he before obeyed as teachers, and as exercising a sort of sovereignty over those rules which have hitherto restrained him. Comparing now no longer the performances of art with each other, but examining the art itself by the standard of nature, he corrects what is erroneous, supplies what is scanty, and adds by his own observation what the industry of his predecessors may have yet left wanting to perfection. Having well established his judgment and stored his memory, he may now without fear try the power of his imagination. The mind that has been thus disciplined may be indulged in the warmest enthusiasm, and venture to play on the borders of the wildest extravagance. The habitual dignity which long converse with the greatest minds has imparted to him will display itself in all his attempts; and he will stand among his instructors, not as an imitator, but a rival.

These are the different stages of the art. But as I now address myself particularly to those students who have been this day rewarded for their happy passage through the first period, I can with no propriety suppose they want any help in the initiatory studies. My present design is to direct your view to distant excellence, and to show you the readiest path that leads to it. Of this I shall speak with such latitude as may leave the province of the professor uninvaded; and shall not anticipate those precepts which it is his business to give and your duty to understand.

It is indisputably evident that a great part of every man's life must be employed in collecting materials for the exercise of genius. Invention, strictly speaking, is little more than a new combination of those images which have been previously gathered and deposited in the memory. Nothing can come of nothing; he who has laid up no materials can produce no combinations.[1]

---

[1] Of the speaker's own art, in contradistinction to that of Gainsborough, a French critic says: "It is by the artifice of a perfected

A student unacquainted with the attempts of former adventurers is always apt to overrate his own abilities, — to mistake the most trifling excursions for discoveries of moment, and every coast new to him for a new-found country. If by chance he passes beyond his usual limits, he congratulates his own arrival at those regions which they who have steered a better course have long left behind them.

The productions of such minds are seldom distinguished by an air of originality; they are anticipated in their happiest efforts; and if they are found to differ in any thing from their predecessors, it is only in irregular sallies and trifling conceits. The more extensive, therefore, your acquaintance is with the works of those who have excelled, the more extensive will be your powers of invention; and what may appear still more like a paradox, the more original will be your conceptions. But the difficulty on this occasion is to determine what ought to be proposed as models of excellence, and who ought to be considered as the properest guides.

To a young man just arrived in Italy, many of the present painters of that country are ready enough to obtrude their precepts, and to offer their own performances as examples of that perfection which they affect to recommend. The modern, however, who recommends himself as a standard, may justly be suspected as ignorant of the true end, and unacquainted

science that Reynolds obtains such striking effects in his portraits. He forged for his own use a complete armory of weapons, a magazine of rules and well tried systems, which he had gathered and selected by a careful study of the old masters." — CHESNEAU, *English Painting*.

with the proper object, of the art which he professes. To follow such a guide will not only retard the student, but mislead him.

On whom, then, can he rely, or who shall show him the path that leads to excellence? The answer is obvious: those great masters who have travelled the same road with success are the most likely to conduct others. The works of those who have stood the test of ages have a claim to that respect and veneration to which no modern can pretend. The duration and stability of their fame is sufficient to evince that it has not been suspended upon the slender thread of fashion and caprice, but bound to the human heart by every tie of sympathetic approbation.

There is no danger of studying too much the works of those great men; but how they may be studied to advantage is an inquiry of great importance.

Some who have never raised their minds to the consideration of the real dignity of the art, and who rate the works of an artist in proportion as they excel or are defective in the mechanical parts, look on theory as something that may enable them to talk but not to paint better; and confining themselves entirely to mechanical practice, very assiduously toil on in the drudgery of copying, and think they make a rapid progress while they faithfully exhibit the minutest part of a favorite picture. This appears to me a very tedious, and, I think, a very erroneous method of proceeding. Of every large composition, even of those which are most admired, a great part may be truly said to be *commonplace*. This, though it takes up much time in copying, conduces little to improvement. I consider general copying as a delusive kind of industry: the student satisfies himself with the appearance of doing something; he falls into the dangerous habit of imitating without selecting, and of laboring without any determinate object; as it requires no effort of the mind, he sleeps over his work; and those powers of invention and composition which ought particularly to be called out and put in action, lie torpid and lose their energy for want of exercise.

How incapable those are of producing anything of their own who have spent much of their time in making finished copies, is well known to all who are conversant with our art.

To suppose that the complication of powers and variety of ideas necessary to that mind which aspires to the first honors in the art of painting can be obtained by the frigid contemplation of a few single models, is no less absurd than it would be in him who wishes to be a poet to imagine that by translatting a tragedy he can acquire to himself sufficient knowledge of the appearances of nature, the operations of the passions, and the incidents of life.

The great use in copying, if it be at all useful, should seem to be in learning to color; yet even coloring will never be perfectly attained by servilely copying the model before you. An eye critically nice can only be formed by observing well-colored pictures with attention; and by close inspection and minute examination you will discover, at last, the manner of handling, the artifices of contrast, glazing, and other expedients by which good colorists have raised the value of their tints, and by which nature has been so happily imitated.

I must inform you, however, that old pictures, deservedly celebrated for their coloring, are often so changed by dirt and varnish that we ought not to wonder if they do not appear equal to their reputation in the eyes of unexperienced painters, or young students. An artist whose judgment is matured by long observation considers rather what the picture once was than what it is at present. He has by habit acquired a power of seeing the brilliancy of tints through the cloud by which it is obscured. An exact imitation, therefore, of those pictures is likely to fill the student's mind with false opinions, and to send him back a colorist of his own formation, with ideas equally remote from nature and from art, from the genuine practice of the masters and the real appearances of things.

Following these rules, and using these precautions, when you have clearly and distinctly learned in what good coloring consists, you cannot do better than have recourse to nature herself, who is always at hand, and in comparison of whose true splendor the best-colored pictures are but faint and feeble.

However, as the practice of copying is not entirely to be excluded, since the mechanical practice of painting is learned in some measure by it, let those choice parts only be selected which have recommended the work to notice. If its excellence consists in its general effect, it would be proper to make slight sketches of the machinery and general management of the picture. Those sketches should be kept always by you for the regulation of your style. Instead of copying the touches of those great masters, copy only their conceptions. Instead of treading in their footsteps, endeavor only to keep the same road. Labor to invent on their general principles and way of thinking. Possess yourself with their spirit. Consider with yourself how a Michael Angelo or a Raphael would have treated this subject, and work yourself into a belief that your picture is to be seen and criticised by them when completed. Even an attempt of this kind will rouse your powers.

But as mere enthusiasm will carry you but a little way, let me recommend a practice that may be equivalent to and will, perhaps, more efficaciously contribute to your advancement than even the verbal corrections of those masters themselves, could they be obtained. What I would propose is that you should enter into a kind of competition, by painting a similar subject, and making a companion to any picture that you consider as a model. After you have finished your work, place it near the model, and compare them carefully together. You will then not only see but feel your own deficiencies more sensibly than by precepts or any other means of instruction. The true principles of painting will mingle with your thoughts. Ideas thus fixed by sensible objects will be certain and definitive, and sinking deep into the mind will not only be more just but more lasting than those presented to you by precepts only, which will always be fleeting, variable, and undetermined.

This method of comparing your own efforts with

those of some great master is, indeed, a severe and mortifying task, to which none will submit but such as have great views, with fortitude sufficient to forego the gratifications of present vanity for future honor. When the student has succeeded in some measure to his own satisfaction, and has felicitated himself on his success, to go voluntarily to a tribunal where he knows his vanity must be humbled, and all self-approbation must vanish, requires not only great resolution but great humility. To him, however, who has the ambition to be a real master, the solid satisfaction which proceeds from a consciousness of his advancement (of which seeing his own faults is the first step) will very abundantly compensate for the mortification of present disappointment. There is, besides, this alleviating circumstance: every discovery he makes, every acquisition of knowledge he attains, seems to proceed from his own sagacity; and thus he acquires a confidence in himself sufficient to keep up the resolution of perseverance.

We all must have experienced how lazily, and consequently how ineffectually, instruction is received when forced upon the mind by others. Few have been taught to any purpose who have not been their own teachers. We prefer those instructions which we have given ourselves, from our affection to the instructor; and they are more effectual from being received into the mind at the very time when it is most open and eager to receive them.

With respect to the pictures that you are to choose for your models, I could wish that you would take the world's opinion rather than your own. In other words, I would have you choose those of established reputation rather than follow your own fancy. If you should not admire them at first, you will, by endeavoring to imitate them, find that the world has not been mistaken.

It is not an easy task to point out those various excellences for your imitation which lie distributed among the various schools. An endeavor to do this may, perhaps, be the subject of some future discourse. I will, therefore, at present, only recommend a model for style in painting, which is a branch of the art more immediately necessary to the young student. Style in painting[1] is the same as in writing, a power over materials, whether words or colors, by which conceptions or sentiments are conveyed. And in this Ludovico Caracci (I mean in his best works) appears to me to approach the nearest to perfection.[2] His unaffected breadth of light and shadow, the simplicity of coloring, which, holding its proper rank, does not draw aside the least part of the attention

---

[1] The following definition is merely technical; in the Third Discourse Reynolds approaches the subject on its intellectual side.

[2] Sir Joshua throughout overrates the Caraccis. Ludovico (1555–1619), with his cousins Agostino and Annibale, founded the Bolognese Eclectic school, which includes Guido Reni, Domenichino, Sassoferrato, and Guercino. As Agostino said, their object was to "acquire the design of Rome, Venetian action and Venetian management of shade, the dignified color of Lombardy, the terrible manner of Michael Angelo, Titian's truth and nature, the sovereign purity of Correggio's style, and the just symmetry of Raphael," — briefly, to select and unite the salient merits of earlier schools; a vaulting ambition, which, as Symonds puts it, "doomed their style to the sterility of hybrids." Let us not, however, underrate these once belauded, now vituperated painters, who, while they fell short of excellence, left many works that refuse to be dogmatized into contempt.

from the subject, and the solemn effect of that twilight which seems diffused over his pictures, appear to me to correspond with grave and dignified subjects better than the more artificial brilliancy of sunshine which enlightens the pictures of Titian, — though Tintoret thought that Titian's coloring was the model of perfection, and would correspond even with the sublime of Michael Angelo; and that if Angelo had colored like Titian, or Titian designed like Angelo, the world would once have had a perfect painter.

It is our misfortune, however, that those works of Caracci which I would recommend to the student are not often found out of Bologna. The "Saint Francis in the Midst of his Friars," "The Transfiguration," "The Birth of Saint John the Baptist," "The Calling of Saint Matthew," the "Saint Jerome," the fresco paintings in the Zampieri palace, are all worthy the attention of the student. And I think those who travel would do well to allot a much greater portion of their time to that city than it has been hitherto the custom to bestow.

In this art, as in others, there are many teachers who profess to show the nearest way to excellence; and many expedients have been invented by which the toil of study might be saved. But let no man be seduced to idleness by specious promises. Excellence is never granted to man but as the reward of labor. It argues, indeed, no small strength of mind to persevere in habits of industry, without the pleasure of perceiving those advances; which, like the hands of a clock, while they make hourly approaches to their point, yet proceed so slowly as to escape observation. A facility of drawing, like that of playing upon a musical instrument, cannot be acquired but by an infinite number of acts. I need not, therefore, enforce by many words the necessity of continual application, nor tell you that the porte-crayon ought to be forever in your hands. Various methods will occur to you by which this power may be acquired. I would particularly recommend that after your return from the Academy (where I suppose your attendance to be constant), you would endeavor to draw the figure by memory. I will even venture to add that by perseverance in this custom you will become able to draw the human figure tolerably correctly, with as little effort of the mind as is required to trace with a pen the letters of the alphabet.

That this facility is not unattainable, some members in this Academy give a sufficient proof. And be assured that if this power is not acquired while you are young, there will be no time for it afterwards; at least, the attempt will be attended with as much difficulty as those experience who learn to read or write after they have arrived at the age of maturity.

But while I mention the porte-crayon as the student's constant companion, he must still remember that the pencil is the instrument by which he must hope to obtain eminence. What, therefore, I wish to impress upon you is that, whenever an opportunity offers, you paint your studies instead of drawing them. This will give you such a facility in using colors that in time they will arrange themselves under the pencil, even without the attention of the hand that conducts it. If one act excluded the other, this advice could not with any propriety be given. But if painting comprises both drawing and coloring, and if, by a short struggle of resolute industry, the same expedition is attainable in painting as in drawing on paper, I cannot see what objection can justly be made to the practice, or why that should be done by parts which may be done all together.

If we turn our eyes to the several schools of painting, and consider their respective excellences, we shall find that those who excel most in coloring pursued this method. The Venetian and Flemish schools, which owe much of their fame to coloring, have enriched the cabinets of the collectors of drawings with very few examples. Those of Titian, Paul Veronese, Tintoret, and the Bassans, are in general slight and undetermined. Their sketches on paper are as rude as their pictures are excellent in regard to harmony of coloring. Correggio and Baroccio have left few, if any, finished drawings behind them. And in the Flemish school Rubens and Vandyck made their designs for the most part either in colors or in chiaroscuro. It is as common to find studies of the Venetian and Flemish painters on canvas as of the schools of Rome and Florence on paper. Not but that many finished drawings are sold under the names of those masters. Those, however, are undoubtedly the productions either of engravers or their scholars, who copied their works.

These instructions I have ventured to offer from my own experience; but as they deviate widely from received opinions I offer them with diffidence, and when better are suggested shall retract them without regret.

There is one precept, however, in which I shall only be opposed by the vain, the ignorant, and the idle. I am not afraid that I shall repeat it too often. You must have no dependence on your own genius. If you have great talents industry will improve them; if you have but moderate abilities industry will supply their deficiency. Nothing is denied to well-directed labor; nothing is to be obtained without it. Not to enter into metaphysical discussions on the nature or essence of genius, I will venture to assert that assiduity unabated by difficulty, and a disposition eagerly directed to the object of its pursuit, will produce effects similar to those which some call the result of natural powers.[1]

Though a man cannot at all times and in all places paint or draw, yet the mind can prepare itself by laying in proper materials at all times and in all places. Both Livy and Plutarch, in describing Philopœmen, one of the ablest generals of antiquity, have given us a striking picture of a mind always intent on its profession, and by assiduity obtaining those excellences which some all their lives vainly expect from nature. I shall quote the passage in Livy at length, as it runs parallel with the practice I would recommend to the painter, sculptor, and architect: —

---

[1] "The true genius is a mind of large general powers, accidentally determined to some particular direction. Sir Joshua Reynolds, the great painter of the present age, had the first fondness for his art excited by the perusal of Richardson's treatise." — DR. JOHNSON, *Life of Cowley.*

"Philopœmen was a man eminent for his sagacity and experience in choosing ground, and in leading armies; to which he formed his mind by perpetual meditation, in times of peace as well as war. When in any occasional journey he came to a strait, difficult passage, if he was alone he considered with himself, and if he was in company he asked his friends what it would be best to do if in this place they had found an enemy, either in the front or in the rear, on the one side or on the other. 'It might happen,' says he, 'that the enemy to be opposed might come on drawn up in regular lines, or in a tumultuous body formed only by the nature of the place.' He then considered a little what ground he should take; what number of soldiers he should use, and what arms he should give them; where he should lodge his carriages, his baggage, and the defenceless followers of his camp; how many guards, and of what kind, he should send to defend them; and whether it would be better to press forward along the pass, or recover by retreat his former station. He would consider likewise where his camp could most commodiously be formed; how much ground he should enclose within his trenches; where he should have the convenience of water, and where he might find plenty of wood and forage; and when he should break up his camp on the following day, through what road he could most safely pass, and in what form he should dispose his troops. With such thoughts and disquisitions he had from his early years so exercised his mind that on these occasions nothing could happen which he had not been already accustomed to consider."

I cannot help imagining that I see a promising young painter equally vigilant, whether at home or abroad, in the streets or in the fields. Every object that presents itself is to him a lesson. He regards all nature with a view to his profession, and combines her beauties or corrects her defects. He examines the countenances of men under the influence of passion, and often catches the most pleasing hints from subjects of turbulence or deformity. Even bad pictures themselves supply him with useful documents; and, as Leonardo da Vinci has observed, he improves upon the fanciful images that are sometimes seen in the fire, or are accidentally sketched upon a discolored wall.

The artist who has his mind thus filled with ideas, and his hand made expert by practice, works with ease and readiness; while he who would have you believe that he is waiting for the inspirations of genius is in reality at a loss how to begin, and is at last delivered of his monsters with difficulty and pain.

The well-grounded painter, on the contrary, has only maturely to consider his subject, and all the mechanical parts of his art follow without his exertion. Conscious of the difficulty of obtaining what he possesses, he makes no pretensions to secrets, except those of closer application. Without conceiving the smallest jealousy against others, he is contented that all shall be as great as himself who have undergone the same fatigue; and as his pre-eminence depends not upon a trick, he is free from the painful suspicions of a juggler who lives in perpetual fear lest his trick should be discovered.

Miss Kitty Fisher as Cleopatra.

DISCOURSE III.

Delivered to the Students of the Royal Academy, on the Distribution of the Prizes, December 14, 1770.

THE GREAT LEADING PRINCIPLES OF THE GRAND STYLE. — OF BEAUTY. — THE GENUINE HABITS OF NATURE TO BE DISTINGUISHED FROM THOSE OF FASHION.

IT is not easy to speak with propriety to so many students of different ages and different degrees of advancement. The mind requires nourishment adapted to its growth; and what may have promoted our earlier efforts might retard us in our nearer approaches to perfection.

The first endeavors of a young painter, as I have remarked in a former discourse, must be employed in the attainment of mechanical dexterity, and confined to the mere imitation of the object before him. Those who have advanced beyond the rudiments may, perhaps, find advantage in reflecting on the advice which I have likewise given them, when I recommended the diligent study of the works of our great predecessors; but I at the same time endeavored to guard them against an implicit submission to the authority of any one master, however excellent, or, by a strict imitation of his manner, precluding themselves from the abundance and variety of nature. I will now add that nature herself is not to be too closely copied. There are excellences in the art of painting beyond what is commonly called the imitation of nature, and these excellences I wish to point out. The students who, having passed through the initiatory exercises, are more advanced in the art, and who, sure of their hand, have leisure to exert their understanding, must now be told that a mere copyist of nature can never produce anything great, can never raise and enlarge the conceptions, or warm the heart of the spectator.

The wish of the genuine painter must be more extensive; instead of endeavoring to amuse mankind with the minute neatness of his imitations, he must endeavor to improve them by the grandeur of his ideas; instead of seeking praise by deceiving the superficial sense of the spectator, he must strive for fame by captivating the imagination.

The principle now laid down, that the perfection of this art does not consist in mere imitation, is far from being new or singular. It is, indeed, supported by the general opinion of the enlightened part of mankind. The poets, orators, and rhetoricians of antiquity are continually enforcing this position, — that all the arts receive their perfection from an ideal beauty, superior to what is to be found in individual nature. They are ever referring to the practice of the painters and sculptors of their times, particularly Phidias (the favorite artist of antiquity), to illustrate their assertions. As if they could not sufficiently express their admiration of his genius by what they knew, they have recourse to poetical enthusiasm;

they call it inspiration, — a gift from heaven. The artist is supposed to have ascended the celestial regions, to furnish his mind with this perfect idea of beauty. "He," says Proclus,[1] "who takes for his model such forms as nature produces, and confines himself to an exact imitation of them, will never attain to what is perfectly beautiful; for the works of nature are full of disproportion, and fall very short of the true standard of beauty. So that Phidias, when he formed his Jupiter, did not copy any object ever presented to his sight, but contemplated only that image which he had conceived in his mind from Homer's description." And thus Cicero, speaking of this same Phidias: "Neither did this artist," says he, "when he carved the image of Jupiter or Minerva, set before him any one human figure, as a pattern which he was to copy; but having a more perfect idea of beauty fixed in his mind, this is steadily contemplated, and to the imitation of this all his skill and labor were directed."

The moderns are not less convinced than the ancients of this superior power existing in the art, nor less sensible of its effects. Every language has adopted terms expressive of this excellence. The *gusto grande* of the Italians, the *beau idéal* of the French, and "great style," "genius," and "taste" among the English, are but different appellations of the same thing.[2] It is this intellectual dignity, they

---

[1] Lib. 2, in Timæum Platonis, as cited by Junius de Pictura Veterum. — R.

[2] "The art is greatest which includes the greatest ideas. . . . Great art is precisely that which never was, nor will be, taught; it is

say, that ennobles the painter's art, — that lays the line between him and the mere mechanic, and produces those great effects in an instant which eloquence and poetry by slow and repeated efforts are scarcely able to attain.

Such is the warmth with which both the ancients and moderns speak of this divine principle of the art; but, as I have formerly observed, enthusiastic admiration seldom promotes knowledge. Though a student by such praise may have his attention roused, and a desire excited of running in this great career, yet it is possible that what has been said to excite may only serve to deter him. He examines his own mind, and perceives there nothing of that divine inspiration with which he is told so many others have been favored. He never travelled to heaven to gather new ideas; and he finds himself possessed of no other qualifications than what mere common observation and a plain understanding can confer. Thus he becomes gloomy amid the splendor of figurative declamation, and thinks it hopeless to pursue an object which he supposes out of the reach of human industry.

But on this, as upon many other occasions, we ought to distinguish how much is to be given to enthusiasm, and how much to reason. We ought to allow for, and we ought to commend that strength of vivid expression which is necessary to convey, in its full force, the highest sense of the most complete effect of art; taking care at the same time not to

pre-eminently and finally the expression of the spirits of great men."
— RUSKIN.

lose in terms of vague admiration that solidity and truth of principle upon which alone we can reason, and may be enabled to practise.

It is not easy to define in what this great style consists; nor to describe, by words, the proper means of acquiring it, — if the mind of the student should be at all capable of such an acquisition. Could we teach taste or genius by rules, they would be no longer taste and genius. But though there neither are, nor can be, any precise invariable rules for the exercise, or the acquisition, of these great qualities, yet we may truly say that they always operate in proportion to our attention in observing the works of nature, to our skill in selecting, and to our care in digesting, methodizing, and comparing our observations. There are many beauties in our art that seem, at first, to lie without the reach of precept, and yet may easily be reduced to practical principles. Experience is all in all; but it is not every one who profits by experience; and most people err, not so much from want of capacity to find their object, as from not knowing what object to pursue. This great ideal perfection and beauty are not to be sought in the heavens, but upon the earth. They are about us, and upon every side of us. But the power of discovering what is deformed in nature, or, in other words, what is particular and uncommon, can be acquired only by experience; and the whole beauty and grandeur of the art consists, in my opinion, in being able to get above all singular forms, local customs, particularities, and details of every kind.

All the objects which are exhibited to our view by

nature, upon close examination will be found to have their blemishes and defects. The most beautiful forms have something about them like weakness, minuteness, or imperfection. But it is not every eye that perceives these blemishes. It must be an eye long used to the contemplation and comparison of these forms, and which, by a long habit of observing what any set of objects of the same kind have in common, has acquired the power of discerning what each wants in particular. This long, laborious comparison should be the first study of the painter who aims at the great style. By this means he acquires a just idea of beautiful forms; he corrects nature by herself, her imperfect state by her more perfect. His eye being enabled to distinguish the accidental deficiencies, excrescences, and deformities of things from their general figures, he makes out an abstract idea of their forms more perfect than any one original; and what may seem a paradox, he learns to design naturally by drawing his figures unlike to any one object. This idea of the perfect state of nature, which the artist calls the ideal beauty, is the great leading principle by which works of genius are conducted. By this Phidias acquired his fame. He wrought upon a sober principle what has so much excited the enthusiasm of the world; and by this method you who have courage to tread the same path may acquire equal reputation.

This is the idea which has acquired, and which seems to have a right to, the epithet of *divine;* as it may be said to preside, like a supreme judge, over all the productions of nature, appearing to be possessed of the will and intention of the Creator, as far as they regard the external form of living beings. When a man once possesses this idea in its perfection there is no danger but that he will be sufficiently warmed by it himself, and be able to warm and ravish every one else.

Thus it is from a reiterated experience, and a close comparison of the objects in nature, that an artist becomes possessed of the idea of that central form, if I may so express it, from which every deviation is deformity. But the investigation of this form, I grant, is painful, and I know but of one method of shortening the road; this is by a careful study of the works of the ancient sculptors; who, being indefatigable in the school of nature, have left models of that perfect form behind them which an artist would prefer as supremely beautiful who had spent his whole life in that single contemplation. But if industry carried them thus far, may not you also hope for the same reward from the same labor? We have the same school opened to us that was opened to them; for nature denies her instructions to none who desire to become her pupils.

This laborious investigation, I am aware, must appear superfluous to those who think everything is to be done by felicity and the powers of native genius. Even the great Bacon treats with ridicule the idea of confining proportion to rules, or of producing beauty by selection. "A man cannot tell," says he, "whether Apelles or Albert Dürer were the more trifler: whereof the one would make a personage by geometrical proportions; the other, by taking the best parts out of divers faces, to make one excellent. . . . The painter," he adds, " must do it by a kind of felicity . . . and not by rule."

It is not safe to question any opinion of so great a writer and so profound a thinker as undoubtedly Bacon was. But he studies brevity to excess; and therefore his meaning is sometimes doubtful. If he means that beauty has nothing to do with rule he is mistaken. There is a rule, obtained out of general nature, to contradict which is to fall into deformity. Whenever anything is done beyond this rule it is in virtue of some other rule which is followed along with it, but which does not contradict it. Everything which is wrought with certainty is wrought upon some principle. If it is not, it cannot be repeated. If by felicity is meant anything of chance or hazard, or something born with a man, and not earned, I cannot agree with this great philosopher. Every object which pleases must give us pleasure upon some certain principles; but as the objects of pleasure are almost infinite, so their principles vary without end, and every man finds them out, not by felicity or successful hazard, but by care and sagacity.

To the principle I have laid down, that the idea of beauty in each species of beings is an invariable one, it may be objected that in every particular species there are various central forms, which are separate and distinct from each other, and yet are undeniably beautiful; that in the human figure, for instance, the beauty of Hercules is one, of the Gladiator another, of the Apollo another; which makes so many different ideas of beauty.

It is true, indeed, that these figures are each perfect in their kind, though of different characters and proportions; but still none of them is the representation of an individual, but of a class. And as there is one general form which, as I have said, belongs to the human kind at large, so in each of these classes there is one common idea and central form which is the abstract of the various individual forms belonging to that class. Thus, though the forms of childhood and age differ exceedingly, there is a common form in childhood, and a common form in age, which is the more perfect as it is more remote from all peculiarities. But I must add, further, that though the most perfect forms of each of the general divisions of the human figure are ideal and superior to any individual form of that class, yet the highest perfection of the human figure is not to be found in any one of them. It is not in the Hercules, nor in the Gladiator, nor in the Apollo; but in that form which is taken from all, and which partakes equally of the activity of the Gladiator, of the delicacy of the Apollo, and of the muscular strength of the Hercules. For perfect beauty in any species must combine all the characters which are beautiful in that species. It cannot consist in any one to the exclusion of the rest; no one, therefore, must be predominant, that no one may be deficient.

The knowledge of these different characters, and the power of separating and distinguishing them, is undoubtedly necessary to the painter, who is to vary his compositions with figures of various forms and proportions, though he is never to lose sight of the general idea of perfection in each kind.

There is, likewise, a kind of symmetry, or proportion, which may properly be said to belong to deformity. A figure lean or corpulent, tall or short, though deviating from beauty, may still have a certain union of the various parts, which may contribute to make them on the whole not unpleasing.

When the artist has by diligent attention acquired a clear and distinct idea of beauty and symmetry, when he has reduced the variety of nature to the abstract idea, his next task will be to become acquainted with the genuine habits of nature, as distinguished from those of fashion. For in the same manner, and on the same principles, as he has acquired the knowledge of the real forms of nature, distinct from accidental deformity, he must endeavor to separate simple, chaste nature from those adventitious, those affected and forced airs or actions, with which she is loaded by modern education.

Perhaps I cannot better explain what I mean than by reminding you of what was taught us by the professor of anatomy, in respect to the natural position and movement of the feet. He observed that the fashion of turning them outwards was contrary to the intent of nature, as might be seen from the structure of the bones, and from the weakness that proceeded from that manner of standing. To this we may add the erect position of the head, the projection of the chest, the walking with straight knees, and many such actions, which we know to be merely the result of fashion, and what nature never warranted, as we are sure that we have been taught them when children.

I have mentioned but a few of those instances in which vanity or caprice have contrived to distort and disfigure the human form; your own recollection will add to these a thousand more of ill-understood methods, which have been practised to disguise nature among our dancing-masters, hairdressers, and tailors, in their various schools of deformity.[1]

However the mechanic and ornamental arts may sacrifice to Fashion, she must be entirely excluded from the art of painting; the painter must never mistake this capricious changeling for the genuine offspring of nature. He must divest himself of all prejudices in favor of his age or country; he must disregard all local and temporary ornaments, and look only on those general habits which are everywhere and always the same.[2] He addresses his works to the people of every country and every age; he calls upon posterity to be his spectators, and says, with Zeuxis, "*In æternitatem pingo.*"

The neglect of separating modern fashions from the habits of nature leads to that ridiculous style which has been practised by some painters, who have given to Grecian heroes the airs and graces practised

[1] "Those," says Quintilian, "who are taken with the outward show of things think that there is more beauty in persons who are trimmed, curled, and painted, than uncorrupt nature can give; as if beauty were merely the effect of the corruption of manners." — R.

[2] "Nearly every word that Reynolds wrote was contrary to his own practice . . . he enforced with his lips generalization and idealism, while with his pencil he was tracing the patterns of the dresses of the belles of the day; he exhorted his pupils to attend only to the invariable, while he himself was occupied in distinguishing every variation of womanly temper; and he denied the existence of the beautiful at the same instant that he arrested it as it passed, and perpetuated it forever." — RUSKIN, *Mod. Painters*, Part iv. c. iii.

in the court of Louis XIV., — an absurdity almost as great as it would have been to have dressed them after the fashion of that court.

To avoid this error, however, and to retain the true simplicity of nature, is a task more difficult than at first sight it may appear. The prejudices in favor of the fashions and customs that we have been used to, and which are justly called a second nature, make it too often difficult to distinguish that which is natural from that which is the result of education; they frequently even give a predilection in favor of the artificial mode; and almost every one is apt to be guided by those local prejudices who has not chastised his mind, and regulated the instability of his affections by the eternal, invariable idea of nature.

Here, then, as before, we must have recourse to the ancients as instructors. It is from a careful study of their works that you will be enabled to attain to the real simplicity of nature; they will suggest many observations which would probably escape you if your study were confined to nature alone. And, indeed, I cannot help suspecting that, in this instance, the ancients had an easier task than the moderns. They had, probably, little or nothing to unlearn, as their manners were nearly approaching to this desirable simplicity; while the modern artist, before he can see the truth of things, is obliged to remove a veil, with which the fashion of the times has thought proper to cover her.

Having gone thus far in our investigation of the great style in painting, if we now should suppose that the artist has found the true idea of beauty, which enables him to give his works a correct and perfect design; if we should suppose, also, that he has acquired a knowledge of the unadulterated habits of nature, which gives him simplicity; the rest of his task is, perhaps, less than is generally imagined. Beauty and simplicity have so great a share in the composition of a great style that he who has acquired them has little else to learn. It must not, indeed, be forgotten that there is a nobleness of conception which goes beyond anything in the mere exhibition even of perfect form; there is an art of animating and dignifying the figures with intellectual grandeur, of impressing the appearance of philosophic wisdom, or heroic virtue. This can only be acquired by him that enlarges the sphere of his understanding by a variety of knowledge, and warms his imagination with the best productions of ancient and modern poetry.

A hand thus exercised, and a mind thus instructed, will bring the art to a higher degree of excellence than, perhaps, it has hitherto attained in this country. Such a student will disdain the humbler walks of painting, which, however profitable, can never assure him a permanent reputation. He will leave the meaner artist servilely to suppose that those are the best pictures which are most likely to deceive the spectator. He will permit the lower painter, like the florist or collector of shells, to exhibit the minute discriminations which distinguish one object of the same species from another; while he, like the philosopher, will consider nature in the abstract, and represent in every one of his figures the character of its species.

If deceiving the eye were the only business of the art, there is no doubt, indeed, but the minute painter would be more apt to succeed; but it is not the eye, it is the mind which the painter of genius desires to address; nor will he waste a moment upon those smaller objects which only serve to catch the sense, to divide the attention, and to counteract his great design of speaking to the heart.

This is the ambition which I wish to excite in your minds; and the object I have had in my view throughout this discourse is that one great idea which gives to painting its true dignity, which entitles it to the name of a liberal art, and ranks it as a sister of poetry.

It may possibly have happened to many young students, whose application was sufficient to overcome all difficulties, and whose minds were capable of embracing the most extensive views, that they have, by a wrong direction originally given, spent their lives in the meaner walks of painting, without ever knowing there was a nobler to pursue. Albert Dürer, as Vasari has justly remarked, would probably have been one of the first painters of his age (and he lived in an era of great artists) had he been initiated into those great principles of the art which were so well understood and practised by his contemporaries in Italy. But, unluckily, having never seen nor heard of any other manner, he, without doubt, considered his own as perfect.

As for the various departments of painting which do not presume to make such high pretensions, they are many. None of them are without their merit, though none enter into competition with this universal presiding idea of the art. The painters who have applied themselves more particularly to low and vulgar characters, and who express with precision the various shades of passion as they are exhibited by vulgar minds (such as we see in the works of Hogarth), deserve great praise; but as their genius has been employed on low and confined subjects, the praise which we give must be as limited as its object. The merrymaking or quarrelling of the boors of Teniers, the same sort of productions of Brouwer or Ostade, are excellent in their kind; and the excellence and its praise will be in proportion as, in those limited subjects and peculiar forms, they introduce more or less of the expression of those passions as they appear in general and more enlarged nature. This principle may be applied to the battle-pieces of Bourgognone, the French gallantries of Watteau, and even beyond the exhibition of animal life, to the landscapes of Claude Lorraine, and the sea views of Vandervelde. All these painters have, in general, the same right, in different degrees, to the name of a painter, which a satirist, an epigrammatist, a sonneteer, a writer of pastorals or descriptive poetry, has to that of a poet.

In the same rank, and perhaps of not so great merit, is the cold painter of portraits. But his correct and just imitation of his object has its merit. Even the painter of still life, whose highest ambition is to give a minute representation of every part of those low objects which he sets before him, deserves praise in proportion to his attainment, because no part of this excellent art, so much the ornament of polished life, is destitute of value and use. These, however, are by no means the views to which the mind of the student ought to be primarily directed. Having begun by aiming at better things, if from particular inclination, or from the taste of the time and place he lives in, or from necessity, or from failure in the highest attempts, he is obliged to descend lower, he will bring into the lower sphere of art a grandeur of composition and character that will raise and ennoble his works far above their natural rank.

A man is not weak, though he may not be able to wield the club of Hercules; nor does a man always practise that which he esteems the best, but does that which he can best do. In moderate attempts there are many walks open to the artist. But as the idea of beauty is of necessity but one, so there can be but one great mode of painting, — the leading principle of which I have endeavored to explain.

I should be sorry if what is here recommended should be at all understood to countenance a careless or undetermined manner of painting. For, though the painter is to overlook the accidental discriminations of nature, he is to exhibit distinctly and with precision the general forms of things. A firm and determined outline is one of the characteristics of the great style in painting; and let me add that he who possesses the knowledge of the exact form which every part of nature ought to have, will be fond of expressing that knowledge with correctness and precision in all his works.

To conclude: I have endeavored to reduce the idea of beauty to general principles; and I had the pleasure to observe that the professor of painting proceeded in the same method, when he showed you that the artifice of contrast was founded but on one principle. I am convinced that this is the only means of advancing science, — of clearing the mind from a confused heap of contradictory observations that do but perplex and puzzle the student when he compares them, or misguide him if he gives himself up to their authority; bringing them under one general head can alone give rest and satisfaction to an inquisitive mind.

Lady Sophia St. Asaph and Child.

DISCOURSE IV.

Delivered to the Students of the Royal Academy, on the Distribution of the Prizes, December 10, 1771.

GENERAL IDEAS, THE PRESIDING PRINCIPLE WHICH REGULATES EVERY PART OF ART; INVENTION, EXPRESSION, COLORING, AND DRAPERY. — TWO DISTINCT STYLES IN HISTORY-PAINTING: THE GRAND, AND THE ORNAMENTAL. — THE SCHOOLS IN WHICH EACH IS TO BE FOUND. — THE COMPOSITE STYLE. — THE STYLE FORMED ON LOCAL CUSTOMS AND HABITS, OR A PARTIAL VIEW OF NATURE.

THE value and rank of every art is in proportion to the mental labor employed in it, or the mental pleasure produced by it. As this principle is observed or neglected, our profession becomes either a liberal art or a mechanical trade. In the hands of one man it makes the highest pretensions, as it is addressed to the noblest faculties; in those of another it is reduced to a mere matter of ornament, and the painter has but the humble province of furnishing our apartments with elegance.

This exertion of mind, which is the only circumstance that truly ennobles our art, makes the great distinction between the Roman and Venetian schools. I have formerly observed that perfect form is produced by leaving out particularities and retaining only general ideas; I shall now endeavor to show that this principle, which I have proved to be metaphysically just, extends itself to every part of the art; that it gives what is called the *grand style* to invention, to composition, to expression, and even to coloring and drapery.

Invention in painting does not imply the invention of the subject, for that is commonly supplied by the poet or historian.[1] With respect to the choice, no subject can be proper that is not generally interesting. It ought to be either some eminent instance of heroic action or heroic suffering. There must be something, either in the action or in the object, in which men are universally concerned, and which powerfully strikes upon the public sympathy.

Strictly speaking, indeed, no subject can be of universal, hardly can it be of general, concern; but there are events and characters so popularly known, in those countries where our art is in request, that they may be considered as sufficiently general for all our purposes. Such are the great events of Greek and Roman fable and history, which early education and the usual course of reading have made familiar and interesting to all Europe, without being degraded by the vulgarism of ordinary life in any country. Such, too, are the capital subjects of Scripture history, which, besides their general notoriety, become venerable by their connection with our religion.

As it is required that the subject selected should be a general one, it is no less necessary that it should be kept unembarrassed with whatever may any way

---

[1] "Invention and novelty in his subjects are far from being the principal things we look for in an artist; a familiar subject furthers and renders more easy the effect of his art."— LESSING.

serve to divide the attention of the spectator. Whenever a story is related every man forms a picture in his mind of the action and expression of the persons employed. The power of representing this mental picture on canvas is what we call invention in a painter. And as, in the conception of this ideal picture, the mind does not enter into the minute peculiarities of the dress, furniture, or scene of action, so, when the painter comes to represent it, he contrives those little necessary concomitant circumstances in such a manner that they shall strike the spectator no more than they did himself in his first conception of the story.

I am very ready to allow that some circumstances of minuteness and particularity frequently tend to give an air of truth to a piece, and to interest the spectator in an extraordinary manner. Such circumstances, therefore, cannot wholly be rejected; but if there be anything in the art which requires peculiar nicety of discernment, it is the disposition of these minute circumstantial parts; which, according to the judgment employed in the choice, become so useful to truth, or so injurious to grandeur.

However, the usual and most dangerous error is on the side of minuteness; and, therefore, I think caution most necessary where most have failed. The general idea constitutes real excellence. All smaller things, however perfect in their way, are to be sacrificed without mercy to the greater. The painter will not inquire what things may be admitted without much censure; he will not think it enough to show that they may be there; he will show that they must be there, — that their absence would render his picture maimed and defective.

Thus, though to the principal group a second or third be added, and a second and third mass of light, care must be taken that these subordinate actions and lights, neither each in particular nor all together, come into any degree of competition with the principal; they should merely make a part of that whole which would be imperfect without them. To every kind of painting this rule may be applied. Even in portraits, the grace, and, we may add, the likeness, consists more in taking the general air than in observing the exact similitude of every feature.

Thus figures must have a ground whereon to stand; they must be clothed; there must be a background; there must be light and shadow; but none of these ought to appear to have taken up any part of the artist's attention. They should be so managed as not even to catch that of the spectator. We know well enough, when we analyze a piece, the difficulty and the subtlety with which an artist adjusts the background drapery and masses of light; we know that a considerable part of the grace and effect of his picture depends upon them; but this art is so much concealed, even to a judicious eye, that no remains of any of these subordinate parts occur to the memory when the picture is not present.

The great end of the art is to strike the imagination. The painter, therefore, is to make no ostentation of the means by which this is done; the spectator is only to feel the result in his bosom. An inferior artist is unwilling that any part of his industry should be lost upon the spectator. He takes as much pains to discover, as the greater artist does to conceal, the marks of his subordinate assiduity. In works of the lower kind everything appears studied and encumbered; it is all boastful art and open affectation. The ignorant often part from such pictures with wonder in their mouths and indifference in their hearts.

But it is not enough in invention that the artist should restrain and keep under all the inferior parts of his subject; he must sometimes deviate from vulgar and strict historical truth in pursuing the grandeur of his design.

How much the great style exacts from its professors to conceive and represent their subjects in a poetical manner, not confined to mere matter of fact, may be seen in the cartoons of Raphael. In all the pictures in which the painter has represented the apostles, he has drawn them with great nobleness; he has given them as much dignity as the human figure is capable of receiving; yet we are expressly told in Scripture they had no such respectable appearance; and of Saint Paul, in particular, we are told by himself that his bodily presence was mean. Alexander is said to have been of a low stature; a painter ought not so to represent him. Agesilaus was low, lame, and of a mean appearance; none of these defects ought to appear in a piece of which he is the hero. In conformity to custom, I call this part of the art History Painting; it ought to be called Poetical, as in reality it is.

All this is not falsifying any fact; it is taking an allowed poetical license. A painter of portraits retains the individual likeness; a painter of history shows the man by showing his action. A painter must compensate the natural deficiencies of his art. He has but one sentence to utter, but one moment to exhibit.[1] He cannot, like the poet or historian, expatiate, and impress the mind with great veneration for the character of the hero or saint he represents, though he lets us know, at the same time, that the saint was deformed or the hero lame. The painter has no other means of giving an idea of the dignity of the mind but by that external appearance which grandeur of thought does generally, though not always, impress on the countenance, and by that correspondence of figure to sentiment and situation which all men wish, but cannot command. The painter who may in this one particular attain with ease what others desire in vain, ought to give all that he possibly can, since there are so many circumstances of true greatness that he cannot give at all. He cannot make his hero talk like a great man; he must make him look like one. For which reason he ought to be well studied in the analysis of those circumstances which constitute dignity of appearance in real life.

As in invention, so likewise in expression, care must be taken not to run into particularities. Those

[1] "Behold, I said, the painter's sphere!
The limits of his art appear . . .
In outward semblance he must give
A moment's life of things that live;
Then let him choose his moment well,
With power divine its story tell."
MATTHEW ARNOLD: *Epilogue to Lessing's Laocoön.*

expressions alone should be given to the figures which their respective situations generally produce. Nor is this enough; each person should also have that expression which men of his rank generally exhibit. The joy or the grief of a character of dignity is not to be expressed in the same manner as a similar passion in a vulgar face. Upon this principle, Bernini, perhaps, may be subject to censure. This sculptor, in many respects admirable, has given a very mean expression to his statue of David, who is represented as just going to throw the stone from the sling; and, in order to give it the expression of energy, he has made him biting his under lip. This expression is far from being general, and still farther from being dignified. He might have seen it in an instance or two; and he mistook accident for generality.

With respect to coloring, though it may appear at first a part of painting merely mechanical, yet it still has its rules, and those grounded upon that presiding principle which regulates both the great and the little in the study of a painter. By this, the first effect of the picture is produced; and as this is performed, the spectator, as he walks the gallery, will stop, or pass along. To give a general air of grandeur at first view, all trifling, or artful play of little lights, or an attention to a variety of tints, is to be avoided; a quietness and simplicity must reign over the whole work; to which a breadth of uniform and simple color will very much contribute. Grandeur of effect is produced by two different ways, which seem entirely opposed to each other. One is, by reducing the colors to little more than chiaro-oscuro, which was often the practice of the Bolognian schools; and the other, by making the colors very distinct and forcible, such as we see in those of Rome and Florence; but still, the presiding principle of both those manners is simplicity. Certainly, nothing can be more simple than monotony; and the distinct blue, red, and yellow colors which are seen in the draperies of the Roman and Florentine schools, though they have not that kind of harmony which is produced by a variety of broken and transparent colors, have that effect of grandeur which was intended. Perhaps these distinct colors strike the mind more forcibly from there not being any great union between them; as martial music, which is intended to rouse the nobler passions, has its effect from the sudden and strongly marked transitions from one note to another which that style of music requires; while in that which is intended to move the softer passions, the notes imperceptibly melt into one another.

In the same manner as the historical painter never enters into the detail of colors, so neither does he debase his conceptions with minute attention to the discriminations of drapery. It is the inferior style that marks the variety of stuffs. With him the clothing is neither woollen, nor linen, nor silk, satin, or velvet: it is drapery; it is nothing more. The art of disposing the foldings of the drapery makes a very considerable part of the painter's study. To make it merely natural is a mechanical operation, to which neither genius nor taste are required; whereas it requires the nicest judgment to dispose the drapery so that the folds shall have an easy communication, and gracefully follow each other with such natural negligence as to look like the effect of chance, and at the same time show the figure under it to the utmost advantage.

Carlo Maratti was of opinion that the disposition of drapery was a more difficult art than even that of drawing the human figure; that a student might be more easily taught the latter than the former; as the rules of drapery, he said, could not be so well ascertained as those for delineating a correct form. This, perhaps, is a proof how willingly we favor our own peculiar excellence. Carlo Maratti is said to have valued himself particularly upon his skill in this part of his art; yet in him the disposition appears so ostentatiously artificial that he is inferior to Raphael, even in that which gave him his best claim to reputation.

Such is the great principle by which we must be directed in the nobler branches of our art. Upon this principle, the Roman, the Florentine, the Bolognese schools have formed their practice; and by this they have deservedly obtained the highest praise. These are the three great schools of the world in the epic style. The best of the French school, Poussin, Le Sueur, and Le Brun, have formed themselves upon these models, and consequently may be said, though Frenchmen, to be a colony from the Roman school. Next to these, but in a very different style of excellence, we may rank the Venetian, together with the Flemish and Dutch schools; all professing to depart from the great purposes of painting, and catching at applause by inferior qualities.

I am not ignorant that some will censure me for placing the Venetians in this inferior class, and many of the warmest admirers of painting will think them unjustly degraded; but I wish not to be misunderstood. Though I can by no means allow them to hold any rank with the nobler schools of painting, they accomplished perfectly the thing they attempted. But as mere elegance is their principal object, as they seem more willing to dazzle than to affect, it can be no injury to them to suppose that their practice is useful only to its proper end. But what may heighten the elegant may degrade the sublime. There is a simplicity, and, I may add, severity, in the great manner, which is, I am afraid, almost incompatible with this comparatively sensual style.

Tintoret, Paul Veronese, and others of the Venetian school, seem to have painted with no other purpose than to be admired for their skill and expertness in the mechanism of painting, and to make a parade of that art, which, as I before observed, the higher style requires its followers to conceal.

In a conference of the French Academy, at which were present Le Brun, Sebastian Bourdon, and all the eminent artists of that age, one of the Academicians desired to have their opinion on the conduct of Paul Veronese, who, though a painter of great consideration, had, contrary to the strict rules of art, in his picture of Perseus and Andromeda, represented the principal figure in shade. To this question no satisfactory answer was then given. But I will venture to say that, if they had considered the class of the artist, and ranked him as an ornamental painter, there would have been no difficulty in answering: "It was unreasonable to expect what was never intended. His intention was solely to produce an effect of light and shadow; everything was to be sacrificed to that intent, and the capricious composition of that picture suited very well with the style which he professed."

Young minds are indeed too apt to be captivated by this splendor of style, and that of the Venetians is particularly pleasing; for by them all those parts of the art that gave pleasure to the eye or sense have been cultivated with care, and carried to the degree nearest to perfection. The powers exerted in the mechanical part of the art have been called "the language of painters;" but we may say that it is but poor eloquence which only shows that the orator can talk. Words should be employed as the means, not as the end; language is the instrument, conviction is the work.[1]

The language of painting must indeed be allowed these masters; but even in that they have shown more copiousness than choice, and more luxuriancy than judgment. If we consider the uninteresting subjects of their invention, or at least the uninteresting

---

[1] "In art, men have frequently fancied that they were becoming rhetoricians and poets when they were only learning to speak melodiously, and the judge has over and over again advanced to the honor of authors those who never were more than ornamental writing masters. . . . No weight, nor mass, nor beauty of execution can outweigh one grain or fragment of thought. Three penstrokes of Raphael are a greater and a better picture than the most finished work that ever Carlo Dolci polished into inanity."

RUSKIN, *Modern Painters.*

manner in which they are treated; if we attend to their capricious composition, their violent and affected contrasts, whether of figures or of light and shadow, the richness of their drapery, and at the same time the mean effect which the discrimination of stuffs gives to their pictures; if to these we add their total inattention to expression; and then reflect on the conceptions and the learning of Michael Angelo, or the simplicity of Raphael, we can no longer dwell on the comparison. Even in coloring, if we compare the quietness and chastity of the Bolognese pencil to the bustle and tumult that fills every part of a Venetian picture, without the least attempt to interest the passions, their boasted art will appear a mere struggle without effect, — "a tale told by an idiot, full of sound and fury, signifying nothing."

Such as suppose that the great style might happily be blended with the ornamental, that the simple, grave, and majestic dignity of Raphael could unite with the glow and bustle of a Paolo or Tintoret, are totally mistaken. The principles by which each is attained are so contrary to each other that they seem, in my opinion, incompatible, and as impossible to exist together, as that in the mind the most sublime ideas and the lowest sensuality should at the same time be united.[1]

---

[1] "Their glory" (the great masters) "is their dissimilarity, and they who propose to themselves in the training of an artist that he should unite the coloring of Tintoret, the finish of Albert Dürer, and the tenderness of Correggio, are no wiser than a horticulturist would be, who made it the object of his labor to produce a fruit which should unite in itself the lusciousness of the grape, the crispness of the nut, and the fragrance of the pine." — RUSKIN, *Modern Painters.*

The subjects of the Venetian painters are mostly such as give them an opportunity of introducing a great number of figures, — such as feasts, marriages, and processions, public martyrdoms, or miracles. I can easily conceive that Paul Veronese, if he were asked, would say that no subject was proper for an historical picture, but such as admitted at least forty figures; for in a less number, he would assert, there could be no opportunity of the painter's showing his art in composition, his dexterity of managing and disposing the masses of light and groups of figures, and of introducing a variety of Eastern dresses and characters in their rich stuffs.

But the thing is very different with a pupil of the greater schools. Annibale Caracci thought twelve figures sufficient for any story; he conceived that more would contribute to no end but to fill space; that they would be but cold spectators of the general action, or, to use his own expression, that they would be *figures to be let*. Besides, it is impossible for a picture composed of so many parts to have that effect so indispensably necessary to grandeur, that of one complete whole. However contradictory it may be in geometry, it is true in taste, that many little things will not make a great one. The sublime impresses the mind at once with one great idea, — it is a single blow; the elegant, indeed, may be produced by repetition, by an accumulation of many minute circumstances.

However great the difference is between the composition of the Venetian and the rest of the Italian schools, there is full as great a disparity in the effect of their pictures as produced by colors. And though in this respect the Venetians must be allowed extraordinary skill, yet even that skill, as they have employed it, will but ill correspond with the great style. Their coloring is not only too brilliant, but, I will venture to say, too harmonious, to produce that solidity, steadiness, and simplicity of effect, which heroic subjects require, and which simple or grave colors only can give to a work. That they are to be cautiously studied by those who are ambitious of treading the great walk of history is confirmed, if it wants confirmation, by the greatest of all authorities, Michael Angelo. This wonderful man, after having seen a picture by Titian, told Vasari, who accompanied him, "that he liked much his coloring and manner;" but then he added that "it was a pity the Venetian painters did not learn to draw correctly in their early youth, and adopt a better *manner of study.*"

By this it appears that the principal attention of the Venetian painters, in the opinion of Michael Angelo, seemed to be engrossed by the study of colors, to the neglect of the ideal beauty of form, or propriety of expression. But if general censure was given to that school from the sight of a picture of Titian, how much more heavily and more justly would the censure fall on Paolo Veronese, and more especially on Tintoret! And here I cannot avoid citing Vasari's opinion of the style and manner of Tintoret.

"Of all the extraordinary geniuses," says he, "that have practised the art of painting, for wild, capricious, extravagant, and fantastical inventions, for furious impetuosity and boldness in the execution of his work, there is none like

Tintoret; his strange whimsies are even beyond extravagance; and his works seem to be produced rather by chance than in consequence of any previous design, as if he wanted to convince the world that the art was a trifle, and of the most easy attainment."

For my own part, when I speak of the Venetian painters, I wish to be understood to mean Paolo Veronese and Tintoret, to the exclusion of Titian; for though his style is not so pure as that of many other of the Italian schools, yet there is a sort of senatorial dignity about him, which, however awkward in his imitators, seems to become him exceedingly. His portraits alone, from the nobleness and simplicity of character which he always gave them, will entitle him to the greatest respect, as he undoubtedly stands in the first rank in this branch of the art.

It is not with Titian, but with the seducing qualities of the two former, that I could wish to caution you against being too much captivated. These are the persons who may be said to have exhausted all the powers of florid eloquence to debauch the young and inexperienced; and have, without doubt, been the cause of turning off the attention of the connoisseur and of the patron of art, as well as that of the painter, from those higher excellences of which the art is capable, and which ought to be required in every considerable production. By them and their imitators, a style merely ornamental has been disseminated throughout all Europe. Rubens carried it to Flanders, Voet to France, and Luca Giordano to Spain and Naples.

The Venetian is indeed the most splendid of the

schools of elegance; and it is not without reason that the best performances in this lower school are valued higher than the second-rate performances of those above them; for every picture has value when it has a decided character, and is excellent in its kind. But the student must take care not to be so much dazzled with this splendor as to be tempted to imitate what must ultimately lead from perfection. Poussin, whose eye was always steadily fixed on the sublime, has been often heard to say, " that a particular attention to coloring was an obstacle to the student in his progress to the great end and design of the art; and that he who attaches himself to this principal end will acquire by practice a reasonably good method of coloring."

Though it be allowed that elaborate harmony of coloring, a brilliancy of tints, a soft and gradual transition from one to another, present to the eye what an harmonious concert of music does to the ear, it must be remembered that painting is not merely a gratification of the sight. Such excellence, though properly cultivated where nothing higher than elegance is intended, is weak and unworthy of regard when the work aspires to grandeur and sublimity.

The same reasons that have been urged to show that a mixture of the Venetian style cannot improve the great style will hold good in regard to the Flemish and Dutch schools. Indeed, the Flemish school, of which Rubens is the head, was formed upon that of the Venetian;[1] like them, he took his figures too

---

[1] "The conditions of art in Flanders — wealthy, *bourgeois*, proud, free — were not dissimilar to those of art in Venice. As Van Eyck

much from the people before him. But it must be allowed in favor of the Venetians, that he was more gross than they, and carried all their mistaken methods to a far greater excess. In the Venetian school itself, where they all err from the same cause, there is a difference in the effect. The difference between Paolo and Bassano seems to be only that one introduced Venetian gentlemen into his pictures, and the other the boors of the district of Bassano, and called them patriarchs and prophets.

The painters of the Dutch school have still more locality. With them a history-piece is properly a portrait of themselves; whether they describe the inside or outside of their houses, we have their own people engaged in their own peculiar occupations, — working or drinking, playing or fighting. The circumstances that enter into a picture of this kind are so far from giving a general view of human life that they exhibit all the minute particularities of a nation differing in several respects from the rest of mankind. Yet let them have their share of more humble praise. The painters of this school are excellent in their own way; they are only ridiculous when they attempt general history on their own narrow principles, and debase great events by the meanness of their characters.

Some inferior dexterity, some extraordinary mechanical power, is apparently that from which they seek distinction. Thus, we see that school alone has the custom of representing candle-light, not as it

is to the Vivarini, so is Rubens to Paolo Veronese. This expresses the amount of likeness and difference." — SYMONDS: iii. 362, *n*.

really appears to us by night, but red, as it would illuminate objects to a spectator by day. Such tricks, however pardonable in the little style, where petty effects are the sole end, are inexcusable in the greater, where the attention should never be drawn aside by trifles, but should be entirely occupied by the subject itself.

The same local principles which characterize the Dutch school extend even to their landscape painters; and Rubens himself, who has painted many landscapes,[1] has sometimes transgressed in this particular. Their pieces in this way are, I think, always a representation of an individual spot, and each in its kind a very faithful but a very confined portrait. Claude Lorrain, on the contrary, was convinced that taking nature as he found it seldom produced beauty. His pictures are a composition of the various draughts which he had previously made from various beautiful scenes and prospects. However, Rubens in some measure has made amends for the deficiency with which he is charged; he has contrived to raise and animate his otherwise uninteresting views by introducing a rainbow, storm, or some particular accidental effect of light. That the practice of Claude Lorrain, in respect to his choice, is to be adopted by landscape-painters in opposition to that of the Flemish and Dutch schools, there can be no doubt, as its

---

[1] Rubens "perhaps furnishes us with the first instances of complete, unconventional, unaffected landscape. His treatment is healthy, manly, rational, not very affectionate, yet often condescending to minute and multitudinous detail; always, as far as it goes, pure, forcible, and refreshing, consummate in composition, and marvellous in color." — RUSKIN, *Modern Painters*.

truth is founded upon the same principle as that by which the historical painter acquires perfect form. But whether landscape-painting has a right to aspire so far as to reject what the painters call accidents of nature, is not easy to determine. It is certain Claude Lorrain seldom, if ever, availed himself of those accidents; either he thought that such peculiarities were contrary to that style of general nature which he professed, or that it would catch the attention too strongly, and destroy that quietness and repose which he thought necessary to that kind of painting.

A portrait-painter likewise, when he attempts history, unless he is upon his guard, is likely to enter too much into the detail. He too frequently makes his historical heads look like portraits; and this was once the custom among those old painters, who revived the art before general ideas were practised or understood. A history-painter paints man in general; a portrait-painter, a particular man, and consequently a defective model.

Thus an habitual practice in the lower exercises of the art will prevent many from attaining the greater. But such of us who move in these humbler walks of the profession are not ignorant that, as the natural dignity of the subject is less, the more all the little ornamental helps are necessary to its embellishment. It would be ridiculous for a painter of domestic scenes, of portraits, landscapes, animals, or still life, to say that he despised those qualities which have made the subordinate schools so famous. The art of coloring, and the skilful management of light and shadow, are essential requisites in his confined labors.

If we descend still lower, what is the painter of fruit and flowers without the utmost art in coloring, and what the painters call handling; that is, a lightness of pencil that implies great practice, and gives the appearance of being done with ease? Some here, I believe, must remember a flower-painter whose boast it was, that he scorned to paint for the *million;* no, he professed to paint in the true Italian taste; and, despising the crowd, called strenuously upon the *few* to admire him. His idea of the Italian taste was to paint as black and dirty as he could, and to leave all clearness and brilliancy of coloring to those who were fonder of money than immortality. The consequence was such as might be expected. For these petty excellences are here essential beauties; and without this merit the artist's work will be more short-lived than the objects of his imitation.

From what has been advanced, we must now be convinced that there are two distinct styles in history-painting, — the grand, and the splendid, or ornamental.

The great style stands alone, and does not require, perhaps does not so well admit, any addition from inferior beauties. The ornamental style also possesses its own peculiar merit. However, though the union of the two may make a sort of composite style, yet that style is likely to be more imperfect than either of those which go to its composition. Both kinds have merit, and may be excellent though in different ranks, if uniformity be preserved, and the general and particular ideas of nature be not mixed. Even the meanest of them is difficult enough to attain; and the first place being already occupied by the great artists in each department, some of those who followed thought there was less room for them; and feeling the impulse of ambition and the desire of novelty, and being at the same time, perhaps, willing to take the shortest way, endeavored to make for themselves a place between both. This they have effected by forming a union of the different orders. But as the grave and majestic style would suffer by a union with the florid and gay, so also has the Venetian ornament in some respect been injured by attempting an alliance with simplicity.

It may be asserted that the great style is always more or less contaminated by any meaner mixture. But it happens in a few instances that the lower may be improved by borrowing from the grand. Thus, if a portrait-painter is desirous to raise and improve his subject, he has no other means than by approaching it to a general idea. He leaves out all the minute breaks and peculiarities in the face, and changes the dress from a temporary fashion to one more permanent, which has annexed to it no ideas of meanness from its being familiar to us. But if an exact resemblance of an individual be considered as the sole object to be aimed at, the portrait-painter will be apt to lose more than he gains by the acquired dignity taken from general nature. It is very difficult to ennoble the character of a countenance but at the expense of the likeness, which is what is most generally required by such as sit to the painter.

Of those who have practised the composite style, and have succeeded in this perilous attempt, perhaps the foremost is Correggio. His style is founded upon modern grace and elegance, to which is superadded something of the simplicity of the grand style. A breadth of light and color, the general ideas of the drapery, an uninterrupted flow of outline, all conspire to this effect. Next to him (perhaps equal to him), Parmegiano has dignified the genteelness of modern effeminacy, by uniting it with the simplicity of the ancients and the grandeur and severity of Michael Angelo. It must be confessed, however, that these two extraordinary men, by endeavoring to give the utmost degree of grace, have sometimes, perhaps, exceeded its boundaries, and have fallen into the most hateful of all hateful qualities, — affectation. Indeed, it is the peculiar characteristic of men of genius to be afraid of coldness and insipidity, from which they think they never can be too far removed. It particularly happens to these great masters of grace and elegance. They often boldly drive on to the very verge of ridicule; the spectator is alarmed, but at the same time admires their vigor and intrepidity.

> "Strange graces still, and stranger flights they had,
> . . . .
> Yet ne'er so sure our passion to create,
> As when they touch'd the brink of all we hate."

The errors of genius, however, are pardonable, and none even of the more exalted painters are wholly free from them; but they have taught us, by the rectitude of their general practice, to correct their own affected or accidental deviation. The very first have not been always upon their guard, and perhaps there is not a fault but what may take shelter under the most venerable authorities; yet that style only is perfect in which the noblest principles are uniformly pursued; and those masters only are entitled to the first rank in our estimation who have enlarged the boundaries of their art, and have raised it to its highest dignity, by exhibiting the general ideas of nature.

On the whole, it seems to me that there is but one presiding principle which regulates and gives stability to every art. The works, whether of poets, painters, moralists, or historians, which are built upon general nature, live forever; while those which depend for their existence on particular customs and habits, a partial view of nature, or the fluctuation of fashion, can only be coeval with that which first raised them from obscurity. Present time and future may be considered as rivals; and he who solicits the one must expect to be discountenanced by the other.

Mrs. Merrick.

DISCOURSE V.

Delivered to the Students of the Royal Academy, on the Distribution of the Prizes, December 10, 1772.

CIRCUMSPECTION REQUIRED IN ENDEAVORING TO UNITE CONTRARY EXCELLENCES. — THE EXPRESSION OF A MIXED PASSION NOT TO BE ATTEMPTED. — EXAMPLES OF THOSE WHO EXCELLED IN THE GREAT STYLE. — RAPHAEL, MICHAEL ANGELO, THOSE TWO EXTRAORDINARY MEN COMPARED WITH EACH OTHER. — THE CHARACTERISTICAL STYLE. — SALVATOR ROSA MENTIONED AS AN EXAMPLE OF THAT STYLE; AND OPPOSED TO CARLO MARATTI. — SKETCH OF THE CHARACTERS OF POUSSIN AND RUBENS. — THESE TWO PAINTERS ENTIRELY DISSIMILAR, BUT CONSISTENT WITH THEMSELVES. — THIS CONSISTENCY REQUIRED IN ALL PARTS OF THE ART.

I PURPOSE to carry on in this discourse the subject which I began in my last. It was my wish upon that occasion to incite you to pursue the higher excellences of the art. But I fear that in this particular I have been misunderstood. Some are ready to imagine, when any of their favorite acquirements in the art are properly classed, that they are utterly disgraced. This is a very great mistake; nothing has its proper lustre but in its proper place. That which is most worthy of esteem in its allotted sphere becomes an object, not of respect, but of derision, when it is forced into a higher, to which it is not suited; and there it becomes doubly a source of disorder, by occupying a situation which is not natural to it, and by putting down from the first place what is in reality of too much magnitude to become with grace and proportion that subordinate station, to which something of less value would be much better suited.

My advice, in a word, is this: keep your principal attention fixed upon the higher excellences. If you compass them, and compass nothing more, you are still in the first class. We may regret the innumerable beauties which you may want; you may be very imperfect; but still you are an imperfect artist of the highest order.

If, when you have got thus far, you can add any, or all, of the subordinate qualifications, it is my wish and advice that you should not neglect them. But this is as much a matter of circumspection and caution at least, as of eagerness and pursuit.

The mind is apt to be distracted by a multiplicity of objects; and that scale of perfection which I wish always to be preserved is in the greatest danger of being totally disordered, and even inverted.

Some excellences bear to be united, and are improved by union; others are of a discordant nature, and the attempt to join them only produces a harsh jarring of incongruent principles. The attempt to unite contrary excellences (of form, for instance) in a single figure can never escape degenerating into the monstrous but by sinking into the insipid, — by taking away its marked character, and weakening its expression.

This remark is true to a certain degree with regard to the passions. If you mean to preserve the most perfect beauty in its most perfect state, you cannot express the passions, all of which produce distortion and deformity, more or less, in the most beautiful faces.[1]

Guido, from want of choice in adapting his subject to his ideas and his powers, or from attempting to preserve beauty where it could not be preserved, has in this respect succeeded very ill. His figures are often engaged in subjects that require great expression; yet his Judith and Holofernes, the daughter of Herodias with the Baptist's head, the Andromeda, and some even of the Mothers of the Innocents, have little more expression than his Venus attired by the Graces.

Obvious as these remarks appear, there are many writers on our art who, not being of the profession, and consequently not knowing what can or cannot be done, have been very liberal of absurd praises in their descriptions of favorite works. They always find in them what they are resolved to find. They praise excellences that can hardly exist together; and, above all things, are fond of describing, with great exactness, the expression of a mixed passion, which more particularly appears to me out of the reach of our art.

Such are many disquisitions which I have read on some of the cartoons and other pictures of Raphael,

[1] There are passions and degrees of passion, which are expressed by the ugliest possible contortions of countenance, and throw the whole body into such a forced position that all the beautiful lines which cover its surface are lost. From all such emotions the ancient masters either abstained entirely, or reduced them to that lower degree in which they are capable of a certain measure of beauty. Rage and despair disgraced none of their productions; I dare maintain that they have never painted a Fury. — LESSING, *The Laocoön.*

where the critics have described their own imaginations; or, indeed, where the excellent master himself may have attempted this expression of passions above the powers of the art, and has, therefore, by an indistinct and imperfect marking, left room for every imagination, with equal probability, to find a passion of his own. What has been, and what can be done in the art, is sufficiently difficult; we need not be mortified or discouraged at not being able to execute the conceptions of a romantic imagination. Art has its boundaries, though imagination has none. We can easily, like the ancients, suppose a Jupiter to be possessed of all those powers and perfections which the subordinate deities were endowed with separately. Yet, when they employed their art to represent him, they confined his character to majesty alone. Pliny, therefore, though we are under great obligations to him for the information he has given us in relation to the works of the ancient artists, is very frequently wrong when he speaks of them, which he does very often, in the style of many of our modern connoisseurs. He observes that in a statue of Paris, by Euphranor, you might discover, at the same time, three different characters: the dignity of a judge of the goddesses, the lover of Helen, and the conqueror of Achilles. A statue in which you endeavor to unite stately dignity, youthful elegance, and stern valor, must surely possess none of these to any eminent degree.

From hence it appears, that there is much difficulty, as well as danger, in an endeavor to concentrate, in a single subject, those various powers which, rising from different points, naturally move in different directions.

The summit of excellence seems to be an assemblage of contrary qualities, but mixed in such proportions that no one part is found to counteract the other. How hard this is to be attained in every art, those only know who have made the greatest progress in their respective professions.

To conclude what I have to say on this part of the subject, which I think of great importance, I wish you to understand that I do not discourage the younger students from the noble attempt of uniting all the excellences of art; but suggest to them, that, besides the difficulties which attend every arduous attempt, there is a peculiar difficulty in the choice of the excellences which ought to be united. I wish to attend to this, that you may try yourselves, whenever you are capable of that trial, what you can and what you cannot do; and that, instead of dissipating your natural faculties over the immense field of possible excellence, you may choose some particular walk, in which you may exercise all your powers in order that each of you may become the first in his way. If any man shall be master of such a transcendent, commanding, and ductile genius, as to enable him to rise to the highest, and to stoop to the lowest, flights of art, and to sweep over all of them, unobstructed and secure, he is fitter to give example than to receive instruction.

Having said thus much on the *union* of excellences, I will next say something of the subordination in which various excellences ought to be kept.

I am of opinion that the ornamental style, which, in my discourse of last year, I cautioned you against considering as *principal*, may not be wholly unworthy the attention even of those who aim at the grand style, when it is properly placed and properly reduced.

But this study will be used with far better effect, if its principles are employed in softening the harshness and mitigating the rigor of the great style, than if it attempt to stand forward with any pretensions of its own to positive and original excellence. It was thus Ludovico Caracci, whose example I formerly recommended to you, employed it. He was acquainted with the works both of Correggio and the Venetian painters, and knew the principles by which they produced those pleasing effects which, at the first glance, prepossess us so much in their favor; but he took only as much from each as would embellish, but not overpower, that manly strength and energy of style which is his peculiar character.

Since I have already expatiated so largely in my former discourse, and in my present, upon the *styles* and *characters* of painting, it will not be at all unsuitable to my subject if I mention to you some particulars relative to the leading principles and capital works of those who excelled in the *great style*, that I may bring you from abstraction nearer to practice, and, by exemplifying the positions which I have laid down, enable you to understand more clearly what I would enforce.

The principal works of modern art are in fresco, a mode of painting which excludes attention to minute elegances; yet these works in fresco are the productions on which the fame of the greatest masters depends. Such are the pictures of Michael Angelo and Raphael in the Vatican; to which we may add the cartoons; which, though not strictly to be called fresco, yet may be put under that denomination; and such are the works of Giulio Romano at Mantua. If these performances were destroyed, with them would be lost the best part of the reputation of those illustrious painters; for these are justly considered as the greatest effort of our art which the world can boast. To these, therefore, we should principally direct our attention for higher excellences. As for the lower arts, as they have been once discovered, they may be easily attained by those possessed of the former.

Raphael, who stands in general foremost of the first painters, owes his reputation, as I have observed, to his excellence in the higher parts of the art; his works in fresco, therefore, ought to be the first object of our study and attention. His easel-works stand in a lower degree of estimation; for though he continually, to the day of his death, embellished his performances more and more with the addition of those lower ornaments which entirely make the merit of some painters, yet he never arrived at such perfection as to make him an object of imitation. He never was able to conquer perfectly that dryness, or even littleness of manner, which he inherited from his master. He never acquired that nicety of taste in colors, that breadth of light and shadow, that art and management of uniting light to light, and shadow to shadow, so as to make the object rise out of the ground, with the plenitude of effect so much admired in the works of Correggio.[1] When he painted in oil, his hand seemed to be so cramped and confined that he not only lost that facility and spirit, but I think even that correctness of form, which is so perfect and admirable in his fresco-works. I do not recollect any pictures of his of this kind, except the "Transfiguration," in which there are not some parts that appear to be even feebly drawn. That this is not a necessary attendant on oil-painting, we have abundant instances in more modern painters. Ludovico Caracci, for instance, preserved in his works in oil the same spirit, vigor, and correctness which he had in fresco. I have no desire to degrade Raphael from the high rank which he deservedly holds; but by comparing him with himself, he does not appear to me to be the same man in oil as in fresco.

From those who have ambition to tread in this great walk of the art, Michael Angelo claims the next attention. He did not possess so many excellences as Raphael, but those which he had were of the highest kind. He considered the art as consisting of little more than what may be attained by sculpture, — correctness of form and energy of character. We ought not to expect more than an artist intends in his work. He never attempted those lesser elegances and graces in the art. Vasari says he never

---

[1] I have no hesitation in saying that, from the technical point of view, Raphael himself never came to maturity as a painter. . . . He advanced with great rapidity as a draughtsman, and brought the art of drawing, as he understood it, to a sudden maturity, but his painting did not advance at the same rate, and the only rational account of him is that he was a draughtsman who colored his drawings delicately. — HAMERTON, *Graphic Arts.*

painted but one picture in oil, and resolved never to paint another, saying it was an employment only fit for women and children.

If any man had a right to look down upon the lower accomplishments as beneath his attention, it was certainly Michael Angelo; nor can it be thought strange that such a mind should have slighted or have been withheld from paying due attention to all those graces and embellishments of art which have diffused such lustre over the works of other painters.

It must be acknowledged, however, that together with these, which we wish he had more attended to, he has rejected all the false, though specious ornaments which disgrace the works even of the most esteemed artists; and I will venture to say that when those higher excellences are more known and cultivated by the artists and the patrons of arts, his fame and credit will increase with our increasing knowledge. His name will then be held in the same veneration as it was in the enlightened age of Leo X.; and it is remarkable that the reputation of this truly great man has been continually declining as the art itself has declined. For I must remark to you that it has long been much on the decline, and that our only hope of its revival will consist in your being thoroughly sensible of its depravation and decay. It is to Michael Angelo that we owe even the existence of Raphael; it is to him Raphael owes the grandeur of his style. He was taught by him to elevate his thoughts, and to conceive his subjects with dignity. His genius, however, formed to blaze and shine, might, like fire in combustible matter, forever have lain dormant if it had not caught a spark by its contact with Michael Angelo; and though it never burst out with *his* extraordinary heat and vehemence, yet it must be acknowledged to be a more pure, regular, and chaste flame. Though our judgment must, upon the whole, decide in favor of Raphael, yet he never takes such a firm hold and entire possession of the mind as to make us desire nothing else, and to feel nothing wanting. The effect of the capital works of Michael Angelo perfectly corresponds to what Bouchardon said he felt from reading Homer; his whole frame appeared to himself to be enlarged, and all nature which surrounded him diminished to atoms.

If we put these great artists in a light of comparison with each other, Raphael had more taste and fancy, Michael Angelo more genius and imagination. The one excelled in beauty, the other in energy. Michael Angelo has more of the poetical inspiration; his ideas are vast and sublime; his people are a superior order of beings; there is nothing about them, nothing in the air of their actions, or their attitudes, or the style and cast of their limbs or features, that reminds us of their belonging to our own species. Raphael's imagination is not so elevated; his figures are not so much disjoined from our own diminutive race of beings, though his ideas are chaste, noble, and of great conformity to their subjects. Michael Angelo's works have a strong, peculiar, and marked character; they seem to proceed from his own mind entirely, and that mind so rich and abundant that he never needed, or seemed to disdain, to look abroad for foreign help. Raphael's materials are generally borrowed, though the noble structure is his own. The excellence of this extraordinary man lay in the propriety, beauty, and majesty of his characters, the judicious contrivance of his composition, his correctness of drawing, purity of taste, and skilful accommodation of other men's conceptions to his own purpose. Nobody excelled him in that judgment with which he united to his own observations on nature the energy of Michael Angelo and the beauty and simplicity of the antique. To the question, therefore, which ought to hold the first rank, Raphael or Michael Angelo, it must be answered that if it is to be given to him who possessed a greater combination of the higher qualities of the art than any other man, there is no doubt but Raphael is the first. But if, as Longinus thinks, the sublime, being the highest excellence that human composition can attain to, abundantly compensates the absence of every other beauty, and atones for all other deficiencies, then Michael Angelo demands the preference.

These two extraordinary men carried some of the higher excellences of the art to a greater degree of perfection than probably they ever arrived at before. They certainly have not been excelled, nor equalled since. Many of their successors were induced to leave this great road as a beaten path, endeavoring to surprise and please by something uncommon or new. When this desire of novelty has proceeded from mere idleness or caprice, it is not worth the trouble of criticism; but when it has been the result of a busy mind of a peculiar complexion, it is always striking and interesting, never insipid.

Such is the great style, as it appears in those who possessed it at its height; in this, search after novelty, in conception or in treating the subject, has no place.

But there is another style, which, though inferior to the former, has still great merit, because it shows that those who cultivated it were men of lively and vigorous imagination. This, which may be called the original or characteristical style, being less referred to any true archetype existing either in general or particular nature, must be supported by the painter's consistency in the principles which he has assumed, and in the union and harmony of his whole design. The excellence of every style, but of the subordinate styles more especially, will very much depend on preserving that union and harmony between all the component parts that they may appear to hang well together, as if the whole proceeded from one mind. It is in the works of art as in the characters of men. The faults or defects of some men seem to become them when they appear to be the natural growth, and of a piece with the rest of their character. A faithful picture of a mind, though it be not of the most elevated kind, though it be irregular, wild, and incorrect, yet if it be marked with that spirit and firmness which characterize works of genius, will claim attention, and be more striking than a combination of excellences that do not seem to unite well together; or we may say, than a work that possesses even all excellences, but those in a moderate degree.

One of the strongest-marked characters of this kind, which must be allowed to be subordinate to the great style, is that of Salvator Rosa. He gives us a peculiar cast of nature, which, though void of all grace, elegance, and simplicity, though it has nothing of that elevation and dignity which belongs to the grand style, yet has that sort of dignity which belongs to savage and uncultivated nature; but what is most to be admired in him is the perfect correspondence which he observed between the subjects which he chose and his manner of treating them. Everything is of a piece; his rocks, trees, sky, even to his handling, have the same rude and wild character which animates his figures.

With him we may contrast the character of Carlo Maratti, who, in my opinion, had no great vigor of mind or strength of original genius. He rarely seizes the imagination by exhibiting the higher excellences, nor does he captivate us by that originality which attends the painter who thinks for himself. He knew and practised all the rules of art, and from a composition of Raphael, Caracci, and Guido, made up a style of which the only fault was that it had no manifest defects and no striking beauties, and that the principles of his composition are never blended together so as to form one uniform body, original in its kind, or excellent in any view.

I will mention two other painters, who, though entirely dissimilar, yet, by being each consistent with himself, and possessing a manner entirely his own, have both gained reputation, though for very opposite accomplishments. The painters I mean are

Rubens and Poussin. Rubens I mention in this place, as I think him a remarkable instance of the same mind being seen in all the various parts of the art. The whole is so much of a piece that one can scarce be brought to believe but that if any one of the qualities he possessed had been more correct and perfect, his works would not have been so complete as they now appear. If we should allow him a greater purity and correctness of drawing, his want of simplicity in composition, coloring, and drapery, would appear more gross.

In his composition his art is too apparent. His figures have expression and act with energy, but without simplicity or dignity. His coloring, in which he is eminently skilled, is, notwithstanding, too much of what we call tinted. Throughout the whole of his works there is a proportionable want of that nicety of distinction and elegance of mind which is required in the higher walks of painting; and to this want it may be in some degree ascribed that those qualities which make the excellence of this subordinate style appear in him with their greatest lustre. Indeed, the facility with which he invented, the richness of his composition, the luxuriant harmony and brilliancy of his coloring, so dazzle the eye, that while his works continue before us, we cannot help thinking that all his deficiencies are fully supplied.

Opposed to this florid, careless, loose, and inaccurate style, that of the simple, careful, pure and correct style of Poussin seems to be a complete contrast. Yet however opposite their characters, in one thing they agreed, both of them always preserving a perfect correspondence between all the parts of their respective manners; insomuch that it may be doubted whether any alteration of what is considered as defective in either would not destroy the effect of the whole.

Poussin lived and conversed with the ancient statues so long that he may be said to have been better acquainted with them than with the people who were about him. I have often thought that he carried his veneration for them so far as to wish to give his works the air of ancient paintings. It is certain he copied some of the antique paintings, particularly the Marriage in the Aldobrandini Palace at Rome, which I believe to be the best relic of those remote ages that has yet been found.

No works of any modern have so much of the air of antique painting as those of Poussin. His best performances have a remarkable dryness of manner, which though by no means to be recommended for imitation, yet seems perfectly correspondent to that ancient simplicity which distinguishes his style. Like Polidoro, he studied the ancients so much that he acquired a habit of thinking in their way, and seemed to know perfectly the actions and gestures they would use on every occasion.

Poussin, in the latter part of his life, changed from his dry manner to one much softer and richer, where there is a greater union between the figures and ground,—as in the Seven Sacraments in the Duke of Orleans's collection; but neither these nor any of his other pictures in this manner, are at all comparable to many in this dry manner which we have in England.

The favorite subjects of Poussin were ancient fables; and no painter was ever better qualified to paint such subjects, not only from his being eminently skilled in the knowledge of the ceremonies, customs, and habits of the ancients, but from his being so well acquainted with the different characters which those who invented them gave to their allegorical figures. Though Rubens has shown great fancy in his Satyrs, Silenuses, and Fauns, yet they are not that distinct, separate class of beings which is carefully exhibited by the ancients, and by Poussin. Certainly, when such subjects of antiquity are represented, nothing in the picture ought to remind us of modern times. The mind is thrown back into antiquity, and nothing ought to be introduced that may tend to awaken it from the illusion.

Poussin seemed to think that the style and the language in which such stories are told is not the worse for preserving some relish of the old way of painting, which seemed to give a general uniformity to the whole, so that the mind was thrown back into antiquity not only by the subject, but the execution.

If Poussin, in imitation of the ancients, represents Apollo driving his chariot out of the sea, by way of representing the sun rising, if he personifies lakes and rivers, it is nowise offensive in him, but seems perfectly of a piece with the general air of the picture. On the contrary, if the figures which people his pictures had a modern air or countenance, if they appeared like our countrymen, if the draperies were like cloth or silk of our manufacture, if the landscape had the appearance of a modern view, how ridiculous would Apollo appear instead of the sun, — and an old man, or a nymph with an urn, to represent a river or a lake!

I cannot avoid mentioning here a circumstance in portrait-painting which may help to confirm what has been said. When a portrait is painted in the historical style, as it is neither an exact minute representation of an individual, nor completely ideal, every circumstance ought to correspond to this mixture. The simplicity of the antique air and attitude, however much to be admired, is ridiculous when joined to a figure in a modern dress. It is not to my purpose to enter into the question at present, whether this mixed style ought to be adopted or not; yet if it is chosen, it is necessary it should be complete, and all of a piece; the difference of stuffs, for instance, which make the clothing, should be distinguished in the same degree as the head deviates from a general idea. Without this union, which I have so often recommended, a work can have no marked and determined character, which is the peculiar and constant evidence of genius. But when this is accomplished to a high degree it becomes in some sort a rival to that style which we have fixed as the highest.

Thus I have given a sketch of the characters of Rubens and Salvator Rosa, as they appear to me to have the greatest uniformity of mind throughout their whole work. But we may add to these all those artists who are at the head of a class, and have had a school of imitators, from Michael Angelo down to Watteau. Upon the whole it appears that, setting aside the ornamental style, there are two different modes, either of which a student may adopt without degrading the dignity of his art. The object of the first is to combine the higher excellences and embellish them to the greatest advantage; of the other, to carry one of these excellences to the highest degree. But those who possess neither must be classed with them who, as Shakspeare says, are "men of no mark or likelihood."

I inculcate as frequently as I can your forming yourselves upon great principles and great models. Your time will be much misspent in every other pursuit. Small excellences should be viewed, not studied; they ought to be viewed, because nothing ought to escape a painter's observation, but for no other reason.

There is another caution which I wish to give you. Be as select in those whom you endeavor to please as in those whom you endeavor to imitate. Without the love of fame you can never do anything excellent; but by an excessive and undistinguishing thirst after it you will come to have vulgar views; you will degrade your style, and your taste will be entirely corrupted. It is certain that the lowest style will be the most popular, as it falls within the compass of ignorance itself; and the vulgar will always be pleased with what is natural, in the confined and misunderstood sense of the word.

One would wish that such depravation of taste should be counteracted with that manly pride which actuated Euripides when he said to the Athenians who criticised his works, "I do not compose my works in order to be corrected by you, but to instruct you." It is true, to have a right to speak thus, a man must be a Euripides. However, thus much may be allowed, that when an artist is sure that he is upon firm ground, supported by the authority and practice of his predecessors of the greatest reputation, he may then assume the boldness and intrepidity of genius; at any rate he must not be tempted out of the right path by any allurement of popularity, which always accompanies the lower styles of painting.

I mention this, because our exhibitions, while they produce such admirable effects by nourishing emulation, and calling out genius, have also a mischievous tendency, by seducing the painter to an ambition of pleasing indiscriminately the mixed multitude of people who resort to them.

Mrs. Lucy Hardinge.

DISCOURSE VI.

Delivered to the Students of the Royal Academy, on the Distribution of the Prizes, December 10, 1774.

IMITATION. — GENIUS BEGINS WHERE RULES END. — INVENTION : ACQUIRED BY BEING CONVERSANT WITH THE INVENTIONS OF OTHERS. — THE TRUE METHOD OF IMITATING. — BORROWING, HOW FAR ALLOWABLE. — SOMETHING TO BE GATHERED FROM EVERY SCHOOL.

WHEN I have taken the liberty of addressing you on the course and order of your studies, I never proposed to enter into a minute detail of the art. This I have always left to the several professors, who pursue the end of our institution with the highest honor to themselves, and with the greatest advantage to the students.

My purpose in the discourses I have held in the Academy has been to lay down certain general positions which seem to me proper for the formation of a sound taste, — principles necessary to guard the pupils against those errors into which the sanguine temper common to their time of life has a tendency to lead them, and which have rendered abortive the hopes of so many successions of promising young men in all parts of Europe. I wished also to intercept and suppress those prejudices which particularly prevail when the mechanism of painting is come to its perfection; and which, when they do prevail, are certain utterly to destroy the higher and more valuable parts of this literate and liberal profession.

These two have been my principal purposes; they are still as much my concern as ever; and if I repeat my own notions on the subject, you who know how fast mistake and prejudice, when neglected, gain ground upon truth and reason, will easily excuse me. I only attempt to set the same thing in the greatest variety of lights.

The subject of this discourse will be imitation, as far as a painter is concerned in it. By imitation, I do not mean imitation in its largest sense, but simply the following of other masters, and the advantage to be drawn from the study of their works.

Those who have undertaken to write on our art, and have represented it as a kind of *inspiration*, as a *gift* bestowed upon peculiar favorites at their birth, seem to insure a much more favorable disposition from their readers, and have a much more captivating and liberal air, than he who attempts to examine, coldly, whether there are any means by which this art may be acquired; how the mind may be strengthened and expanded, and what guides will show the way to eminence.

It is very natural for those who are unacquainted with the *cause* of anything extraordinary to be astonished at the *effect*, and to consider it as a kind of magic. They who have never observed the gradation by which art is acquired, who see only what is the full result of long labor and application of an infinite number and infinite variety of acts, are apt to conclude, from their entire inability to do the same at once, that it is not only inaccessible to themselves, but can be done by those only who have some gift of the nature of inspiration bestowed upon them.

The travellers into the East tell us that when the ignorant inhabitants of those countries are asked concerning the ruins of stately edifices yet remaining among them, the melancholy monuments of their former grandeur and long-lost science, they always answer that they were built by magicians. The untaught mind finds a vast gulf between its own powers and those works of complicated art which it is utterly unable to fathom; and it supposes that such a void can be passed only by supernatural powers.

And, as for artists themselves, it is by no means their interest to undeceive such judges, however conscious they may be of the very natural means by which their extraordinary powers were acquired; though our art, being intrinsically imitative, rejects this idea of inspiration, more perhaps than any other.

It is to avoid this plain confession of the truth, as it should seem, that this imitation of masters, indeed almost all imitation, which implies a more regular and progressive method of attaining the ends of painting, has ever been particularly inveighed against with great keenness, both by ancient and modern writers.

To derive all from native power, to owe nothing to another, is the praise which men who do not much think on what they are saying, bestow sometimes upon others, and sometimes on themselves; and their imaginary dignity is naturally heightened by a supercilious censure of the low, the barren, the grovelling, the servile imitator. It would be no wonder if a student, frightened by these terrific and disgraceful epithets, with which the poor imitators are so often loaded, should let fall his pencil in mere despair, — conscious as he must be how much he has been indebted to the labors of others, how little, how very little of his art was born with him, — and consider it as hopeless to set about acquiring by the imitation of any human master what he is taught to suppose is matter of inspiration from heaven.

Some allowance must be made for what is said in the gayety of rhetoric. We cannot suppose that any one can really mean to exclude all imitation of others. A position so wild would scarce deserve a serious answer; for it is apparent, if we were forbid to make use of the advantages which our predecessors afford us, the art would be always to begin, and consequently remain always in its infant state; and it is a common observation that no art was ever invented and carried to perfection at the same time.

But to bring us entirely to reason and sobriety, let it be observed, that a painter must not only be of necessity an imitator of the works of nature, which alone is sufficient to dispel this phantom of inspiration, but he must be as necessarily an imitator of the works of other painters. This appears more humiliating, but is equally true; and no man can be an artist, whatever he may suppose, upon any other terms.

However, those who appear more moderate and reasonable allow that our study is to begin by imitation, but maintain that we should no longer use the thoughts of our predecessors when we are become able to think for ourselves. They hold that imitation is as hurtful to the more advanced student as it was advantageous to the beginner.

For my own part, I confess, I am not only very much disposed to maintain the absolute necessity of imitation in the first stages of the art, but am of opinion that the study of other masters, which I here call imitation, may be extended throughout our whole lives without any danger of the inconveniences with which it is charged, of enfeebling the mind, or preventing us from giving that original air which every work undoubtedly ought always to have.

I am on the contrary persuaded that by imitation only, variety, and even originality of invention, is produced. I will go further; even genius, at least what generally is so called, is the child of imitation. But as this appears to be contrary to the general opinion, I must explain my position before I enforce it.

Genius is supposed to be a power of producing excellences which are out of the reach of the rules of art, — a power which no precepts can teach, and which no industry can acquire.

This opinion of the impossibility of acquiring those beauties which stamp the work with the character of genius supposes that it is something more fixed than in reality it is; and that we always do, and ever did agree in opinion, with respect to what should be considered as the characteristic of genius. But the truth is that the degree of excellence which proclaims genius is different in different times and different places; and what shows it to be so is that mankind have often changed their opinion upon this matter.

When the arts were in their infancy the power of merely drawing the likeness of any object was considered as one of its greatest efforts. The common people, ignorant of the principles of art, talk the same language even to this day. But when it was found that every man could be taught to do this, and a great deal more, merely by the observance of certain precepts, the name of genius then shifted its application, and was given only to him who added the peculiar character of the object he represented, — to him who had invention, expression, grace, or dignity; in short, those qualities, or excellences, the power of producing which could not then be taught by any known and promulgated rules.

We are very sure that the beauty of form, the expression of the passions, the art of composition, even the power of giving a general air of grandeur to a work, is at present very much under the dominion of rules. These excellences were, heretofore, considered merely as the effect of genius; and justly, if genius is not taken for inspiration, but as the effect of close observation and experience.

He who first made any of these observations, and digested them, so as to form an invariable principle for himself to work by, had that merit, but probably no one went very far at once; and generally, the first who gave the hint, did not know how to pursue it steadily and methodically, — at least not in the beginning. He himself worked on it, and improved it; others worked more, and improved further; until the secret was discovered, and the practice made as general as refined practice can be made. How many more principles may be fixed and ascertained we cannot tell; but as criticism is likely to go hand in hand with the art which is its subject, we may venture to say that, as that art shall advance, its powers will be still more and more fixed by rules.

But by whatever strides criticism may gain ground, we need be under no apprehension that invention will ever be annihilated or subdued; or intellectual energy be brought entirely within the restraint of written law. Genius will still have room enough to expatiate, and keep always at the same distance from narrow comprehension and mechanical performance.

What we now call genius begins, not where rules abstractedly taken end, but where known vulgar and trite rules have no longer any place. It must of necessity be that even works of genius, like every other effect, as they must have their cause, must likewise have their rules; it cannot be by chance that excellences are produced with any constancy or any certainty, for this is not the nature of chance; but the rules by which men of extraordinary parts, and such as are called men of genius, work, are either such as they discover by their own peculiar observations, or of such a nice texture as not easily to admit being expressed in words; especially as artists are not very frequently skilful in that mode of communicating ideas. Unsubstantial, however, as these rules may seem, and difficult as it may be to convey them in writing, they are still seen and felt in the mind of the artist; and he works from them with as much certainty as if they were embodied, as I may say, upon paper. It is true, these refined principles cannot be always made palpable, like the more gross rules of art; yet it does not follow but that the mind may be put in such a train that it shall perceive, by a kind of scientific sense, that propriety which words, particularly words of unpractised writers such as we are, can but very feebly suggest.

Invention is one of the great marks of genius; but if we consult experience we shall find that it is by being conversant with the inventions of others that we learn to invent, as by reading the thoughts of others we learn to think.

Whoever has so far formed his taste as to be able to relish and feel the beauties of the great masters has gone a great way in his study; for, merely from a consciousness of this relish of the right, the mind swells with an inward pride, and is almost as powerfully affected as if it had itself produced what it admires. Our hearts, frequently warmed in this manner by the contact of those whom we wish to resemble, will undoubtedly catch something of their way of thinking; and we shall receive in our own bosoms some radiation at least of their fire and splendor. That disposition, which is so strong in children, still continues with us, of catching involuntarily the general air and manner of those with whom we are most conversant, — with this difference only, that a young mind is naturally pliable and imitative, but in a more advanced state it grows rigid, and must be warmed and softened before it will receive a deep impression.

From these considerations, which a little of your

own reflection will carry a great way further, it appears of what great consequence it is that our minds should be habituated to the contemplation of excellence; and that, far from being contented to make such habits the discipline of our youth only, we should, to the last moment of our lives, continue a settled intercourse with all the true examples of grandeur. Their inventions are not only the food of our infancy, but the substance which supplies the fullest maturity of our vigor.

The mind is but a barren soil — a soil which is soon exhausted, and will produce no crop, or only one, unless it be continually fertilized and enriched with foreign matter.

When we have had continually before us the great works of art to impregnate our minds with kindred ideas, we are then, and not till then, fit to produce something of the same species. We behold all about us with the eyes of those penetrating observers whose works we contemplate; and our minds, accustomed to think the thoughts of the noblest and brightest intellects, are prepared for the discovery and selection of all that is great and noble in nature. The greatest natural genius cannot subsist on its own stock; he who resolves never to ransack any mind but his own, will be soon reduced from mere barrenness to the poorest of all imitations; he will be obliged to imitate himself, and to repeat what he has before often repeated. When we know the subject designed by such men, it will never be difficult to guess what kind of work is to be produced.

It is vain for painters or poets to endeavor to invent without materials on which the mind may work, and from which invention must originate. Nothing can come of nothing.

Homer is supposed to be possessed of all the learning of his time; and we are certain that Michael Angelo and Raphael were equally possessed of all the knowledge in the art which had been discovered in the works of their predecessors.[1]

A mind enriched by an assemblage of all the treasures of ancient and modern art will be more elevated and fruitful in resources, in proportion to the number of ideas which have been carefully collected and thoroughly digested. There can be no doubt but that he who has the most materials has the greatest means of invention; and if he has not the power of using them, it must proceed from a feebleness of intellect, or from the confused manner in which those collections have been laid up in his mind.

The addition of other men's judgment is so far from weakening our own, as is the opinion of many, that it will fashion and consolidate those ideas of excellence which lay in embryo — feeble, ill-shaped, and confused — but which are finished and put in order by the authority and practice of those whose works may be said to have been consecrated by having stood the test of ages.

The mind, or genius, has been compared to a spark of fire, which is smothered by a heap of fuel, and

---

[1] Michael Angelo, in his old age, said of Raphael that industry, not genius, was the cause of his success; certainly, an intense power of assimilation, of learning all things from all men, furthered incalculably his natural gifts.

prevented from blazing into a flame. This simile, which is made use of by the younger Pliny, may be easily mistaken for argument or proof. But there is is no danger of the mind being overburdened with knowledge, or the genius extinguished by any addition of images; on the contrary, these acquisitions may as well, perhaps better, be compared, if comparisons signified anything in reasoning, to the supply of living embers, which will contribute to strengthen the spark, that without the association of more fuel would have died away. The truth is, he whose feebleness is such as to make other men's thoughts an incumbrance to him, can have no very great strength of mind or genius of his own to be destroyed; so that not much harm will be done at worst.

We may oppose to Pliny the greater authority of Cicero, who is continually enforcing the necessity of this method of study. In his dialogue on oratory, he makes Crassus say that one of the first and most important precepts is to choose a proper model for our imitation: *Hoc sit primum in præceptis meis, ut demonstremus quem imitemur.*

When I speak of the habitual imitation and continued study of masters, it is not to be understood that I advise any endeavor to copy the exact peculiar color and complexion of another man's mind; the success of such an attempt must always be like his who imitates exactly the air, manner, and gestures of him whom he admires. His model may be excellent, but the copy will be ridiculous; this ridicule does not arise from his having imitated, but from his not having chosen the right mode of imitation.

It is a necessary and warrantable pride to disdain to walk servilely behind any individual, however elevated his rank. The true and liberal ground of imitation is an open field, where though he who precedes has had the advantage of starting before you, you may always propose to overtake him; it is enough, however to pursue his course; you need not tread in his footsteps, and you certainly have a right to outstrip him if you can.

Nor, while I recommend studying the art from artists, can I be supposed to mean that nature is to be neglected; I take this study in aid, and not in exclusion of the other. Nature is and must be the fountain which alone is inexhaustible, and from which all excellences must originally flow.

The great use of studying our predecessors is, to open the mind, to shorten our labor, and to give us the result of the selection made by those great minds of what is grand or beautiful in nature; her rich stores are all spread out before us; but it is an art, and no easy art, to know how or what to choose, and how to attain and secure the object of our choice. Thus, the highest beauty of form must be taken from nature; but it is an art of long deduction and great experience to know how to find it. We must not content ourselves with merely admiring and relishing; we must enter into the principles on which the work is wrought; these do not swim on the superficies, and consequently are not open to superficial observers.

Art in its perfection is not ostentatious; it lies hid and works its effect, itself unseen. It is the proper study and labor of an artist to uncover and find out the latent cause of conspicuous beauties, and from thence form principles of his owr conduct. Such an examination is a continual exertion of the mind; as great, perhaps, as that of the artist whose works he is thus studying.

The sagacious imitator does not content himself with merely remarking what distinguishes the different manner or genius of each master; he enters into the contrivance in the composition, how the masses of lights are disposed, the means by which the effect is produced, how artfully some parts are lost in the ground, others boldly relieved, and how all these are mutually altered and interchanged according to the reason and scheme of the work. He admires not the harmony of coloring alone, but examines by what artifice one color is a foil to its neighbor. He looks close into the tints, examines of what colors they are composed, till he has formed clear and distinct ideas, and has learned to see in what harmony and good coloring consists. What is learned in this manner from the works of others becomes really our own, sinks deep, and is never forgotten; nay, it is by seizing on this clue that we proceed forward, and get further and further in enlarging the principles and improving the practice of our art.

There can be no doubt but the art is better learned from the works themselves than from the precepts which are formed upon those works; but if it is difficult to choose proper models for imitation, it requires no less circumspection to separate and distinguish what in those models we ought to imitate.

I cannot avoid mentioning here, though it is not my

intention at present to enter into the art and method of study, an error which students are too apt to fall into. He that is forming himself must look with great caution and wariness on those peculiarities, or prominent parts, which at first force themselves upon view, and are the marks, or what is commonly called the manner, by which that individual artist is distinguished.

Peculiar marks I hold to be, generally, if not always, defects, — however difficult it may be wholly to escape them.

Peculiarities in the works of art are like those in the human figure; it is by them that we are cognizable, and distinguished one from another, but they are always so many blemishes; which, however, both in real life and in painting, cease to appear deformities to those who have them continually before their eyes. In the works of art, even the most enlightened mind, when warmed by beauties of the highest kind, will by degrees find a repugnance within him to acknowledge any defects; nay, his enthusiasm will carry him so far as to transform them into beauties and objects of imitation.

It must be acknowledged that a peculiarity of style, either from its novelty or by seeming to proceed from a peculiar turn of mind, often escapes blame; on the contrary, it is sometimes striking and pleasing; but this it is a vain labor to endeavor to imitate, because novelty and peculiarity being its only merit, when it ceases to be new it ceases to have value.

A manner, therefore, being a defect, and every painter, however excellent, having a manner, it seems to follow that all kinds of faults, as well as beauties, may be learned under the sanction of the greatest authorities. Even the great name of Michael Angelo may be used to keep in countenance a deficiency, or rather neglect, of coloring, and every other ornamental part of the art. If the young student is dry and hard, Poussin is the same. If his work has a careless and unfinished air, he has most of the Venetian school to support him. If he makes no selection of objects, but takes individual nature just as he finds it, he is like Rembrandt. If he is incorrect in the proportions of his figures, Correggio was likewise incorrect. If his colors are not blended and united, Rubens was equally crude. In short, there is no defect that may not be excused, if it is a sufficient excuse that it can be imputed to considerable artists; but it must be remembered that it was not by these defects they acquired their reputation; they have a right to our pardon, but not to our admiration.

However, to imitate peculiarities, or mistake defects for beauties, that man will be most liable who confines his imitation to one favorite master; and even though he chooses the best, and is capable of distinguishing the real excellences of his model, it is not by such narrow practice that a genius or mastery in the art is acquired. A man is as little likely to form a true idea of the perfection of the art by studying a single artist, as he would be to produce a perfectly beautiful figure by an exact imitation of any individual living model. And as the painter, by bringing together in one piece those beauties which are dispersed among a great variety of individuals, produces a figure more beautiful than can be found in nature, so that artist who can unite in himself the excellences of the various great painters, will approach nearer to perfection than any one of his masters. He who confines himself to the imitation of an individual, as he never proposes to surpass, so he is not likely to equal, the object of his imitation. He professes only to follow; and he that follows must necessarily be behind.

We should imitate the conduct of the great artists in the course of their studies, as well as the works which they produced when they were perfectly formed. Raphael began by imitating implicitly the manner of Pietro Perugino, under whom he studied; hence his first works are scarce to be distinguished from his master's; but soon forming higher and more extensive views, he imitated the grand outline of Michael Angelo; he learned the manner of using colors from the works of Leonardo da Vinci, and Fra Bartolomeo; to all this he added the contemplation of all the remains of antiquity that were within his reach, and employed others to draw for him what was in Greece and distant places. And it is from his having taken so many models that he became himself a model for all succeeding painters; always imitating, and always original.

If your ambition, therefore, be to equal Raphael, you must do as Raphael did, take many models, and not even *him* for your guide alone, to the exclusion of others. And yet the number is infinite of those who seem, if one may judge by their style, to have seen no other works but those of their master, or of some favorite, whose *manner* is their first wish, and their last.

I will mention a few that occur to me of this narrow, confined, illiberal, unscientific, and servile kind of imitators. Guido was thus meanly copied by Elizabetta, Sirani, and Simone Cantarini; Poussin, by Verdier and Cheron; Parmegiano by Jeronimo Mazzuoli. Paolo Veronese and Iacomo Bassan had for their imitators their brothers and sons. Pietro da Cortona was followed by Ciro Ferri, and Romanelli; Rubens, by Jacques Jordaens and Diepenbeke; Guercino, by his own family, the Gennari. Carlo Maratti was imitated by Giuseppe Chiari, and Pietro de Pietri; and Rembrandt, by Bramer, Eeckhout, and Flink. All these, to whom may be added a much longer list of painters, whose works among the ignorant pass for those of their masters, are justly to be censured for barrenness and servility.

To oppose to this list a few that have adopted a more liberal style of imitation, — Pellegrino Tibaldi, Rosso, and Primaticcio did not coldly imitate, but caught something of the fire that animates the works of Michael Angelo. The Caraccis formed their style from Pellegrino Tibaldi, Correggio, and the Venetian school. Domenichino, Guido, Lanfranco, Albano, Guercino, Cavidone, Schidone, Tiarini, though it is sufficiently apparent that they came from the school of the Caraccis, have yet the appearance of men who extended their views beyond the model that lay before them, and have shown that they had opinions of their own, and thought for themselves after they had made themselves masters of the general principles of their schools.

Le Suer's first manner resembles very much that of his master Voüet; but as he soon excelled him, so he differed from him in every part of the art. Carlo Maratti succeeded better than those I have first named, and, I think, owes his superiority to the extension of his views; beside his master Andrea Sacchi, he imitated Raphael, Guido, and the Caraccis. It is true, there is nothing very captivating in Carlo Maratti; but this proceeded from a want which cannot be completely supplied; that is, want of strength of parts. In this certainly men are not equal; and a man can bring home wares only in proportion to the capital with which he goes to market. Carlo, by diligence, made the most of what he had; but there was undoubtedly a heaviness about him, which extended itself, uniformly, to his invention, expression, his drawing, coloring, and the general effect of his pictures. The truth is, he never equalled any of his patterns in any one thing, and he added little of his own.

But we must not rest contented even in this general study of the moderns; we must trace back the art to its fountain-head, — to that source from whence they drew their principal excellences, the monuments of pure antiquity. All the inventions and thoughts of the ancients, whether conveyed to us in statues, bas-reliefs, intaglios, cameos, or coins, are to be sought after and carefully studied; the genius that hovers over these venerable relics may be called the father of modern art.

From the remains of the works of the ancients the modern arts were revived, and it is by their means that they must be restored a second time. However it may mortify our vanity, we must be forced to allow them our masters; and we may venture to prophesy that when they shall cease to be studied, arts will no longer flourish, and we shall again relapse into barbarism.

The fire of the artist's own genius, operating upon these materials which have been thus diligently collected, will enable him to make new combinations, perhaps superior to what had ever before been in the possession of the art; as in the mixture of the variety of metals, which are said to have been melted and run together at the burning of Corinth, a new and till then unknown metal was produced, equal in value to any of those that had contributed to its composition. And though a curious refiner should come with his crucibles, analyse and separate its various component parts, yet Corinthian brass would still hold its rank among the most beautiful and valuable of metals.

We have hitherto considered the advantages of imitation as it tends to form the taste, and as a practice by which a spark of that genius may be caught which illumines those noble works that ought always to be present to our thoughts.

We come now to speak of another kind of imitation, — the borrowing a particular thought, an action, attitude, or figure, and transplanting it into your own work. This will either come under the charge of plagiarism, or be warrantable, and deserve commendation, according to the address with which it is performed.[1] There is some difference, likewise, whether it is upon the ancients or moderns that these depredations are made. It is generally allowed, that no man need be ashamed of copying the ancients; their works are considered as a magazine of common property, always open to the public, whence every man has a right to take what materials he pleases; and if he has the art of using them they are supposed to become to all intents and purposes his own property. The collection of the thoughts of the ancients which Raphael made with so much trouble is a proof of his opinion on this subject. Such collections may be made with much more ease by means of an art scarce known in his time; I mean that of engraving; by which, at an easy rate, every man may now avail himself of the inventions of antiquity.

It must be acknowledged that the works of the moderns are more the property of their authors. He who borrows an idea from an ancient, or even from a modern artist not his contemporary, and so accommodates it to his own work that it makes a part of it, with no seam or joining appearing, can hardly be

[1] The principles advanced by Sir Joshua in this discourse were consistently adhered to in his practice. An able critic, Mr. Thomas Phillips, said: "The numberless instances in which he is known to have borrowed thoughts, both in actions of figures, and effects of color, seem to impeach his power of invention. But surely it could not proceed from want of a sufficient portion of that high and necessary quality that he who produced so many novel combinations adopted that shorthand path to composition. . . . These (his best portraits) are composed in a taste far surpassing all that had ever been done by his predecessors; uniting the grandeur, simplicity, and fulness of Titian, and the grace and nature of Van Dyck, with the artful and attractive effects of Rembrandt."

charged with plagiarism; poets practise this kind of borrowing without reserve. But an artist should not be contented with this only; he should enter into a competition with his original, and endeavor to improve what he is appropriating to his own work. Such imitation is so far from having anything in it of the servility of plagiarism that it is a perpetual exercise of the mind, a continual invention. Borrowing or stealing with such art and caution will have a right to the same lenity as was used by the Lacedæmonians, who did not punish theft, but the want of artifice to conceal it.

In order to encourage you to imitation, to the utmost extent, let me add, that very finished artists in the inferior branches of the art will contribute to furnish the mind and give hints, of which a skilful painter, who is sensible of what he wants, and is in no danger of being infected by the contact of vicious models, will know how to avail himself. He will pick up from dunghills what, by a nice chemistry, passing through his own mind, shall be converted into pure gold; and under the rudeness of Gothic essays he will find original, rational, and even sublime inventions.

The works of Albert Dürer, Lucas Van Leyden, the numerous inventions of Tobias Stimmer, and Jost Ammon, afford a rich mass of genuine materials, which, wrought up, and polished to elegance, will add copiousness to what, perhaps, without such aid, could have inspired only to justness and propriety.

In the luxuriant style of Paul Veronese, in the capricious compositions of Tintoret, he will find something that will assist his invention, and give points from which his own imagination shall rise and take flight, when the subject which he treats will with propriety admit of splendid effects.

In every school, whether Venetian, French, or Dutch, he will find either ingenious compositions, extraordinary effects, some peculiar expressions, or some mechanical excellence, well worthy of his attention, and, in some measure, of his imitation. Even in the lower class of the French painters, great beauties are often found, united with great defects. Though Coypel wanted a simplicity of taste, and mistook a presumptuous and assuming air for what is grand and majestic, yet he frequently has good sense and judgment in his manner of telling his stories, great skill in his compositions, and is not without a considerable power of expressing the passions. The modern affectation of grace in his works, as well as in those of Bosch and Watteau, may be said to be separated by a very thin partition from the more simple and pure grace of Correggio and Parmegiano.

Among the Dutch painters, the correct, firm, and determined pencil, which was employed by Bamboccio and Jean Miel, on vulgar and mean subjects, might, without any change, be employed on the highest; to which, indeed, it seems more properly to belong. The greatest style, if that style is confined to small figures, such as Poussin generally painted, would receive an additional grace by the elegance and precision of pencil so admirable in the works of Teniers; and though the school to which he belonged more particularly excelled in the mechanism of painting, yet it produced many who have shown great abilities in expressing what must be ranked above mechanical excellences. In the works of Franz Hals, the portrait-painter may observe the composition of a face, the features well put together, as the painters express it; from whence proceeds that strong-marked character of individual nature which is so remarkable in his portraits, and is not found in an equal degree in any other painter. If he had joined to this most difficult part of the art a patience in finishing what he had so correctly planned, he might justly have claimed the place which Van Dyck, all things considered, so justly holds as the first of portrait-painters.

Others of the same school have shown great power in expressing the character and passions of those vulgar people which were the subjects of their study and attention. Among those, Jan Steen seems to be one of the most diligent and accurate observers of what passed in those scenes which he frequented, and which were to him an academy. I can easily imagine that if this extraordinary man had had the good fortune to have been born in Italy, instead of Holland, had he lived in Rome, instead of Leyden, and been blessed with Michael Angelo and Raphael for his masters, instead of Brouwer and Van Goyen, the same sagacity and penetration which distinguished so accurately the different characters and expression in his vulgar figures would, when exerted in the selection and imitation of what was great and elevated in nature, have been equally successful; and he now would have ranged with the great pillars and supporters of our art.[1]

Men who, although thus bound down by the almost invincible powers of early habits, have still exerted extraordinary abilities within their narrow and confined circle, and have, from the natural vigor of their mind, given a very interesting expression, and great force and energy to their works, though they cannot be recommended to be exactly imitated, may yet invite an artist to endeavor to transfer, by a kind of parody, their excellences to his own performances. Whoever has acquired the power of making this use of the Flemish, Venetian, and French schools is a real genius, and has sources of knowledge open to him which were wanting to the great artists who lived in the great age of painting.

To find excellences, however dispersed, to discover beauties, however concealed by the multitude of defects with which they are surrounded, can be the work only of him who, having a mind always alive to his art, has extended his views to all ages and to all schools, and has acquired from that comprehensive mass which he has thus gathered to himself a well-digested and perfect idea of his art, to which everything is referred. Like a sovereign judge and arbiter of art, he is possessed of that presiding power which

[1] In the house I lodged in at Leyden there once lived Jan Steen, the great Jan Steen, whom I hold to be as great as Raphael. Even as a sacred painter Jan was as great, and that will be clearly seen when the religion of sorrow has passed away, and the religion of joy has torn off the thick veil that covers the rose-bushes of the earth, and the nightingales dare at last to sing joyously out their long-concealed raptures. But no nightingale will ever sing so joyously as Jan Steen painted. — HEINRICH HEINE.

separates and attracts every excellence from every school; selects both from what is great, and what is little; brings home knowledge from the East and from the West, — making the universe tributary towards furnishing his mind, and enriching his works with originality and variety of inventions.

Thus I have ventured to give my opinion of what appears to me the true and only method by which an artist makes himself master of his profession; which I hold ought to be one continued course of imitation, that is not to cease but with his life.

Those who, either from their own engagements and hurry of business, or from indolence, or from conceit and vanity, have neglected looking out of themselves, as far as my experience and observation reaches, have from that time not only ceased to advance, and improve in their performances, but have gone backward. They may be compared to men who have lived upon their principal till they are reduced to beggary, and left without resources.

I can recommend nothing better, therefore, than that you endeavor to infuse into your works what you learn from the contemplation of the works of others. To recommend this has the appearance of needless and superfluous advice; but it has fallen within my own knowledge that artists, though they were not wanting in a sincere love for their art, though they had great pleasure in seeing good pictures, and were well skilled to distinguish what was excellent or defective in them, yet have gone on in their own manner, without any endeavor to give a little of those beauties which they admired in others to their own works. It is difficult to conceive how the present Italian painters, who live in the midst of the treasures of art, should be contented with their own style. They proceed in their commonplace inventions, and never think it worth while to visit the works of those great artists with which they are surrounded.

I remember, several years ago, to have conversed at Rome with an artist of great fame throughout Europe; he was not without a considerable degree of abilities, but those abilities were by no means equal to his own opinion of them. From the reputation he had acquired, he too fondly concluded that he stood in the same rank when compared with his predecessors as he held with regard to his miserable contemporary rivals. In conversation about some particulars of the works of Raphael, he seemed to have, or to affect to have, a very obscure memory of them. He told me that he had not set his foot in the Vatican for fifteen years together; that he had been in treaty to copy a capital picture of Raphael, but that the business had gone off; however, if the agreement had held, his copy would have greatly exceeded the original. The merit of this artist, however great we may suppose it, I am sure would have been far greater, and his presumption would have been far less, if he had visited the Vatican, as in reason he ought to have done, at least once every month of his life.

I address myself, gentlemen, to you who have made some progress in the art, and are to be, for the future, under the guidance of your own judgment and discretion. I consider you as arrived to that period when you have a right to think for yourselves, and to presume that every man is fallible; to study the masters with a suspicion that great men are not always exempt from great faults; to criticise, compare, and rank their works in your own estimation, as they approach to, or recede from, that standard of perfection which you have formed in your own minds, but which those masters themselves, it must be remembered, have taught you to make, and which you will cease to make with correctness when you cease to study them. It is their excellences which have taught you their defects.

I would wish you to forget where you are, and who it is that speaks to you. I only direct you to higher models and better advisers. We can teach you here but very little; you are henceforth to be your own teachers. Do this justice, however, to the English Academy, — to bear in mind that in this place you contracted no narrow habits, no false ideas, nothing that could lead you to the imitation of any living master who may be the fashionable darling of the day. As you have not been taught to flatter us, do not learn to flatter yourselves. We have endeavored to lead you to the admiration of nothing but what is truly admirable. If you choose inferior patterns, or if you make your own *former* works your patterns for your *latter*, it is your own fault.

The purport of this discourse, and, indeed, of most of my other discourses, is to caution you against that false opinion, but too prevalent among artists, of the imaginary powers of native genius, and its sufficiency in great works. This opinion, according to the temper of mind it meets with, almost always produces either a vain confidence or a sluggish despair, — both equally fatal to all proficiency.

Study, therefore, the great works of the great masters forever. Study, as nearly as you can, in the order, in the manner, and on the principles, on which they studied. Study nature attentively, but always with those masters in your company; consider them as models which you are to imitate, and at the same time as rivals with whom you are to contend.

Lady Louisa Manners.
Countess Dysart.

DISCOURSE VII.

Delivered to the Students of the Royal Academy, on the Distribution of the Prizes, December 10, 1776.

THE REALITY OF A STANDARD OF TASTE, AS WELL AS OF CORPORAL BEAUTY. — BESIDES THIS IMMEDIATE TRUTH, THERE ARE SECONDARY TRUTHS, WHICH ARE VARIABLE; BOTH REQUIRING THE ATTENTION OF THE ARTIST, IN PROPORTION TO THEIR STABILITY OR THEIR INFLUENCE.

IT has been my uniform endeavor, since I first addressed you from this place, to impress you strongly with one ruling idea. I wished you to be persuaded that success in your art depends almost entirely on your own industry; but the industry which I principally recommended is not the industry of the hands, but of the mind.

As our art is not a divine gift, so neither is it a mechanical trade. Its foundations are laid in solid science; and practice, though essential to perfection, can never attain that to which it aims, unless it works under the direction of principle.

Some writers upon art carry this point too far, and suppose that such a body of universal and profound learning is requisite that the very enumeration of its kinds is enough to frighten a beginner. Vitruvius, after going through the many accomplishments of nature, and the many acquirements of learning necessary to an architect, proceeds with great gravity to assert that he ought to be well skilled in the civil law, that he may not be cheated in the title of the ground he builds on. But without such exaggeration, we may go so far as to assert that a painter stands in need of more knowledge than is to be picked off his pallet, or collected by looking on his model, whether it be in life or in picture. He can never be a great artist who is grossly illiterate.

Every man whose business is description ought to be tolerably conversant with the poets, in some language or other,— that he may imbibe a poetical spirit, and enlarge his stock of ideas. He ought to acquire a habit of comparing and digesting his notions. He ought not to be wholly unacquainted with that part of philosophy which gives an insight into human nature, and relates to the manners, characters, passions, and affections. He ought to know something concerning the mind as well as a great deal concerning the body of man. For this purpose it is not necessary that he should go into such a compass of reading as must, by distracting his attention, disqualify him for the practical part of his profession, and make him sink the performer in the critic. Reading, if it can be made the favorite recreation of his leisure hours, will improve and enlarge his mind, without retarding his actual industry. What such partial and desultory reading cannot afford may be supplied by the conversation of learned and ingenious men, which is the best of all substitutes for those who have not the means or opportunities of deep study. There are many such men in this age; and they will be pleased with communicating their ideas to artists, when they see them curious and docile, if they are treated with that respect and deference which is so justly their due. Into such society, young artists, if they make it the point of their ambition, will, by degrees, be admitted. There, without formal teaching, they will insensibly come to feel and reason like those they live with, and find a rational and systematic taste imperceptibly formed in their minds, which they will know how to reduce to a standard by applying general truth to their own purposes, better, perhaps, than those to whom they owed the original sentiment.

Of these studies, and this conversation, the desire and legitimate offspring is a power of distinguishing right from wrong; which power, applied to works of art, is denominated " taste."[1] Let me, then, without further introduction, enter upon an examination whether taste be so far beyond our reach as to be unattainable by care; or be so very vague and capricious, that no care ought to be employed about it.

It has been the fate of arts to be enveloped in mysterious and incomprehensible language, as if it was thought necessary that even the terms should correspond to the idea entertained of the instability and uncertainty of the rules which they expressed.

To speak of genius and taste as in any way connected with reason or common-sense would be, in the opinion of some towering talkers, to speak like a man who possessed neither; who had never felt that

---

[1] Genius is the power of producing excellence; taste is the power of perceiving the excellence thus produced in its several sorts and degrees, with all their force, refinement, distinctions, and connections. — HAZLITT, *Essay on Taste.*

enthusiasm, or, to use their own inflated language, was never warmed by that Promethean fire, which animates the canvas and vivifies the marble.

If, in order to be intelligible, I appear to degrade art by bringing her down from the visionary situation in the clouds, it is only to give her a more solid mansion upon the earth. It is necessary that at some time or other we should see things as they really are, and not impose on ourselves by that false magnitude with which objects appear when viewed indistinctly as through a mist.

We will allow a poet to express his meaning, when his meaning is not well known to himself, with a certain degree of obscurity, as it is one sort of the sublime. But when, in plain prose, we gravely talk of courting the Muse in shady bowers; waiting the call and inspiration of Genius, finding out where he inhabits, and where he is to be invoked with the greatest success; of attending to times and seasons when the imagination shoots with the greatest vigor, whether at the summer solstice or the vernal equinox; sagaciously observing how much the wild freedom and liberty of imagination is cramped by attention to established rules; and how this same imagination begins to grow dim in advanced age, smothered and deadened by too much judgment; when we talk such language, or entertain such sentiments as these, we generally rest contented with mere words, or at best entertain notions not only groundless but pernicious.

If all this means, what it is very possible was originally intended only to be meant, that in order to cultivate an art a man secludes himself from the commerce of the world and retires into the country at particular seasons; or that at one time of the year his body is in better health, and consequently his mind fitter for the business of hard thinking than at another time; or that the mind may be fatigued and grow confused by long and unremitted application; this I can understand. I can likewise believe that a man, eminent when young for possessing poetical imagination, may, from having taken another road, so neglect its cultivation as to show less of its powers in his later life. But I am persuaded that scarce a poet is to be found, from Homer down to Dryden, who preserved a sound mind in a sound body, and continued practising his profession to the very last, whose later works are not as replete with the fire of imagination, as those which were produced in his more youthful days.

To understand literally these metaphors, or ideas expressed in poetical language, seems to be equally absurd as to conclude that because painters sometimes represent poets writing from the dictates of a little winged boy or genius, this same genius did really inform him in a whisper what he was to write; and that he is himself but a mere machine, unconscious of the operations of his own mind.

Opinions generally received and floating in the world, whether true or false, we naturally adopt and make our own; they may be considered as a kind of inheritance to which we succeed and are tenants for life, and which we leave to our posterity very nearly in the condition in which we received it, it not being much in any one man's power either to impair or improve it. The greatest part of these opinions, like current coin in its circulation, we are used to take without weighing or examining; but by this inevitable inattention many adulterated pieces are received, which, when we seriously estimate our wealth, we must throw away. So the collector of popular opinions, when he embodies his knowledge, and forms a system, must separate those which are true from those which are only plausible. But it becomes more peculiarly a duty to the professors of art not to let any opinions relating to that art pass unexamined. The caution and circumspection required in such examination we shall presently have an opportunity of explaining.

Genius and taste, in their common acceptation, appear to be very nearly related; the difference lies only in this, that genius has superadded to it a habit or power of execution; or we may say that taste, when this power is added, changes its name, and is called genius. They both, in the popular opinion, pretend to an entire exemption from the restraint of rules. It is supposed that their powers are intuitive; that under the name of genius great works are produced, and under the name of taste an exact judgment is given, without our knowing why, and without our being under the least obligation to reason, precept, or experience.

One can scarce state these opinions without exposing their absurdity; yet they are constantly in the mouths of men, and particularly of artists. They who have thought seriously on this subject do not carry the point so far; yet I am persuaded that, even among those few who may be called thinkers, the prevalent opinion allows less than it ought to the powers of reason, and considers the principles of taste, which give all their authority to the rules of art, as more fluctuating, and as having less solid foundations, than we shall find upon examination they really have.

The common saying that "tastes are not to be disputed" owes its influence and its general reception to the same error which leads us to imagine this faculty of too high an original to submit to the authority of an earthly tribunal. It likewise corresponds with the notions of those who consider it as a mere phantom of the imagination, so devoid of substance as to elude all criticism.

We often appear to differ in sentiments from each other, merely from the inaccuracy of terms, as we are not obliged to speak always with critical exactness. Something of this too may arise from want of words in the language in which we speak to express the more nice discrimination which a deep investigation discovers. A great deal, however, of this difference vanishes when each opinion is tolerably explained and understood by constancy and precision in the use of terms.

We apply the term "taste" to that act of the mind by which we like or dislike, whatever be the subject. Our judgment upon an airy nothing, a fancy which has no foundation, is called by the same name which we give to our determination concerning those truths which refer to the most general and most unalterable principles of human nature, — to the works which are only to be produced by the greatest effort of the human understanding. However inconvenient this may be, we are obliged to take words as we find them; all we can do is to distinguish the things to which they are applied.

We may let pass those things which are at once subjects of taste and sense, and which, having as much certainty as the senses themselves, give no occasion to inquiry or dispute. The natural appetite or taste of the human mind is for truth; whether that truth results from the real agreement or equality of original ideas among themselves, from the agreement of the representation of any object with the thing represented, or from the correspondence of the several parts of any arrangement with each other. It is the very same taste which relishes a demonstration in geometry, that is pleased with the resemblance of a picture to an original and touched with the harmony of music.

All these have unalterable and fixed foundations in nature, and are therefore equally investigated by reason, and known by study, — some with more, some with less clearness, but all exactly in the same way. A picture that is unlike is false. Disproportionate ordonnance of parts is not right; because it cannot be true, until it ceases to be a contradiction to assert that the parts have no relation to the whole. Coloring is true, when it is naturally adapted to the eye, from brightness, from softness, from harmony, from resemblance; because these agree with their object, nature, and therefore are true, — as true as mathematical demonstration, but known to be true only to those who study these things.

But besides real, there is also apparent truth, or opinion, or prejudice. With regard to real truth, when it is known, the taste which conforms to it is, and must be, uniform. With regard to the second sort of truth, which may be called truth upon sufferance, or truth by courtesy, it is not fixed, but variable. However, while these opinions and prejudices on which it is founded continue, they operate as truth; and the art whose office it is to please the mind, as well as instruct it, must direct itself according to opinion, or it will not attain its end.

In proportion as these prejudices are known to be generally diffused, or long received, the taste which conforms to them approaches nearer to certainty, and to a sort of resemblance to real science, even where opinions are found to be no better than prejudices. And since they deserve, on account of their duration and extent, to be considered as really true, they become capable of no small degree of stability and determination, by their permanent and uniform nature.

As these prejudices become more narrow, more local, more transitory, this secondary taste becomes more and more fantastical; recedes from real science; is less to be approved by reason, and less followed by practice, — though in no case perhaps to be wholly neglected, where it does not stand, as it sometimes does, in direct defiance of the most respectable opinions received among mankind.

Having laid down these positions, I shall proceed with less method, because less will serve to explain and apply them.

We will take it for granted that reason is something invariable and fixed in the nature of things; and without endeavoring to go back to an account of first principles, which forever will elude our search, we will conclude that whatever goes under the name of taste, which we can fairly bring under the dominion of reason, must be considered as equally exempt from change. If, therefore, in the course of this inquiry, we can show that there are rules for the conduct of the artist which are fixed and invariable, it follows, of course, that the art of the connoisseur, or, in other words, taste, has likewise invariable principles.

Of the judgment which we make on the works of art, and the preference that we give to one class of art over another, if a reason be demanded, the question is perhaps evaded by answering, "I judge from my taste;" but it does not follow that a better answer cannot be given, though for common gazers this may be sufficient. Every man is not obliged to investigate the cause of his approbation or dislike.

The arts would lie open forever to caprice and casualty if those who are to judge of their excellences had no settled principles by which they are to regulate their decisions, and the merit or defect of performances were to be determined by unguided fancy. And indeed we may venture to assert that whatever speculative knowledge is necessary to the artist is equally and indispensably necessary to the connoisseur.

The first idea that occurs in the consideration of what is fixed in art, or in taste, is that presiding principle of which I have so frequently spoken in former discourses, — the general idea of nature. The beginning, the middle, and the end of everything that is valuable in taste is comprised in the knowledge of what is truly nature; for whatever notions are not conformable to those of nature, or universal opinion, must be considered as more or less capricious.

My notion of nature comprehends not only the forms which nature produces, but also the nature and internal fabric and organization, as I may call it, of the human mind and imagination. The terms "beauty," or "nature," which are general ideas, are but different modes of expressing the same thing, whether we apply these terms to statues, poetry, or pictures. Deformity is not nature, but an accidental deviation from her accustomed practice. This general idea, therefore, ought to be called nature; and nothing else, correctly speaking, has a right to that name. But we are surely so far from speaking, in common conversation, with any such accuracy that, on the contrary, when we criticise Rembrandt and other Dutch painters who introduced into their historical pictures exact representations of individual objects with all their imperfections, we say, "Though it is not in a good taste, yet it is nature"

This misapplication of terms must be very often perplexing to the young student. Is not art, he may say, an imitation of nature? Must he not, therefore, who imitates her with the greatest fidelity be the best artist? By this mode of reasoning Rembrandt has a higher place than Raphael. But a very little reflection will serve to show us that these particularities cannot be nature; for how can that be the nature of man in which no two individuals are the same?

It plainly appears that as a work is conducted under the influence of general ideas, or partial, it is principally to be considered as the effect of a good or a bad taste.

As beauty, therefore, does not consist in taking what lies immediately before you, so neither, in our pursuit of taste, are those opinions which we first received and adopted the best choice, or the most natural to the mind and imagination. In the infancy of our knowledge we seize with greediness the good that is within our reach; it is by after-consideration, and in consequence of discipline, that we refuse the present for a greater good at a distance. The nobility or elevation of all arts, like the excellence of virtue itself, consists in adopting this enlarged and comprehensive idea; and all criticism built upon the more confined view of what is natural may properly be called *shallow* criticism, rather than false; its defect is that the truth is not sufficiently extensive.

It has sometimes happened that some of the greatest men in our art have been betrayed into errors by this confined mode of reasoning. Poussin, who upon the whole may be adduced as an artist strictly attentive to the most enlarged and extensive ideas of nature, from not having settled principles on this point, has, in one instance at least, I think, deserted truth for prejudice. He is said to have vindicated the conduct of Julio Romano for his inattention to the masses of light and shade, or grouping the figures in "The Battle of Constantine," as if designedly neglected, the better to correspond with the hurry and confusion of a battle. Poussin's own conduct in many of his pictures makes us more easily give credit to this report. That it was too much his own practice, "The Sacrifice to Silenus," and "The Triumph of Bacchus and Ariadne," may be produced as instances; but this principle is still more apparent, and may be said to be even more ostentatiously displayed in his "Perseus and Medusa's Head."

This is undoubtedly a subject of great bustle and tumult, and that the first effect of the picture may correspond to the subject, every principle of composition is violated; there is no principal figure, no principal light, no groups; everything is dispersed, and in such a state of confusion that the eye finds no repose anywhere. In consequence of the forbidding appearance, I remember turning from it with disgust, and should not have looked a second time if I had not been called back to a closer inspection. I then indeed found, what we may expect always to find in the works of Poussin, correct drawing, forcible expression, and just character; in short, all the excellences which so much distinguish the works of this learned painter.

This conduct of Poussin I hold to be entirely improper to imitate. A picture should please at first sight, and appear to invite the spectator's attention; if, on the contrary, the general effect offends the eye, a second view is not always sought, whatever more substantial and intrinsic merit it may possess.

Perhaps no apology ought to be received for offences committed against the vehicle (whether it be the organ of seeing or of hearing) by which our pleasures are conveyed to the mind. We must take care that the eye be not perplexed and distracted by a confusion of equal parts, or equal lights, or offended by an unharmonious mixture of colors, as we should guard against offending the ear by unharmonious sounds. We may venture to be more confident of the truth of this observation, since we find that Shakspeare, on a parallel occasion, has made Hamlet recommend to the players a precept of the same kind, — never to offend the ear by harsh sounds. "In the very torrent, tempest, and whirlwind of your passion," says he, "you must acquire and beget a temperance that may give it smoothness." And yet, at the same time he very justly observes, " The end of playing, both at the first, and now, was, and is, to hold, as 't were, the mirror up to nature." No one can deny that violent passions will naturally emit harsh and disagreeable tones; yet this great poet and critic thought that this imitation of nature would cost too much if purchased at the expense of disagreeable sensations, or, as he expresses it, of "splitting the ear." The poet and actor, as well as the painter of genius, who is well acquainted with all the variety and sources of pleasure in the mind and imagination, has little regard or attention to common nature, or creeping after common-sense. By overleaping those narrow bounds, he more effectually seizes the whole mind, and more powerfully accomplishes his purpose. This success is ignorantly imagined to proceed from inattention to all rules, and a defiance of reason and judgment; whereas it is in truth acting according to the best rules and the justest reason.

He who thinks nature, in the narrow sense of the word, is alone to be followed, will produce but a scanty entertainment for the imagination; everything is to be done with which it is natural for the mind to be pleased, whether it proceeds from simplicity or variety, uniformity or irregularity; whether the scenes are familiar or exotic, rude and wild, or enriched and cultivated; for it is natural for the mind to be pleased with all these in their turn. In short, whatever pleases has in it what is analogous to the mind, and is, therefore, in the highest and best sense of the word, natural.

It is the sense of nature or truth which ought more particularly to be cultivated by the professors of art; and it may be observed that many wise and learned men, who have accustomed their minds to admit nothing for truth but what can be proved by mathematical demonstration, have seldom any relish for those arts which address themselves to the fancy, the rectitude and truth of which is known by another kind of proof; and we may add that the acquisition of this knowledge requires as much circumspection and sagacity as is necessary to attain those truths which are more capable of demonstration. Reason must ultimately determine our choice on every occasion; but this reason may still be exerted ineffectually by applying to taste principles which, though right as far as they go, yet do not reach the object. No man, for instance, can deny that it seems at first view very reasonable that a statue which is to carry down to posterity the resemblance of an individual should be dressed in the fashion of the times, in the dress which he himself wore. This would certainly be true if the dress were part of the man; but after a time the dress is only an amusement for an antiquarian, and if it obstructs the general design of the piece it is to be disregarded by the artist. Common-sense must here give way to a higher sense. In the naked form, and in the disposition of the drapery, the difference between one artist and another is principally seen. But if he is compelled to exhibit the modern dress, the naked form is entirely hid, and the drapery is already disposed by the skill of the tailor. Were a Phidias to obey such absurd commands, he would please no more than an ordinary sculptor; in the inferior parts of every art the learned and the ignorant are nearly upon a level.

These were probably among the reasons that induced the sculptor of that wonderful figure of Laocoön, to exhibit him naked, notwithstanding he was surprised in the act of sacrificing to Apollo, and consequently ought to have been shown in his sacerdotal habits, if those greater reasons had not preponderated.[1] Art is not yet in so high estimation with us, as to obtain so great a sacrifice as the ancients made, especially the Grecians, who suffered themselves to be represented naked, whether they were generals, lawgivers, or kings.

[1] Had he left Laocoön only the fillet, he would in a great degree have weakened the expression; for the brow, which is the seat of it, would have been in part concealed. Thus, as formerly in the case of the shriek he sacrificed expression to beauty, he here offers up conventionality to expression. — LESSING, *Laocoön*, chap. v.

Under this head of balancing and choosing the greater reason, or of two evils taking the less, we may consider the conduct of Rubens in the Luxembourg gallery, where he has mixed allegorical figures with the representations of real personages, which must be acknowledged to be a fault; yet, if the artist considered himself as engaged to furnish this gallery with a rich, various, and splendid ornament, this could not be done, at least in an equal degree, without peopling the air and water with these allegorical figures; he therefore accomplished all that he purposed. In this case all lesser considerations, which tend to obstruct the great end of the work, must yield and give way.

The variety which portraits and modern dresses, mixed with allegorical figures, produce, is not to be slightly given up upon a punctilio of reason, when that reason deprives the art in a manner of its very existence. It must always be remembered that the business of a great painter is to produce a great picture; he must therefore take especial care not to be cajoled by specious arguments out of his materials.

What has been so often said to the disadvantage of allegorical poetry — that it is tedious and uninteresting — cannot with the same propriety be applied to painting, where the interest is of a different kind. If allegorical painting produces a greater variety of ideal beauty, a richer, a more various and delightful composition, and gives to the artist a greater opportunity of exhibiting his skill, all the interest he wishes for is accomplished; such a picture not only attracts, but fixes the attention.

If it be objected that Rubens judged ill at first in thinking it necessary to make his work so very ornamental, this puts the question upon new ground. It was his peculiar style; he could paint in no other; and he was selected for that work, probably because it was his style. Nobody will dispute but some of the best of the Roman or Bolognian schools would have produced a more learned and more noble work.

This leads us to another important province of taste, — that of weighing the value of the different classes of the art, and of estimating them accordingly.

All arts have means within them of applying themselves with success both to the intellectual and sensitive part of our natures. It cannot be disputed, supposing both these means put in practice with equal abilities, to which we ought to give the preference, — to him who represents the heroic arts and more dignified passions of man, or to him who, by the help of meretricious ornaments, however elegant and graceful, captivates the sensuality, as it may be called, of our taste. Thus the Roman and Bolognian schools are reasonably preferred to the Venetian, Flemish, or Dutch schools, as they address themselves to our best and noblest faculties.[1]

Well-turned periods in eloquence, or harmony of numbers in poetry, which are in those arts what coloring is in painting, however highly we may esteem

[1] Here Reynolds emerges from his metaphysical cloud-land, and hits the nail precisely on the head. "It is not in making the eye a microscope, but in making it the interpreter and organ of all that can touch the soul and the affections, that the perfection of fine art is shown" (Hazlitt).

them, can never be considered as of equal importance with the art of unfolding truths that are useful to mankind, and which make us better or wiser. Nor can those works which remind us of the poverty and meanness of our nature be considered as of equal rank with what excites ideas of grandeur, or raises and dignifies humanity; or, in the words of a late poet, which makes the beholder " learn to venerate himself as man." [1]

It is reason and good sense, therefore, which ranks and estimates every art, and every part of that art, according to its importance, from the painter of animated down to inanimate nature. We will not allow a man who shall prefer the inferior style to say it is his taste; taste here has nothing, or at least ought to have nothing, to do with the question. He wants not taste, but sense and soundness of judgment.

Indeed, perfection in an inferior style may be reasonably preferred to mediocrity in the highest walks of art. A landscape of Claude Lorrain may be preferred to a history by Luca Giordano; but hence appears the necessity of the connoisseur's knowing in what consists the excellence of each class, in order to judge how near it approaches to perfection.

Even in works of the same kind, as in history-painting, which is composed of various parts, excellence of an inferior species, carried to a very high degree, will make a work very valuable, and in some measure compensate for the absence of the higher kinds of merit. It is the duty of the connoisseur to know and esteem, as much as it may deserve, every

[1] Dr. Goldsmith.

part of painting; he will not then think even Bassano unworthy of his notice, who, though totally devoid of expression, sense, grace, or elegance, may be esteemed on account of his admirable taste of colors, which, in his best works, are little inferior to those of Titian.

Since I have mentioned Bassano, we must do him likewise the justice to acknowledge that though he did not aspire to the dignity of expressing the characters and passions of men, yet, with respect to facility and truth in his manner of touching animals of all kinds, and giving them what painters call "their character," few have excelled him.

To Bassano we may add Paul Veronese and Tintoret, for their entire inattention to what is justly thought the most essential part of our art, the expression of the passions. Notwithstanding these glaring deficiencies, we justly esteem their works; but it must be remembered that they do not please from those defects, but from their great excellences of another kind, and in spite of such transgressions. These excellences, too, as far as they go, are founded in the truth of general nature; they tell the truth, though not the whole truth.

By these considerations, which can never be too frequently impressed, may be obviated two errors, which I observed to have been, formerly at least, the most prevalent, and to be most injurious to artists; that of thinking taste and genius to have nothing to do with reason, and that of taking particular living objects for nature.

I shall now say something on that part of taste

which, as I have hinted to you before, does not belong so much to the external form of things, but is addressed to the mind, and depends on its original frame, or, to use the expression, the organization of the soul; I mean the imagination and the passions. The principles of these are as invariable as the former, and are to be known and reasoned upon in the same manner, by an appeal to common-sense, deciding upon the common feelings of mankind. This sense, and these feelings, appear to me of equal authority, and equally conclusive. Now this appeal implies a general uniformity and agreement in the minds of men. It would be else an idle and vain endeavor to establish rules of art; it would be pursuing a phantom, to attempt to move affections with which we were entirely unacquainted. We have no reason to suspect there is a greater difference between our minds than between our forms; of which, though there are no two alike, yet there is a general similitude that goes through the whole race of mankind; and those who have cultivated their taste can distinguish what is beautiful or deformed, or, in other words, what agrees with or deviates from the general idea of nature, in one case, as well as in the other.

The internal fabric of our minds, as well as the external form of our bodies, being nearly uniform, it seems then to follow of course that, as the imagination is incapable of producing anything originally of itself, and can only vary and combine those ideas with which it is furnished by means of the senses, there will be necessarily an agreement in the imaginations, as in the senses of men. There being this agreement, it follows that in all cases, in our lightest amusements as well as in our most serious actions and engagements of life, we must regulate our affections of every kind by that of others. The well-disciplined mind acknowledges this authority, and submits its own opinion to the public voice. It is from knowing what are the general feelings and passions of mankind that we acquire a true idea of what imagination is; though it appears as if we had nothing to do but to consult our own particular sensations, and these were sufficient to ensure us from all error and mistake.

A knowledge of the disposition and character of the human mind can be acquired only by experience; a great deal will be learned, I admit, by a habit of examining what passes in our bosoms, what are our own motives of action, and of what kind of sentiments we are conscious on any occasion. We may suppose a uniformity, and conclude that the same effect will be produced by the same cause in the minds of others. This examination will contribute to suggest to us matters of inquiry; but we can never be sure that our own sentiments are true and right, till they are confirmed by more extensive observation. One man opposing another determines nothing; but a general union of minds, like a general combination of the forces of all mankind, makes a strength that is irresistible. In fact, as he who does not know himself does not know others, so it may be said with equal truth that he who does not know others knows himself but very imperfectly.

A man who thinks he is guarding himself against

prejudices by resisting the authority of others, leaves open every avenue to singularity, vanity, self-conceit, obstinacy, and many other vices, all tending to warp the judgment, and prevent the natural operation of his faculties. This submission to others is a deference which we owe, and indeed, are forced involuntarily to pay. In fact, we never are satisfied with our opinions, whatever we may pretend, till they are ratified and confirmed by the suffrages of the rest of mankind. We dispute and wrangle forever; we endeavor to get men to come to us when we do not go to them.

He, therefore, who is acquainted with the works which have pleased different ages and different countries, and has formed his opinion on them, has more materials, and more means of knowing what is analogous to the mind of man, than he who is conversant only with the works of his own age or country. What has pleased, and continues to please, is likely to please again; hence are derived the rules of art, and on this immovable foundation they must ever stand.

This search and study of the history of the mind ought not to be confined to one art only. It is by the analogy that one art bears to another that many things are ascertained which either were but faintly seen, or perhaps would not have been discovered at all if the inventor had not received the first hints from the practices of a sister art on a similar occasion.[1] The frequent allusions which every man who

[1] Nulla ars, non alterius artis, aut mater, aut propinqua est.— TERTULL. as cited by JUNIUS.

treats of any art is obliged to make to others, in order to illustrate and confirm his principles, sufficiently show their near connection and inseparable relation.

All arts having the same general end, which is to please, and addressing themselves to the same faculties through the medium of the senses, it follows that their rules and principles must have as great affinity as the different materials and the different organs or vehicles by which they pass to the mind will permit them to retain.[1]

We may therefore conclude that the real substance, as it may be called, of what goes under the name of taste is fixed and established in the nature of things; that there are certain and regular causes by which the imagination and passions of men are affected; and that the knowledge of these causes is acquired by a laborious and diligent investigation of nature, and by the same slow progress as wisdom or knowledge of every kind, however instantaneous its operations may appear when thus acquired.

It has been often observed that the good and virtuous man alone can acquire this true or just relish even of works of art. This opinion will not appear entirely without foundation when we consider that the same habit of mind which is acquired by our search after truth in the more serious duties of life, is only transferred to the pursuit of lighter amusements. The same disposition, the same desire to find some-

---

[1] Omnes artes quæ ad humanitatem pertinent habent quoddam commune vinculum, et quasi cognatione inter se continentur. — CICERO.

thing steady, substantial, and durable, on which the mind can lean, as it were, and rest with safety, actuates us in both cases. The subject only is changed. We pursue the same method in our search after the idea of beauty and perfection in each, — of virtue, by looking forward beyond ourselves to society, and to the whole; of arts, by extending our views in the same manner to all ages and all times.

Every art, like our own, has in its composition fluctuating as well as fixed principles. It is an attentive inquiry into their difference that will enable us to determine how far we are influenced by custom and habit, and what is fixed in the nature of things.

To distinguish how much has solid foundation, we may have recourse to the same proof by which some hold that wit ought to be tried, — whether it preserves itself when translated. That wit is false which can subsist only in one language; and that picture which pleases only one age or one nation owes its reception to some local or accidental association of ideas.

We may apply this to every custom and habit of life. Thus, the general principles of urbanity, politeness, or civility, have been the same in all nations; but the mode in which they are dressed is continually varying. The general idea of showing respect is by making yourself less; but the manner, whether by bowing the body, kneeling, prostration, pulling off the upper part of our dress, or taking away the lower is a matter of custom.

Thus, in regard to ornaments, it would be unjust to conclude that because they were at first arbitrarily contrived, they are therefore undeserving of our attention; on the contrary, he who neglects the cultivation of those ornaments acts contrary to nature and reason. As life would be imperfect without its highest ornaments, the arts, so these arts themselves would be imperfect without *their* ornaments. Though we by no means ought to rank with these positive and substantial beauties, yet it must be allowed that a knowledge of both is essentially requisite towards forming a complete, whole, and perfect taste. It is in reality from their ornaments that arts receive their peculiar character and complexion; we may add that in them we find the characteristical mark of a national taste, — as, by throwing up a feather in the air, we know which way the wind blows, better than by a more heavy matter.

The striking distinction between the works of the Roman, Bolognian, and Venetian schools consists more in that general effect which is produced by colors than in the more profound excellences of the art; at least it is from thence that each is distinguished and known at first sight. Thus it is the ornaments rather than the proportions of architecture which at the first glance distinguish the different orders from each other; the Doric is known by its triglyphs, the Ionic by its volutes, and the Corinthian by its acanthus.

What distinguishes oratory from a cold narration is a more liberal, though chaste, use of those ornaments which go under the name of figurative and metaphorical expressions; and poetry distinguishes itself from oratory by words and expressions still more ardent and glowing. What separates and distinguishes poetry is more particularly the ornament of verse; it is this which gives it its character, and is an essential without which it cannot exist. Custom has appropriated different metre to different kinds of composition, in which the world is not perfectly agreed. In England the dispute is not yet settled which is to be preferred, rhyme or blank verse. But however we disagree about what these metrical ornaments shall be, that some metre is essentially necessary is universally acknowledged.

In poetry or eloquence, to determine how far figurative or metaphorical language may proceed, and when it begins to be affectation or beside the truth, must be determined by taste; though this taste, we must never forget, is regulated and formed by the presiding feelings of mankind, — by those works which have approved themselves to all times and all persons. Thus, though eloquence has undoubtedly an essential and intrinsic excellence, and immovable principles common to all languages, and founded in the nature of our passions and affections, yet it has its ornaments and modes of address which are merely arbitrary. What is approved in the eastern nations as grand and majestic would be considered by the Greeks and Romans as turgid and inflated; and they in return, would be thought by the Orientals to express themselves in a cold and insipid manner.

We may add, likewise, to the credit of ornaments, that it is by their means that art itself accomplishes its purpose. Fresnoy calls coloring, which is one of the chief ornaments of painting, *lena sororis*, that which procures lovers and admirers to the more valuable excellences of the art.

It appears to be the same right turn of mind which enables a man to acquire the truth, or the just idea of what is right, in the ornaments, as in the more stable principles of art. It has still the same centre of perfection, though it is the centre of a smaller circle.

To illustrate this by the fashion of dress, in which there is allowed to be a good or bad taste. The component parts of dress are continually changing from great to little, from short to long; but the general form still remains; it is still the same general dress, which is comparatively fixed, though on a very slender foundation; but it is on this which fashion must rest. He who invents with the most success, or dresses in the best taste, would probably, from the same sagacity employed to greater purposes, have discovered equal skill, or have formed the same correct taste, in the highest labors of art.

I have mentioned taste in dress, which is certainly one of the lowest subjects to which this word is applied; yet, as I have before observed, there is a right even here, however narrow its foundation, respecting the fashion of any particular nation. But we have still more slender means of determining to which of the different customs of different ages or countries we ought to give the preference, since they seem to be all equally removed from nature. If a European, when he has cut off his beard, and put false hair on his head, or bound up his own natural hair in regular hard knots, as unlike nature as he can possibly make it, and after having rendered them immovable by the help of the fat of hogs, has covered the whole with flour, laid on by a machine with the utmost regularity, — if, when thus attired, he issues forth, and meets a Cherokee Indian, who has bestowed as much time at his toilet, and laid on with equal care and attention his yellow and red ochre on particular parts of his forehead or cheeks, as he judges most becoming, whoever of these two despises the other for this attention to the fashion of his country, whichever first feels himself provoked to laugh, is the barbarian.

All these fashions are very innocent; neither worth disquisition, nor any endeavor to alter them; as the change would, in all probability, be equally distant from nature. The only circumstance against which indignation may reasonably be moved is where the operation is painful or destructive of health, — such as some of the practices at Otaheite, and the strait-lacing of the English ladies; of the last of which practices, how destructive it must be to health and long life the professor of anatomy took an opportunity of proving a few days since in this Academy.

It is in dress as in things of greater consequence. Fashions originate from those only who have the high and powerful advantages of rank, birth, and fortune. Many of the ornaments of art, those at least for which no reason can be given, are transmitted to us, are adopted, and acquire their consequence from the company in which we have been used to see them. As Greece and Rome are the fountains from whence have flowed all kinds of excellence, to that veneration which they have a right to claim for the pleasure and knowledge which they have afforded us we voluntarily add our approbation of every ornament and every custom that belonged to them, even to the fashion of their dress. For it may be observed that, not satisfied with them in their own place, we make no difficulty of dressing statues of modern heroes or senators in the fashion of the Roman armor or peaceful robe; we go so far as hardly to bear a statue in any other drapery.

The figures of the great men of those nations have come down to us in sculpture. In sculpture remain almost all the excellent specimens of ancient art. We have so far associated personal dignity to the persons thus represented, and the truth of art to their manner of representation, that it is not in our power any longer to separate them. This is not so in painting; because, having no excellent ancient portraits, that connection was never formed. Indeed, we could no more venture to paint a general officer in a Roman military habit than we could make a statue in the present uniform. But since we have no ancient portraits, to show how ready we are to adopt this kind of prejudices, we make the best authority among the moderns serve the same purpose. The great variety of excellent portraits with which Van Dyck has enriched this nation, we are not content to admire for their real excellence, but extend our approbation even to the dress which happened to be the fashion of that age. We all very well remember how common it was a few years ago for portraits to be drawn in this fantastic dress; and this custom is not yet entirely laid aside. By this means it must be acknowledged very ordinary pictures acquired something of the air and effect of the works of Van Dyck, and appeared therefore at first sight to be better pictures than they really were; they appeared so, however, to those only who had the means of making this association; and when made, it was irresistible. But this association is nature, and refers to that secondary truth that comes from conformity to general prejudice and opinion; it is therefore not merely fantastical. Besides the prejudice which we have in favor of ancient dresses, there may be likewise other reasons for the effect which they produce; among which we may justly rank the simplicity of them, consisting of little more than one single piece of drapery, without those whimsical, capricious forms by which all other dresses are embarrassed.

Thus, though it is from the prejudice we have in favor of the ancients, who have taught us architecture, that we have adopted likewise their ornaments; and though we are satisfied that neither nature nor reason is the foundation of those beauties which we imagine we see in that art, yet if any one, persuaded of this truth, should therefore invent new orders of equal beauty, which we will suppose to be possible, they would not please; nor ought he to complain, since the old has that great advantage of having custom and prejudice on its side. In this case we leave what has every prejudice in its favor, to take that which will have no advantage over what we have left, but novelty, — which soon destroys itself, and at any rate is but a weak antagonist against custom.

Ancient ornaments, having the right of possession, ought not to be removed, unless to make room for that which not only has higher pretensions, but such pretensions as will balance the evil and confusion which innovation always brings with it.

To this we may add that even the durability of the materials will often contribute to give a superiority to one object over another. Ornaments in buildings, with which taste is principally concerned, are composed of materials which last longer than those of which dress is composed; the former, therefore, make higher pretensions to our favor and prejudice.

Some attention is surely due to what we can no more get rid of than we can go out of ourselves. We are creatures of prejudice; we neither can nor ought to eradicate it; we must only regulate it by reason, which kind of regulation is indeed little more than obliging the lesser, the local and temporal prejudices, to give way to those which are more durable and lasting.

He, therefore, who in his practice of portrait-painting wishes to dignify his subject, which we will suppose to be a lady, will not paint her in the modern dress, the familiarity of which alone is sufficient to destroy all dignity.[1] He takes care that his work shall correspond to those ideas and that imagination which he knows will regulate the judgment of others,

---

[1] Yet Reynolds himself in his portraits "renders with astonishing facility the most fugitive freaks of fashion, giving them the immortal stamp of art" (Chesneau).

and, therefore, dresses his figure something with the general air of the antique for the sake of dignity, and preserves something of the modern for the sake of likeness. By this conduct his works correspond with those prejudices which we have in favor of what we continually see; and the relish of the antique simplicity corresponds with what we may call the more learned and scientific prejudice.

There was a statue made not long since of Voltaire, which the sculptor, not having that respect for the prejudices of mankind which he ought to have had, made entirely naked, and as meagre and emaciated as the original is said to be. The consequence was what might have been expected; it remained in the sculptor's shop, though it was intended as a public ornament, and a public honor to Voltaire, for it was procured at the expense of his contemporary wits and admirers.

Whoever would reform a nation, supposing a bad taste to prevail in it, will not accomplish his purpose by going directly against the stream of their prejudices. Men's minds must be prepared to receive what is new to them. Reformation is a work of time. A national taste, however wrong it may be, cannot be totally changed at once; we must yield a little to the prepossession which has taken hold on the mind, and we may then bring people to adopt what would offend them if endeavored to be introduced by violence. When Battista Franco was employed, in conjunction with Titian, Paul Veronese, and Tintoret, to adorn the library of St. Mark, his work, Vasari says, gave less satisfaction than any of the others; the dry manner of the Roman school was very ill calculated to please eyes that had been accustomed to the luxuriance, splendor, and richness of Venetian coloring. Had the Romans been the judges of this work, probably the determination would have been just contrary; for in the more noble parts of the art Battista Franco was perhaps not inferior to any of his rivals.

It has been the main scope and principal end of this discourse to demonstrate the reality of a standard in taste as well as in corporeal beauty; that a false or depraved taste is a thing as well known, as easily discovered, as any thing that is deformed, misshapen, or wrong in our form or outward make; and that this knowledge is derived from the uniformity of sentiments among mankind, from whence proceeds the knowledge of what are the general habits of nature, the result of which is an idea of perfect beauty.

If what has been advanced be true, that besides this beauty or truth which is formed on the uniform, eternal, and immutable laws of nature, and which of necessity can be but *one*, — that besides this one immutable verity there are likewise what we have called apparent or secondary truths, proceeding from local and temporary prejudices, fancies, fashions, or accidental connection of ideas; if it appears that these last have still their foundation, however slender, in the original fabric of our minds, — it follows that all these truths or beauties deserve and require the attention of the artist, in proportion to their stability or duration, or as their influence is more or less extensive. And let me add that, as they ought not to pass their just bounds, so neither do they, in a well-regulated taste, at all prevent or weaken the influence of those general principles which alone can give to art its true and permanent dignity.

To form this just taste is undoubtedly in your own power; but it is to reason and philosophy that you must have recourse; from them you must borrow the balance, by which is to be weighed and estimated the value of every pretension that intrudes itself on your notice.

The general objection which is made to the introduction of philosophy into the regions of taste is that it checks and restrains the flights of the imagination, and gives that timidity which an over-carefulness not to err or act contrary to reason is likely to produce. It is not so. Fear is neither reason nor philosophy. The true spirit of philosophy, by giving knowledge, gives a manly confidence, and substitutes rational firmness in the place of vain presumption. A man of real taste is always a man of judgment in other respects; and those inventions which either disdain or shrink from reason are generally, I fear, more like the dreams of a distempered brain than the exalted enthusiasm of a sound and true genius. In the midst of the highest flights of fancy or imagination, reason ought to preside from first to last, though I admit her more powerful operation is upon reflection.

Let me add that some of the greatest names of antiquity, and those who have most distinguished themselves in works of genius and imagination, were equally eminent for their critical skill. Plato, Aristotle, Cicero, and Horace; and among the moderns, Boileau, Corneille, Pope, and Dryden, are at least instances of genius not being destroyed by attention or subjection to rules and science. I should hope, therefore, that the natural consequence of what has been said would be to excite in you a desire of knowing the principles and conduct of the great masters of our art, and respect and veneration for them when known.

Mrs. Robinson.

DISCOURSE VIII.

Delivered to the Students of the Royal Academy, on the Distribution of the Prizes, December 10, 1778.

THE PRINCIPLES OF ART, WHETHER POETRY OR PAINTING, HAVE THEIR FOUNDATION IN THE MIND; SUCH AS NOVELTY, VARIETY, AND CONTRAST; THESE IN THEIR EXCESS BECOME DEFECTS.— SIMPLICITY, ITS EXCESS DISAGREEABLE. — RULES NOT TO BE ALWAYS OBSERVED IN THEIR LITERAL SENSE: SUFFICIENT TO PRESERVE THE SPIRIT OF THE LAW. — OBSERVATIONS ON THE PRIZE PICTURES.

I HAVE recommended in former[1] discourses that artists should learn their profession by endeavoring to form an idea of perfection from the different excellences which lie dispersed in the various schools of painting. Some difficulty will still occur to know what is beauty, and where it may be found; one would wish not to be obliged to take it entirely on the credit of fame, — though to this, I acknowledge, the younger students must unavoidably submit. Any suspicion in them of the chance of their being deceived will have more tendency to obstruct their advancement than even an enthusiastic confidence in the perfection of their models. But to the more advanced in the art, who wish to stand on more stable and firmer ground, and to establish principles on a stronger foundation than authority, however venera-

[1] Discourses II. and VI.

ble or powerful, it may be safely told that there is still a higher tribunal, to which those great masters themselves must submit, and to which, indeed, every excellence in art must be ultimately referred. He who is ambitious to enlarge the boundaries of his art must extend his views beyond the precepts which are found in books or may be drawn from the practice of his predecessors, to a knowledge of those precepts in the mind, those operations of intellectual nature, to which everything that aspires to please must be proportioned and accommodated.

Poetry, having a more extensive power than our art, exerts its influence over almost all the passions; among those may be reckoned one of our most prevalent dispositions,—anxiety for the future. Poetry operates by raising our curiosity, engaging the mind by degrees to take an interest in the event, keeping that event suspended, and surprising at last with an unexpected catastrophe.

The painter's art is more confined, and has nothing that corresponds with, or perhaps is equivalent to, this power and advantage of leading the mind on, till attention is totally engaged. What is done by painting must be done at one blow; curiosity has received at once all the satisfaction it can ever have.[1]

---

[1] "— the poet is not compelled to concentrate his picture into the space of a single moment. He has it in his power to take up every action of his hero at its source, and pursue it to its issue, through all possible variations. Each of these, which would cost the artist a separate work, costs the poet but a single trait; and should this trait, if viewed by itself, offend the imagination of the hearer, either such preparation has been made for it by what has preceded, or it will be so softened and compensated by what follows, that its solitary

There are, however, other intellectual qualities and dispositions which the painter can satisfy and affect as powerfully as the poet. Among those we may reckon our love of novelty, variety, and contrast; these qualities, on examination, will be found to refer to a certain activity and restlessness which has a pleasure and delight in being exercised and put in motion. Art, therefore, only administers to those wants and desires of the mind.

It requires no long disquisition to show that the dispositions which I have stated actually subsist in the human mind. Variety reanimates the attention, which is apt to languish under a continual sameness. Novelty makes a more forcible impression on the mind than can be made by the representation of what we have often seen before; and contrasts rouse the power of comparison by opposition. All this is obvious; but, on the other hand, it must be remembered that the mind, though an active principle, has likewise a disposition to indolence; and though it loves exercise, loves it only to a certain degree, beyond which it is very unwilling to be led or driven; the pursuit, therefore, of novelty and variety may be carried to excess. When variety entirely destroys the pleasure proceeding from uniformity and repetition, and when novelty counteracts and shuts out the pleasure arising from old habits and customs, they oppose too much the indolence of our disposition; the mind, therefore, can bear with pleasure but a

---

impression is lost, and the combination produces the best possible effect. . . . Time is the department of the poet, as space is that of the painter." — LESSING, *Laocoön*.

small portion of novelty at a time. The main part of the work must be in the mode to which we have been used. An affection to old habits and customs I take to be the predominant disposition of the mind, and novelty comes as an exception; where all is novelty, the attention, the exercise of the mind is too violent. Contrast, in the same manner, when it exceeds certain limits, is as disagreeable as a violent and perpetual opposition; it gives to the senses in their progress a more sudden change than they can bear with pleasure.

It is, then, apparent that those qualities, however they contribute to the perfection of art when kept within certain bounds, if they are carried to excess become defects, and require correction; a work consequently will not proceed better and better as it is more varied. Variety can never be the groundwork and principle of the performance, — it must be only employed to recreate and relieve.

To apply these general observations, which belong equally to all arts, to ours in particular. In a composition, when the objects are scattered and divided into many equal parts, the eye is perplexed and fatigued from not knowing where to find the principal action, or which is the principal figure; for where all are making equal pretensions to notice, all are in equal danger of neglect.

The expression which is used very often on these occasions is, "The piece wants repose;" a word which perfectly expresses a relief of the mind from that state of hurry and anxiety which it suffers when looking at a work of this character.

On the other hand, absolute unity — that is, a large work consisting of one group or mass of light only — would be as defective as an heroic poem without episode, or any collateral incidents to recreate the mind with that variety which it always requires.

An instance occurs to me of two painters (Rembrandt and Poussin), of characters totally opposite to each other in every respect, but in nothing more than in their mode of composition, and management of light and shadow. Rembrandt's manner is absolute unity; he often has but one group, and exhibits little more then one spot of light in the midst of a large quantity of shadow; if he has a second mass, that second bears no proportion to the principal. Poussin, on the contrary, has scarce any principal mass of light at all, and his figures are often too much dispersed, without sufficient attention to place them in groups.

The conduct of these two painters is entirely the reverse of what might be expected from their general style and character, — the works of Poussin being as much distinguished for simplicity as those of Rembrandt for combination. Even this conduct of Poussin might proceed from two great an affection to simplicity of *another kind*, — too great a desire to avoid that ostentation of art, with regard to light and shadow, on which Rembrandt so much wished to draw the attention; however, each of them ran into contrary extremes, and it is difficult to determine which is the most reprehensible, both being equally distant from the demands of nature and the purposes of art.

The same just moderation must be observed in regard to ornaments; nothing will contribute more to destroy repose than profusion, of whatever kind, whether it consists in the multiplicity of objects, or the variety and brightness of colors. On the other hand, a work without ornament, instead of simplicity, to which it makes pretensions, has rather the appearance of poverty. The degree to which ornaments are admissible must be regulated by the professed style of the work; but we may be sure of this truth, — that the most ornamental style requires repose to set off even its ornaments to advantage. I cannot avoid mentioning here an instance of repose in that faithful and accurate painter of nature, Shakespeare, — the short dialogue between Duncan and Banquo, while they are approaching the gates of Macbeth's castle. Their conversation very naturally turns upon the beauty of its situation, and the pleasantness of the air; and Banquo, observing the martlets' nests in every recess of the cornice, remarks that where those birds most breed and haunt the air is delicate. The subject of this quiet and easy conversation gives that repose so necessary to the mind after the tumultuous bustle of the preceding scenes, and perfectly contrasts the scene of horror that immediately succeeds. It seems as if Shakespeare asked himself, "What is a prince likely to say to his attendants on such an occasion?" The modern writers seem, on the contrary, to be always searching for new thoughts such as never could occur to man in the situation represented. This is also frequently the practice of Homer, who from the midst of battles and horrors relieves and refreshes the mind of the reader, by introducing some quiet rural image, or picture of familiar domestic life. The writers of every age and country where taste has begun to decline, paint and adorn every object they touch; are always on the stretch; never deviate or sink a moment from the pompous and the brilliant. Lucan, Statius, and Claudian (as a learned critic has observed) are examples of this bad taste and want of judgment; they never soften their tones, or condescend to be natural; all is exaggeration and perpetual splendor, without affording repose of any kind.

As we are speaking of excesses, it will not be remote from our purpose to say a few words upon simplicity; which in one of the senses in which it is used, is considered as the general corrector of excess. We shall at present forbear to consider it as implying that exact conduct which proceeds from an intimate knowledge of simple, unadulterated nature, as it is then only another word for perfection, which neither stops short of nor oversteps reality and truth.

In our inquiry after simplicity, as in many other inquiries of this nature, we can best explain what is right by showing what is wrong; and, indeed, in this case it seems to be absolutely necessary; simplicity, being only a negative virtue, cannot be described or defined. We must therefore explain its nature, and show the advantage and beauty which are derived from it, by showing the deformity which proceeds from its neglect.

Though instances of this neglect might be expected to be found in practice, we should not expect to find in the works of critics precepts that bid defiance to simplicity and everything that relates to it. De Piles recommends to us portrait-painters to add grace and dignity to the characters of those whose pictures we draw. So far he is undoubtedly right; but, unluckily, he descends to particulars, and gives his own idea of grace and dignity. "If," says he, "you draw persons of high character and dignity, they ought to be drawn in such an attitude that the portraits must seem to speak to us of themselves, and, as it were, to say to us, 'Stop, take notice of me, I am that invincible king, surrounded by majesty;' 'I am that valiant commander who struck terror everywhere;' 'I am that great minister who knew all the springs of politics:' 'I am that magistrate of consummate wisdom and probity.'" He goes on in this manner with all the characters he can think on. We may contract the tumor of this presumptuous loftiness with the natural, unaffected air of the portraits of Titian, where dignity, seeming to be natural and inherent, draws spontaneous reverence, and instead of being thus vainly assumed, has the appearance of an unalienable adjunct; whereas such pompous and labored insolence of grandeur is so far from creating respect that it betrays vulgarity and meanness, and new-acquired consequence.

The painters, many of them at least, have not been backward in adopting the notions contained in these precepts. The portraits of Rigaud are perfect examples of an implicit observance of these rules of De Piles; so that though he was a painter of great merit in many respects, yet that merit is entirely overpowered by a total absence of simplicity in every sense.

Not to multiply instances which might be produced for this purpose from the works of history-painters, I shall mention only one, — a picture which I have seen of the Supreme Being, by Coypell.

This subject the Roman Catholic painters have taken the liberty to represent, however indecent the attempt, and however obvious the impossibility of any approach to an adequate representation; but here the air and character which the painter has given — and he has doubtless given the highest he could conceive — are so degraded by an attempt at such dignity as De Piles has recommended, that we are enraged at the folly and presumption of the artist, and consider it as little less than profanation.

As we have passed to a neighboring nation for instances of want of this quality, we must acknowledge at the same time that they have produced great examples of simplicity in Poussin and Le Sueur. But as we are speaking of the most refined and subtle notion of perfection, may we not inquire whether a curious eye cannot discern some faults even in those great men? I can fancy that even Poussin, by abhorring that affectation and that want of simplicity which he observed in his countrymen, has, in certain particulars, fallen into the contrary extreme, so far as to approach to a kind of affectation, — to what in writing would be called pedantry.

When simplicity, instead of being a corrector, seems to set up for herself; that is, when an artist seems to value himself solely upon this quality, such an ostentatious display of simplicity becomes then as disagreeable and nauseous as any other kind of affectation. He is, however, in this case likely enough to sit down contented with his own work; for though he finds the world look at it with indifference or dislike, as being destitute of every quality that can recreate or give pleasure to the mind, yet he consoles himself that it has simplicity, a beauty of too pure and chaste a nature to be relished by vulgar minds.

It is in art as in morals; no character would inspire us with an enthusiastic admiration of his virtue, if that virtue consisted only in an absence of vice. Something more is required; a man must do more than merely his duty, to be a hero.

Those works of the ancients which are in the highest esteem have something besides mere simplicity to recommend them. The Apollo, the Venus, the Laocoön, the Gladiator, have a certain composition of action, have contrasts sufficient to give grace and energy in a high degree; but it must be confessed of the many thousand antique statues which we have, that their general characteristic is bordering at least on inanimate insipidity.[1]

Simplicity, when so very inartificial as to seem to evade the difficulties of art, is a very suspicious virtue.

I do not, however, wish to degrade simplicity from the high estimation in which it has been ever justly

---

[1] This "inanimate insipidity," when seen through Winckelman's eyes, becomes a noble simplicity and quiet grandeur. "As," says he, "the depths of the sea always remain calm, however much the surface may be raging, so the expression in the figures of the Greeks, under every form of passion, shows a great and self-collected soul."

held. It is our barrier against that great enemy to truth and nature, affectation, which is ever clinging to the pencil, and ready to drop in and poison everything it touches.

Our love and affection to simplicity proceeds in a great measure from our aversion to every kind of affectation. There is likewise another reason why so much stress is laid upon this virtue, — the propensity which artists have to fall into the contrary extreme; we therefore set a guard on that side which is most assailable. When a young artist is first told that his composition and his attitudes must be contrasted; that he must turn the head contrary to the position of the body, in order to produce grace and animation; that his outline must be undulating and swelling, to give grandeur; and that the eye must be gratified with a variety of colors; when he is told this, with certain animating words of "spirit," "dignity," "energy," "grace," "greatness of style," and "brilliancy of tints," he becomes suddenly vain of his newly-acquired knowledge, and never thinks he can carry those rules too far. It is then that the aid of simplicity ought to be called in to correct the exuberance of youthful ardor.

The same may be said in regard to coloring, which in its pre-eminence is particularly applied to flesh. An artist, in his first essay of imitating nature, would make the whole mass of one color, as the oldest painters did, till he is taught to observe not only the variety of tints which are in the object itself, but the differences produced by the gradual decline of light to shadow; he then immediately puts his instruction in practice, and introduces a variety of distinct colors. He must then be again corrected and told, that though there is this variety, yet the effect of the whole upon the eye must have the union and simplicity of the coloring of nature.

And here we may observe that the progress of an individual student bears a great resemblance to the progress and advancement of the art itself. Want of simplicity would probably be not one of the defects of an artist who had studied nature only, as it was not of the old masters, who lived in the time preceding the great art of painting; on the contrary, their works are too simple and too inartificial.

The art in its infancy, like the first work of a student, was dry, hard, and simple. But this kind of barbarous simplicity would be better named penury, as it proceeds from mere want, — from want of knowledge, want of resources, want of abilities to be otherwise; their simplicity was the offspring, not of choice, but necessity.

In the second stage they were sensible of this poverty; and those who were the most sensible of the want were the best judges of the measure of the supply. There were painters who emerged from poverty without falling into luxury. Their success induced others, who probably never would of themselves have had strength of mind to discover the original defect, to endeavor at the remedy by an abuse; and they ran into the contrary extreme. But however they may have strayed, we cannot recommend to them to return to that simplicity which they have justly quitted, but to deal out their abundance with a more sparing hand, with that dignity which makes no parade either of its riches or of its art. It is not easy to give a rule which may serve to fix this just and correct medium; because, when we may have fixed, or nearly fixed, the middle point, taken as a general principle, circumstances may oblige us to depart from it, either on the side of simplicity, or on that of variety and decoration.

I thought it necessary in a former discourse, speaking of the difference of the sublime and ornamental style of painting — in order to excite your attention to the more manly, noble, and dignified manner — to leave perhaps an impression too contemptuous of those ornamental parts of our art, for which many have valued themselves, and many works are much valued and esteemed.

I said then what I thought it was right at that time to say. I supposed the disposition of young men more inclinable to splendid negligence than perseverance in laborious application to acquire correctness, and therefore did as we do in making what is crooked straight, by bending it the contrary way, in order that it may remain straight at last.

For this purpose, then, and to correct excess or neglect of any kind, we may here add that it is not enough that a work be learned; it must be pleasing; the painter must add grace to strength, if he desires to secure the first impression in his favor. Our taste has a kind of sensuality about it, as well as a love of the sublime; both these qualities of the mind are to have their proper consequence, as far as they do not counteract each other; for that is the grand error which much care ought to be taken to avoid.

There are some rules whose absolute authority, like that of our nurses, continues no longer than while we are in a state of childhood. One of the first rules, for instance, that I believe every master would give to a young pupil, respecting his conduct and management of light and shadow, would be what Leonardo da Vinci has actually given, — that you must oppose a light ground to the shadowed side of your figure, and a dark ground to the light side. If Leonardo had lived to see the superior splendor and effect which has been since produced by the exactly contrary conduct, — by joining light to light and shadow to shadow, — though without doubt he would have admired it, yet, as it ought not, so probably it would not be the first rule with which he would have begun his instructions.

Again; in the artificial management of the figures, it is directed that they shall contrast each other according to the rules generally given; that if one figure opposes his front to the spectator, the next figure is to have his back turned, and that the limbs of each individual figure be contrasted, — that is, if the right leg be put forward, the right arm is to be drawn back.

It is very proper that those rules should be given in the Academy; it is proper the young students should be informed that some research is to be made, and that they should be habituated to consider every excellence as reducible to principles. Besides, it is the natural progress of instruction to teach first what is obvious and perceptible to the senses, and from hence proceed gradually to notions large, liberal, and complete, such as comprise the more refined and higher excellences in art. But when students are more advanced, they will find that the greatest beauties of character and expression are produced without contrast; nay more, that this contrast would ruin and destroy that natural energy of men engaged in real action, unsolicitous of grace. Saint Paul preaching at Athens, in one of the cartoons, far from any affected academical contrast of limbs, stands equally on both legs, and both hands are in the same attitude; add contrast, and the whole energy and unaffected grace of the figure is destroyed. Elymas the sorcerer stretches both hands forward in the same direction, which gives perfectly the expression intended. Indeed, you never will find in the works of Raphael any of those school-boy affected contrasts. Whatever contrast there is appears without any seeming agency of art, by the natural chance of things.

What has been said of the evil of excesses of all kinds, whether of simplicity, variety, or contrast, naturally suggests to the painter the necessity of a general inquiry into the true meaning and cause of rules, and how they operate on those faculties to which they are addressed. By knowing their general purpose and meaning he will often find that he need not confine himself to the literal sense; it will be sufficient if he preserve the spirit of the law.

Critical remarks are not always understood without examples; it may not be improper, therefore, to give instances where the rule itself, though generally received, is false, or where a narrow conception of it may lead the artists into great errors.

It is given as a rule by Fresnoy that "the principal figure of a subject must appear in the midst of the picture, under the principal light, to distinguish it from the rest." A painter who should think himself obliged secretly to follow this rule, would encumber himself with needless difficulties; he would be confined to great uniformity of composition, and be deprived of many beauties which are incompatible with its observance. The meaning of this rule extends, or ought to extend, no further than this, — that the principal figure should be immediately distinguished at the first glance of the eye; but there is no necessity that the principal light should fall on the principal figure, or that the principal figure should be in the middle of the picture. It is sufficient that it be distinguished by its place, or by the attention of other figures pointing it out to the spectator. So far is this rule from being indispensable that it is very seldom practised, — other considerations of greater consequence often standing in the way. Examples in opposition to this rule are found in the cartoons in "Christ's Charge to Peter," the "Preaching of Saint Paul," and "Elymas the Sorcerer," who is undoubtedly the principal object in that picture. In none of those compositions is the principal figure in the midst of the picture. In the very admirable composition of the "Tent of Darius," by Le Brun, Alexander is not in the middle of the picture, nor does the principal light fall on him; but the attention of all the other figures immediately distinguishes him, and distinguishes him more properly; the greatest light falls on the daughter of Darius, who is in the middle of the picture, where it is more necessary the principal light should be placed.

It is very extraordinary that Felibien, who has given a very minute description of this picture, but indeed such a description as may be called rather panegyric than criticism, thinking it necessary (according to the precept of Fresnoy) that Alexander should possess the principal light, has accordingly given it to him; he might with equal truth have said that he was placed in the middle of the picture, as he seemed resolved to give this piece every kind of excellence which he conceived to be necessary to perfection. His generosity is here unluckily misapplied, as it would have destroyed, in a great measure, the beauty of the composition.

Another instance occurs to me, where equal liberty may be taken in regard to the management of light. Though the general practice is to make a large mass about the middle of the picture surrounded by shadow, the reverse may be practised, and the spirit of the rule may still be preserved. Examples of this principle reversed may be found very frequently in the works of the Venetian school. In the great composition of Paul Veronese, "The Marriage at Cana," the figures are, for the most part, in half shadow; the great light is in the sky; and, indeed, the general effect of this picture, which is so striking, is no more than what we often see in landscapes, in small pictures of fairs and country feasts; but those principles of light and shadow being transferred to a large scale, to a space containing near a hundred figures as large as life, and conducted to all appearance with as much facility, and with an attention as steadily fixed upon *the whole together*, as if it were a small picture immediately under the eye, the work justly excites our admiration, — the difficulty being increased as the extent is enlarged.

The various modes of composition are infinite; sometimes it shall consist of one large group in the middle of the picture, and the smaller groups on each side; or a plain space in the middle, and the groups of figures ranked round this vacuity.

Whether this principal broad light be in the middle space of ground, as in " The School of Athens; " or in the sky, as in " The Marriage at Cana," in " The Andromeda," and in the most of the pictures of Paul Veronese; or whether the light be on the groups; whatever mode of composition is adopted, every variety and license is allowable. This only is indisputably necessary: that to prevent the eye from being distracted and confused by a multiplicity of objects of equal magnitude, those objects, whether they consist of lights, shadows, or figures, must be disposed in large masses and groups properly varied and contrasted; that to a certain quantity of action a proportioned space of plain ground is required; that light is to be supported by sufficient shadow; and we may add that a certain quantity of cold colors is necessary to give value and lustre to the warm colors. What those proportions are cannot be so well learned by precept as by observation on pictures, and in this knowledge bad pictures will instruct, as well as good. Our inquiry why pictures have a bad effect may be as advantageous as the inquiry why they have a good effect; each will corroborate the principles that are suggested by the other.

Though it is not my business to enter into the detail of our art, yet I must take this opportunity of mentioning one of the means of producing that great effect which we observe in the works of the Venetian painters, as I think it is not generally known or observed. It ought, in my opinion, to be indispensably observed that the masses of light in a picture be always of a warm mellow color, yellow, red, or a yellowish-white; and that the blue, the gray, or the green colors be kept almost entirely out of these masses, and be used only to support and set off these warm colors; and for this purpose a small portion of cold colors will be sufficient.

Let this conduct be reversed; let the light be cold, and the surrounding colors warm, as we often see in the works of the Roman and Florentine painters, and it will be out of the power of art, even in the hands of Rubens or Titian, to make a picture splendid and harmonious.

Le Brun and Carlo Maratti were two painters of great merit, and particularly what may be called academical merit, but were both deficient in this management of colors; the want of observing this rule is one of the causes of that heaviness of effect which is so observable in their works. The principal light in the picture of Le Brun, which I just now mentioned, falls on Statira, who is dressed very injudiciously in a pale blue drapery. It is true, he has heightened his blue with gold, but that is not enough; the whole picture has a heavy air, and by no means answers the expectations raised by the print. Poussin often made a spot of blue drapery, when the general hue of the picture was inclinable to brown or yellow; which shows sufficiently that harmony of coloring was not a part of the art that had much engaged the attention of that great painter.

The conduct of Titian in the picture of "Bacchus and Ariadne"[1] has been much celebrated, and justly, for the harmony of coloring. To Ariadne is given (say the critics) a red scarf, to relieve the figure from the sea, which is behind her. It is not for that reason alone, but for another of much greater consequence; for the sake of the general harmony and effect of the picture. The figure of Ariadne is separated from the great group, and is dressed in blue, which, added to the color of the sea, makes that quantity of cold color which Titian thought necessary for the support and brilliancy of the great group; which group is composed, with very little exception, entirely of mellow colors. But as the picture in this case would be divided into two distinct parts, one half cold, and the other warm, it was necessary to carry some of the mellow colors of the great group into the cold part of the picture, and a part of the cold into the great group; accordingly, Titian gave

---

[1] One of the gems of the British National Gallery, a marvel of poetic realization and technical excellence. Ruskin says: "The two pictures which I would last part with out of it (the National Gallery) would be Titian's Bacchus and Correggio's Venus."

Ariadne a red scarf, and to one of the Bacchante a little blue drapery.[1]

The light of the picture, as I observed, ought to be of a warm color, for though white may be used for the principal light, as was the practice of many of the Dutch and Flemish painters, yet it is better to suppose that white illumined by the yellow rays of the setting sun, as was the manner of Titian. The superiority of which manner is never more striking than when in a collection of pictures we chance to see a portrait of Titian's hanging by the side of a Flemish picture (even though that should be by the hand of Van Dyck), which, however admirable in other respects, becomes cold and grey in the comparison.

The illuminated parts of objects are in nature of a warmer tint than those that are in the shade; what I have recommended, therefore, is no more than that the same conduct be observed in the whole which is acknowledged to be necessary in every individual part. It is presenting to the eye the same effect as that which it has been accustomed to feel, which, in this case, as in every other, will always produce beauty; no principle, therefore, in our art can be more certain, or is derived from a higher source.

What I just now mentioned of the supposed reason why Ariadne has part of her drapery red gives me occasion here to observe that this favorite quality of giving objects relief, and which De Piles and all the

---

[1] Diogenes refuted the Sophist, who proved to him dialectically that he could not walk, by getting up and walking round his tub; Gainsborough refuted Reynolds, who argued that blue cannot be the dominant color in a picture, by painting his masterpiece, "The Blue Boy."

critics have considered as a requisite of the utmost importance, was not one of those objects which much engaged the attention of Titian; painters of an inferior rank have far exceeded him in producing this effect. This was a great object of attention when art was in its infant state, as it is at present with the vulgar and ignorant, who feel the highest satisfaction in seeing a figure, which, as they say, looks as if they could walk round it. But however low I may rate this pleasure of deception, I should not oppose it, did it not oppose itself to a quality of a much higher kind, by counteracting entirely that fulness of manner which is so difficult to express in words, but which is found in perfection in the best works of Correggio, and we may add, of Rembrandt. This effect is produced by melting and losing the shadows in a ground still darker than those shadows; whereas that relief is produced by opposing and separating the ground from the figure, either by light, or shadow, or color. This conduct of in-laying, as it may be called, figures on their ground in order to produce relief, was the practice of the old painters, — such as Andrea Mantegna, Pietro Perugino, and Albert Dürer; and to these we may add the first manner of Leonardo da Vinci, Giorgione, and even Correggio; but these three were among the first who began to correct themselves in dryness of style, by no longer considering relief as a principal object. As those two qualities, relief, and fulness of effect, can hardly exist together, it is not very difficult to determine to which we ought to give the preference. An artist is obliged forever to hold a balance in his hand, by which he must determine the value of different qualities, that, when *some* fault must be committed, he may choose the least. Those painters who have best understood the art of producing a good effect have adopted one principle that seems perfectly conformable to reason, — that a part may be sacrificed for the good of the whole. Thus, whether the masses consist of light or shadow, it is necessary that they should be compact and of a pleasing shape; to this end some parts may be made darker, and some lighter, and reflections stronger than nature would warrant. Paul Veronese took great liberties of this kind. It is said that, being once asked why certain figures were painted in shade, as no cause was seen in the picture itself, he turned off the inquiry by answering, " *Una nuevola che passa,*" — "A cloud is passing which has overshadowed them."

But I cannot give a better instance of this practice than a picture which I have of Rubens; it is a representation of a moonlight. Rubens has not only diffused more light over the picture than is in nature, but has bestowed on it those warm, glowing colors by which his works are so much distinguished. It is so unlike what any other painters have given us of moonlight that it might be easily mistaken, if he had not likewise added stars, for a fainter setting sun. Rubens thought the eye ought to be satisfied in this case above all other considerations; he might, indeed, have made it more natural, but it would have been at the expense of what he thought of much greater consequence, — the harmony proceeding from the contrast and variety of colors.

This same picture will furnish us with another instance where we must depart from nature for a greater advantage. The moon in this picture does not preserve so great a superiority in regard to its lightness over the subject which it illumines as it does in nature; this is likewise an intended deviation, and for the same reason. If Rubens had preserved the same scale of gradation of light between the moon and the objects which is found in nature, the picture must have consisted of one small spot of light only, and at a little distance from the picture nothing but this spot would have been seen. It may be said, indeed, that, this being the case, it is a subject that ought not to be painted; but then, for the same reason, neither armor, nor anything shining, ought ever to be painted; for though pure white is used in order to represent the greatest light of shining objects, it will not in the picture preserve the same superiority over flesh as it has in nature, without keeping that flesh color of a very low tint. Rembrandt, who thought it of more consequence to paint light than the objects that are seen by it, has done this in a picture of Achilles which I have. The head is kept down to a very low tint in order to preserve this due gradation and distinction between the armor and the face; the consequence of which is that, upon the whole, the picture is too black. Surely too much is sacrificed here to this narrow conception of nature; allowing the contrary conduct a fault, yet it must be acknowledged a less fault than making a picture so dark that it cannot be seen without a peculiar light, and then with difficulty. The merit or demerit of the different conduct of Rubens and Rembrandt in those instances which I have given, is not to be determined by the narrow principles of nature, separated from its effect on the human mind. Reason and common-sense tell us that before and above all other considerations it is necessary that the work should be seen, not only without difficulty or inconvenience, but with pleasure and satisfaction; and every obstacle which stands in the way of this pleasure and convenience must be removed.

The tendency of this Discourse, with the instances which have been given, is not so much to place the artist above rules, as to teach him their reason; to prevent him from entertaining a narrow, confined conception of art; to clear his mind from a perplexed variety of rules and their exceptions, by directing his attention to an intimate acquaintance with the passions and affections of the mind, from which all rules arise, and to which they are all referable. Art effects its purpose by their means; an accurate knowledge, therefore, of those passions and dispositions of the mind is necessary to him who desires to affect them upon sure and solid principles.

A complete essay or inquiry into the connection between the rules of art and the eternal and immutable dispositions of our passions would be indeed going at once to the foundation of criticism;[1] but I am too well convinced what extensive knowledge, what subtle and penetrating judgment, would be required to engage in such an undertaking; it is enough for me if, in the language of painters, I have produced

[1] This was inadvertently said. I did not recollect the admirable treatise on "The Sublime and Beautiful."—R.

a slight sketch of a part of this vast composition, but that sufficiently distinct to show the usefulness of such a theory, and its practicability.

Before I conclude, I cannot avoid making one observation on the pictures now before us. I have observed that every candidate has copied the celebrated invention of Timanthes in hiding the face of Agamemnon in his mantle; indeed, such lavish encomiums have been bestowed on this thought, and that too by men of the highest character in critical knowledge, — Cicero, Quintilian, Valerius, Maximus, and Pliny, — and have been since re-echoed by almost every modern that has written on the arts, that your adopting it can neither be wondered at nor blamed. It appears now to be so much connected with the subject, that the spectator would perhaps be disappointed in not finding united in the picture what he always united in his mind, and considered as indispensably belonging to the subject. But it may be observed that those who praise this circumstance were not painters. They use it as an illustration only of their own art; it served their purpose, and it was certainly not their business to enter into the objections that lie against it in another art. I fear *we* have but very scanty means of exciting those powers over the imagination which make so very considerable and refined a part of poetry. It is a doubt with me whether we should even make the attempt. The chief, if not the only occasion, which the painter has for this artifice is when the subject is improper to be more fully represented, either for the sake of decency, or to avoid what would be disagreeable to be seen; and this is not to raise or increase the passions, which is the reason that is given for this practice, but, on the contrary, to diminish their effect.

It is true, sketches, or such drawings as painters generally make for their works, give this pleasure of imagination to a high degree. From a slight, undetermined drawing, where the ideas of the composition and character are, as I may say, only just touched upon, the imagination supplies more than the painter himself, probably, could produce; and we accordingly often find that the finished work disappoints the expectation that was raised from the sketch; and this power of the imagination is one of the causes of the great pleasure we have in viewing a collection of drawings by great painters. These general ideas which are expressed in sketches, correspond very well to the art often used in poetry. A great part of the beauty of the celebrated description of Eve in Milton's "Paradise Lost" consists in using only general, indistinct expressions, every reader making out the detail according to his own particular imagination, — his own idea of beauty, grace, expression, dignity, or loveliness; but a painter, when he represents Eve on a canvas, is obliged to give a determined form, and his own idea of beauty distinctly expressed.

We cannot on this occasion, nor indeed on any other, recommend an indeterminate manner or vague ideas of any kind, in a complete and finished picture. This notion, therefore, of leaving anything to the imagination, opposes a very fixed and indispensable rule in our art — that everything shall be carefully and distinctly expressed, as if the painter knew, with correctness and precision, the exact form and character of whatever is introduced into the picture. This is what with us is called science and learning; which must not be sacrificed and given up for an uncertain and doubtful beauty, which, not naturally belonging to our art, will probably be sought for without success.

Mr. Falconet has observed, in a note on this passage in his translation of Pliny that the circumstance of covering the face of Agamemnon was probably not in consequence of any fine imagination of the painter — which he considers as a discovery of the critics, — but merely copied from the description of the sacrifice, as it is found in Euripides.

The words from which the picture is supposed to be taken are these: "Agamemnon saw Iphigenia advance towards the fatal altar; he groaned, he turned aside his head, he shed tears, and covered his face with his robe."

Falconet does not at all acquiesce in the praise that is bestowed on Timanthes; not only because it is not his invention, but because he thinks meanly of this trick of concealing, except in instances of blood, where the objects would be too horrible to be seen; but, says he, "in an afflicted father, in a king, in Agamemnon, you, who are a painter, conceal from me the most interesting circumstances, and then put me off with sophistry and a veil. You are [he adds] a feeble painter, without resource; you do not know even those of your art. I care not what veil it is, whether closed hands, arms raised, or any other action that conceals from me the countenance of the hero. You think of veiling Agamemnon; you have unveiled your own ignorance. A painter who represents Agamemnon veiled is as ridiculous as a poet would be who, in a pathetic situation, in order to satisfy my expectations and rid himself of the business, should say that the sentiments of his hero are so far above whatever can be said on the occasion, that he shall say nothing."[1]

To what Falconet has said, we may add that, supposing this method of leaving the expression of grief to the imagination to be, as it was thought to be, the invention of the painter, and that it deserves all the praise that has been given it, still it is a trick that will serve but once; whoever does it a second time will not only want novelty, but be justly suspected of using artifice to evade difficulties. If difficulties overcome make a great part of the merit of art, difficulties evaded can deserve but little commendation.

[1] An acuter critic says: "But Timanthes knew the limits within which the Graces had confined his art. He knew that the grief which became Agamemnon, as a father, must have been expressed by contortions, at all times ugly; but so far as dignity and beauty could be combined with the expression of such a feeling, so far he pushed it. True, he would fain have passed over the ugly, fain have softened it; but since his piece did not admit either of its omission or diminution, what was left him but its concealment? He left to conjecture what he might not paint. In short, this concealment is a sacrifice which the artist made to beauty, and is an instance, not how expression may exceed the capacity of art, but how it should be subjected to art's first law, the law of beauty." — LESSING, *The Laocoön*, chap. ii.

Sir Joseph Banks.

DISCOURSE IX.

Delivered at the Opening of the Royal Academy, in Somerset Place, October 16, 1780.

ON THE REMOVAL OF THE ROYAL ACADEMY TO SOMERSET PLACE. — THE ADVANTAGES TO SOCIETY FROM CULTIVATING INTELLECTUAL PLEASURE.

THE honor which the arts acquire by being permitted to take possession of this noble habitation is one of the most considerable of the many instances we have received of his Majesty's protection, and the strongest proof of his desire to make the Academy respectable.

Nothing has been left undone that might contribute to excite our pursuit or to reward our attainments. We have already the happiness of seeing the arts in a state to which they never before arrived in this nation. This building, in which we are now assembled, will remain to many future ages an illustrious specimen of the architect's[1] abilities. It is our duty to endeavor that those who gaze with wonder at the structure may not be disappointed when they visit the apartments. It will be no small addition to the glory which this nation has already acquired from having given birth to eminent men in every part of science, if it should be enabled to pro-

[1] Sir William Chambers.

duce, in consequence of this institution, a school of English artists. The estimation in which we stand in respect to our neighbors, will be in proportion to the degree in which we excel or are inferior to them in the acquisition of intellectual excellence, of which trade and its consequential riches must be acknowledged to give the means; but a people whose whole attention is absorbed in those means, and who forget the end, can aspire but little above the rank of a barbarous nation. Every establishment that tends to the cultivation of the pleasures of the mind, as distinct from those of sense, may be considered as an inferior school of morality, where the mind is polished and prepared for higher attainments.

Let us for a moment take a short survey of the progress of the mind towards what is, or ought to be, its true object of attention. Man, in his lowest state, has no pleasures but those of sense, and no wants but those of appetite; afterwards, when society is divided into different ranks, and some are appointed to labor for the support of others, those whom their superiority sets free from labor begin to look for intellectual entertainments. Thus, while the shepherds were attending their flocks, their masters made the first astronomical observations; so music is said to have had its origin from a man at leisure listening to the strokes of a hammer.

As the senses, in the lowest state of nature, are necessary to direct us to our support, when that support is once secure there is danger in following them further; to him who has no rule of action but the gratification of the senses, plenty is always dangerous; it is therefore necessary to the happiness of individuals, and still more necessary to the security of society, that the mind should be elevated to the idea of general beauty, and the contemplation of general truth; by this pursuit the mind is always carried forward in search of something more excellent than it finds, and obtains its proper superiority over the common senses of life, by learning to feel itself capable of higher aims and nobler enjoyments. In this gradual exaltation of human nature every art contributes its contingent towards the general supply of mental pleasure. Whatever abstracts the thoughts from sensual gratifications, whatever teaches us to look for happiness within ourselves, must advance in some measure the dignity of our nature.

Perhaps there is no higher proof of the excellence of man than this: that to a mind properly cultivated, whatever is bounded is little. The mind is continually laboring to advance, step by step, through successive gradations of excellence, towards perfection, which is dimly seen at a great, though not hopeless, distance, and which we must always follow because we never can attain; but the pursuit rewards itself; one truth teaches another, and our store is always increasing, though nature can never be exhausted. Our art, like all arts which address the imagination, is applied to a somewhat lower faculty of the mind, which approaches nearer to sensuality; but through sense and fancy it must make its way to reason; for such is the progress of thought that we perceive by sense, we combine by fancy, and distinguish by reason; and without carrying our art out of its natural and true character, the more we purify it from everything that is gross in sense, in that proportion we advance its use and dignity; and in proportion as we lower it to mere sensuality, we pervert its nature, and degrade it from the rank of a liberal art; and this is what every artist ought well to remember. Let him remember also that he deserves just so much encouragement in the State as he makes himself a member of it virtuously useful, and contributes in his sphere to the general purpose and perfection of society.

The art which we profess has beauty for its object; this it is our business to discover and to express. The beauty of which we are in quest is general and intellectual; it is an idea that subsists only in the mind; the sight never beheld it, nor has the hand expressed it; it is an idea residing in the breast of the artist, which he is always laboring to impart, and which he dies at last without imparting; but which he is yet so far able to communicate as to raise the thoughts and extend the views of the spectator; and which, by a succession of art, may be so far diffused that its effects may extend themselves imperceptibly into public benefits, and be among the means of bestowing on whole nations refinement of taste; which, if it does not lead directly to purity of manners, obviates at least their greatest depravation, by disentangling the mind from appetite, and conducting the thoughts through successive stages of excellence, till that contemplation of universal rectitude and harmony which began by taste, may, as it is exalted and refined, conclude in virtue.

Saint Agnes.

DISCOURSE X.

Delivered to the Students of the Royal Academy, on the Distribution of the Prizes, December 11, 1780.

SCULPTURE: — HAS BUT ONE STYLE. — ITS OBJECTS, FORM, AND CHARACTER. — INEFFECTUAL ATTEMPTS OF THE MODERN SCULPTORS TO IMPROVE THE ART. — ILL EFFECTS OF MODERN DRESS IN SCULPTURE.

I SHALL now, as it has been customary on this day, and on this occasion, communicate to you such observations as have occurred to me on the theory of art.

If these observations have hitherto referred principally to painting, let it be remembered that this art is much more extensive and complicated than sculpture, and affords, therefore, a more ample field for criticism; and as the greater includes the less, the leading principles of sculpture are comprised in those of painting.

However, I wish now to make some remarks with particular relation to sculpture; to consider wherein or in what manner its principles and those of painting agree or differ; what is within its power of performing, and what it is vain or improper to attempt, that it may be clearly and distinctly known what ought to be the great purpose of the sculptor's labors.

Sculpture is an art of much more simplicity and uniformity than painting; it cannot with propriety, and the best effect, be applied to many subjects. The object of its pursuit may be comprised in two words, — Form and Character; and those qualities are presented to us but in one manner, or in one style only; whereas the powers of painting, as they are more various and extensive, so they are exhibited in as great a variety of manners. The Roman, Lombard, Florentine, Venetian, and Flemish schools all pursue the same end by different means. But sculpture having but one style, can only to one style of painting have any relation; and to this (which is indeed the highest and most dignified that painting can boast) it has a relation so close that it may be said to be almost the same art operating upon different materials. The sculptors of the last age, from not attending sufficiently to this discrimination of the different styles of painting, have been led into many errors. Though they well knew that they were allowed to imitate or take ideas for the improvement of their own art from the grand style of painting, they were not aware that it was not permitted to borrow in the same manner from the ornamental. When they endeavor to copy the picturesque effects, contrasts, or petty excellences of whatever kind, which not improperly find a place in the inferior branches of painting, they doubtless imagine themselves improving and extending the boundaries of their art by this imitation; but they are in reality violating its essential character by giving a different direction to its operations, and proposing to themselves either what is unattainable, or at best a meaner object of pursuit. The grave and austere character of sculpture requires the utmost degree of formality in composition; picturesque contrasts have here no place; everything is carefully weighed and measured, one side making almost an exact equipoise to the other; a child is not a proper balance to a full-grown figure, nor is a figure sitting or stooping a companion to an upright figure.

The excellence of every art must consist in the complete accomplishment of its purpose; and if by a false imitation of nature, or mean ambition of producing a picturesque effect or illusion of any kind, all the grandeur of ideas which this art endeavors to excite be degraded or destroyed, we may boldly oppose ourselves to any such innovation. If the producing of a deception is the summit of this art, let us at once give to statues the addition of color, which will contribute more towards accomplishing this end than all those artifices which have been introduced and professedly defended, on no other principle but that of rendering the work more natural. But as color is universally rejected, every practice liable to the same objection must fall with it. If the business of sculpture were to administer pleasure to ignorance, or a mere entertainment to the senses, the Venus de Medicis might certainly receive much improvement by color; but the character of sculpture makes it her duty to afford delight of a different, and, perhaps, of a higher kind, the delight resulting from the contemplation of perfect beauty; and this, which is in truth an intellectual pleasure, is in many respects incompatible with what is merely addressed to the senses, such as that with which ignorance and levity contemplate elegance of form.

The sculptor may be safely allowed to practise every means within the power of his art to produce a deception, provided this practice does not interfere with or destroy higher excellences; on these conditions he will be forced, however loath, to acknowledge that the boundaries of his art have long been fixed, and that all endeavors will be vain that hope to pass beyond the best works which remain of ancient sculpture.

Imitation is the means, and not the end of art. It is employed by the sculptor as the language by which his ideas are presented to the mind of the spectator. Poetry and elocution of every sort make use of signs, but those signs are arbitrary and conventional. The sculptor employs the representation of the thing itself; but still as a means to a higher end,— as a gradual ascent, always advancing towards faultless form and perfect beauty. It may be thought at the first view that even this form, however perfectly represented, is to be valued and take its rank only for the sake of a still higher object,— that of conveying sentiment and character, as they are exhibited by attitude and expression of the passions. But we are sure from experience that the beauty of form alone, without the assistance of any other quality, makes of itself a great work, and justly claims our esteem and admiration. As a proof of the high value we set on the mere excellence of form, we may adduce the greatest part of the works of Michael Angelo, both in painting and sculpture, as well as most of the antique statues, which are justly esteemed in a very high degree, though no very marked or striking character or expression of any kind is represented.

But, as a stronger instance that this excellence alone inspires sentiment, what artist ever looked at the "Torso" without feeling a warmth of enthusiasm, as from the highest efforts of poetry ? From whence does this proceed ? What is there in this fragment that produces this effect, but the perfection of this science of abstract form ?

A mind elevated to the contemplation of excellence perceives in this defaced and shattered fragment *disjecta membra poetæ*, the traces of superlative genius, the relics of a work on which succeeding ages can only gaze with inadequate admiration.

It may be said that this pleasure is reserved only to those who have spent their whole life in the study and contemplation of this art; but the truth is that all would feel its effects if they could divest themselves of the expectation of *deception*, and look only for what it really is — a *partial*, representation of nature. The only impediment of their judgment must then proceed from their being uncertain to what rank, or rather, kind of excellence, it aspires, and to what sort of approbation it has a right. This state of darkness is, without doubt, irksome to every mind; but by attention to works of this kind the knowledge of what is aimed at comes of itself, without being taught, and almost without being perceived.

The sculptor's art is limited in comparison with others, but it has its variety and intricacy within its proper bounds. Its essence is correctness; and when to correct and perfect form is added the ornament of grace, dignity of character, and appropriate expression, as in the "Apollo," the "Venus," the "Laocoön," the "Moses" of Michael Angelo, and many others, this art may be said to have accomplished its purpose.

What grace is, how it is to be acquired or conceived, are in speculation difficult questions; but *causa latet, res est notissima;* without any perplexing inquiry, the effect is hourly perceived. I shall only observe that its natural foundation is correctness of design; and though grace may be sometimes united with incorrectness, it cannot proceed from it.

But to come nearer to our present subject. It has been said that the grace of the "Apollo" depends on a certain degree of incorrectness; that the head is not anatomically placed between the shoulders; and that the lower half of the figure is longer than just proportion allows.

I know that Correggio and Parmegiano are often produced as authorities to support this opinion; but very little attention will convince us that the incorrectness of some parts which we find in their works does not contribute to grace, but rather tends to destroy it. The Madonna, with the sleeping infant and beautiful group of angels, by Parmegiano, in the Palazzo Pitti, would not have lost any of its excellence if the neck, fingers, and, indeed, the whole figure of the Virgin, instead of being so very long and incorrect, had preserved their due proportion.

In opposition to the first of these remarks, I have the authority of a very able sculptor of this Academy who has copied that figure, and consequently measured and carefully examined it, to declare that the criticism is not true. In regard to the last, it must be remembered that Apollo is here in the exertion of one of his peculiar powers, which is swiftness; he has therefore that proportion which is best adapted to that character. This is no more incorrectness than when there is given to a Hercules an extraordinary swelling and strength of muscles.

The art of discovering and expressing grace is difficult enough of itself, without perplexing ourselves with what is incomprehensible. A supposition of such a monster as Grace, begot by Deformity, is poison to the mind of a young artist, and may make him neglect what is essential to his art — correctness of design — in order to pursue a phantom, which has no existence but in the imagination of affected and refined speculators.

I cannot quit the "Apollo" without making one observation on the character of this figure. He is supposed to have just discharged his arrow at the python; and, by the head retreating a little towards the right shoulder, he appears attentive to its effect. What I would remark is the difference of this attention from that of the "Discobolus," who is engaged in the same purpose, watching the effect of his discus. The graceful, negligent, though animated air of the one, and the vulgar eagerness of the other, furnish a signal instance of the judgment of the ancient sculptors in their nice discrimination of character. They are both equally true to nature, and equally admirable.

It may be remarked that grace, character, and expression, though words of different sense and meaning, and so understood when applied to the works of painters, are indiscriminately used when we speak of sculpture. This indecision we may suspect to proceed from the undetermined effects of the art itself; those qualities are exhibited in sculpture rather by form and attitude than by the features, and can therefore be expressed but in a very general manner.

Though the Laocoön and his two sons have more expression in the countenance than perhaps any other antique statues, yet it is only the general expression of pain; and this passion is still more strongly expressed by the writhing and contortion of the body than by the features.[1]

It has been observed in a late publication, that if the attention of the father in this group had been occupied more by the distress of his children than by his own sufferings, it would have raised a much greater interest in the spectator. Though this observation comes from a person whose opinion in everything relating to the arts carries with it the highest authority, yet I cannot but suspect that such refined expression is scarce within the province of this art; and in attempting it the artist will run great

---

[1] This great work is finely characterized by Byron:—

>   Or, turning to the Vatican, go see
>   Laocoön's torture dignifying pain—
>   A father's love and mortal's agony
>   With an immortal's patience blending:—Vain
>   The struggle; vain, against the coiling strain
>   And gripe, and deepening of the dragon's grasp,
>   The old man's clench; the long envenom'd chain
>   Rivets the living links,—the enormous asp
>   Enforces pang on pang, and stifles gasp on gasp.
>   *Childe Harold.*

risk of enfeebling expression, and making it less intelligible to the spectator.

As the general figure presents itself in a more conspicuous manner than the features, it is there we must principally look for expression or character; *patuit in corpore vultus;* and in this respect, the sculptor's art is not unlike that of dancing, where the attention of the spectator is principally engaged by the attitude and action of the performer, and it is there he must look for whatever expression that art is capable of exhibiting. The dancers themselves acknowledge this, by often wearing masks with little diminution in the expression. The face bears so very inconsiderable a proportion to the effect of the whole figure that the ancient sculptors neglected to animate the features, even with the general expression of the passions. Of this the group of the "Boxers" is a remarkable instance; they are engaged in the most animated action with the greatest serenity of countenance. This is not recommended for imitation (for there can be no reason why the countenance should not correspond with the attitude and expression of the figure), but is mentioned in order to infer from hence that this frequent deficiency in ancient sculpture could proceed from nothing but a habit of inattention to what was considered as comparatively immaterial.

Those who think sculpture can express more than we have allowed may ask by what means we discover, at the first glance, the character that is represented in a bust, cameo, or intaglio. I suspect it will be found, on close examination, by him who is resolved not to see more than he really does see, that the figures are distinguished by their *insignia* more than by any variety of form or beauty. Take from Apollo his lyre, from Bacchus his thyrsus and vine-leaves, and from Meleager the boar's head, and there will remain little or no difference in their characters. In a Juno, Minerva, or Flora, the idea of the artist seems to have gone no further than representing perfect beauty, and afterwards adding the proper attributes, with a total indifference to which they gave them. Thus John de Bologna, after he had finished a group of a young man holding up a young woman in his arms, with an old man at his feet, called his friends together, to tell him what name he should give it, and it was agreed to call it " The Rape of the Sabines; " and this is the celebrated group which now stands before the Palazzo Vecchio at Florence.[1] The figures have the same general expression which is to be found in most of the antique sculpture; and yet it would be no wonder if future critics should find out delicacy of expression which was never intended, and go so far as to see, in the old man's countenance, the exact relation which he bore to the woman who appears to be taken from him.

Though painting and sculpture are, like many other arts, governed by the same general principles, yet in the detail, or what may be called the by-laws of each art, there seems to be no longer any connection between them. The different materials upon which those two arts exert their powers must infallibly create a proportional difference in their practice.

[1] In the Loggia dei Lanzi at Florence.

There are many petty excellences which the painter attains with ease, but which are impracticable in sculpture; and which, even if it could accomplish them, would add nothing to the true value and dignity of the work.

Of the ineffectual attempts which the modern sculptors have made by way of improvement, these seem to be the principal: the practice of detaching drapery from the figure, in order to give the appearance of flying in the air;

Of making different plans in the same bas-relievos;

Of attempting to represent the effects of perspective.

To these we may add the ill effect of figures clothed in a modern dress.

The folly of attempting to make stone sport and flutter in the air is so apparent that it carries with it its own reprehension; and yet to accomplish this seemed to be the great ambition of many modern sculptors, particularly Bernini;[1] his art was so much set on overcoming this difficulty that he was forever attempting it, though by that attempt he risked everything that was valuable in the art.

Bernini stands in the first class of modern sculptors, and therefore it is the business of criticism to prevent the ill effects of so powerful an example.

From his very early work of " Apollo and Daphne," the world justly expected he would rival the best pro-

[1] Many curious attempts at impossible aerial effects, and the overthrow of the boundaries of painting and sculpture may be seen in the famous Campo Santo of Genoa, where the fantastic spirit of Bernini seems to run riot.

ductions of ancient Greece; but he soon strayed from the right path. And though there is in his works something which always distinguishes him from the common herd, yet he appears in his latter performances to have lost his way. Instead of pursuing the study of that ideal beauty with which he had so successfully begun, he turned his mind to an injudicious quest of novelty, attempted what was not within the province of the art, and endeavored to overcome the hardness and obstinacy of his materials; which even supposing he had accomplished so far as to make this species of drapery appear natural, the ill effect and confusion occasioned by its being detached from the figure to which it belongs ought to have been alone a sufficient reason to have deterred him from that practice.

We have not, I think, in our Academy, any of Bernini's works, except a cast of the head of his Neptune; this will be sufficient to serve us for an example of the mischief produced by this attempt of representing the effects of the wind. The locks of the hair are flying abroad in all directions, insomuch that it is not a superficial view that can discover what the object is which is represented, or distinguish those flying locks from the features, as they are all of the same color, of equal solidity, and consequently project with equal force.

The same entangled confusion which is here occasioned by the hair is produced by drapery flying off; which the eye must, for the same reason, inevitably mingle and confound with the principal parts of the figure.

It is a general rule, equally true in both arts that the form and attitude of the figure should be seen clearly and without any ambiguity at the first glance of the eye. This the painter can easily do by color, by losing parts in the ground, or keeping them so obscure as to prevent them from interfering with the more principal objects. The sculptor has no other means of preventing this confusion than by attaching the drapery for the greater part close to the figure; the folds of which following the order of the limbs whenever the drapery is seen, the eye is led to trace the form and attitude of the figure at the same time.

The drapery of the Apollo, though it makes a large mass, and is separated from the figure, does not affect the present question, from the very circumstance of its being so completely separated; and from the regularity and simplicity of its form, it does not in the least interfere with a distinct view of the figure. In reality, it is no more a part of it than a pedestal, a trunk of a tree, or an animal, which we often see joined to statues.

The principal use of those appendages is to strengthen and preserve the statue from accidents; and many are of opinion that the mantle which falls from the Apollo's arm is for the same end; but surely it answers a much greater purpose, by preventing that dryness of effect which would inevitably attend a naked arm, extended almost at full length, to which we may add the disagreeable effect which would proceed from the body and arm making a right angle.

The Apostles, in the Church of Saint John Lateran,

appear to me to fall under the censure of an injudicious imitation of the manner of the painters. The drapery of those figures, from being disposed in large masses, gives undoubtedly that air of grandeur which magnitude or quantity is sure to produce. But though it should be acknowledged that it is managed with great skill and intelligence, and contrived to appear as light as the materials will allow, yet the weight and solidity of stone were not to be overcome.

Those figures are much in the style of Carlo Maratti, and such as we may imagine he would have made if he had attempted sculpture; and when we know he had the superintendence of that work, and was an intimate friend of one of the principal sculptors, we may suspect that his taste had some influence, if he did not even give the designs. No man can look at those figures without recognizing the manner of Carlo Maratti. They have the same defect which his works so often have, of being overlaid with drapery, and that too artificially disposed. I cannot but believe that if Ruscono, Le Gros, Monot, and the rest of the sculptors employed in that work, had taken for their guide the simple dress, such as we see in the antique statues of the philosophers, it would have given more real grandeur to their figures, and would certainly have been more suitable to the characters of the Apostles.

Though there is no remedy for the ill effect of those solid projections which flying drapery in stone must always produce in statues, yet in bas-relievos it is totally different; those detached parts of drapery the sculptor has here as much power over as the painter, by uniting and losing it in the ground, so that it shall not in the least entangle and confuse the figure.

But here again the sculptor, not content with this successful imitation, if it may be so called, proceeds to represent figures, or groups of figures, on different plans; that is, some on the foreground, and some at a greater distance, in the manner of painters in historical compositions. To do this he has no other means than by making the distant figures of less dimensions, and relieving them in a less degree from the surface; but this is not adequate to the end; they will still appear only as figures on a less scale, but equally near the eye with those in the front of the piece.

Nor does the mischief of this attempt, which never accomplishes its intention, rest here; by this division of the work into many minute parts, the grandeur of its general effect is inevitably destroyed.

Perhaps the only circumstance in which the modern have excelled the ancient sculptors is the management of a single group in basso-relievo, — the art of gradually raising the group from the flat surface, till it imperceptibly emerges into alto-relievo. Of this there is no ancient example remaining that discovers any approach to the skill which Le Gros has shown in an altar in the Jesuits' Church at Rome. Different plans or degrees of relief in the same group have, as we see in this instance, a good effect, though the contrary happens when the groups are separated. and are at some distance behind each other.

This improvement in the art of composing a group in basso-relievo was probably first suggested by the practice of the modern painters, who relieve their figures, or groups of figures, from their ground, by the same gentle gradation; and it is accomplished in every respect by the same general principles; but as the marble has no color, it is the composition itself that must give its light and shadow. The ancient sculptors could not borrow this advantage from their painters, for this was an art with which they appear to have been entirely unacquainted; and in the bas-relievos of Lorenzo Ghiberti, the casts of which we have in the Academy, this art is no more attempted than it was by the painters of his age.

The next imaginary improvement of the moderns is the representing the effects of perspective in bas-relief. Of this little need be said; all must recollect how ineffectual has been the attempt of modern sculptors to turn the buildings which they have introduced as seen from their angle, with a view to make them appear to recede from the eye in perspective. This, though it may show indeed their eager desire to encounter difficulties, shows at the same time how inadequate their materials are even to this their humble ambition.

The ancients, with great judgment, represented only the elevation of whatever architecture they introduced into their bas-reliefs, which is composed of little more than horizontal or perpendicular lines; whereas the interruption of crossed lines, or whatever causes a multiplicity of subordinate parts, destroys that regularity and firmness of effect on which grandeur of style so much depends.

We come now to the last consideration; in what

manner statues are to be dressed, which are made in honor of men, either now living or lately departed.

This is a question which might employ a long discourse of itself; I shall at present only observe, that he who wishes not to obstruct the artist, and prevent his exhibiting his abilities to their greatest advantage, will certainly not desire a modern dress.

The desire of transmitting to posterity the shape of modern dress must be acknowledged to be purchased at a prodigious price, even the price of everything that is valuable in art.

Working in stone is a very serious business; and it seems to be scarce worth while to employ such durable materials in conveying to posterity a fashion of which the longest existence scarce exceeds a year.

However agreeable it may be to the antiquary's principles of equity and gratitude, that as he has received great pleasure from the contemplation of the fashions of dress of former ages, he wishes to give the same satisfaction to future antiquaries, yet, methinks, pictures of an inferior style, or prints, may be considered as quite sufficient, without prostituting this great art to such mean purposes.

In this town may be seen an equestrian statue in a modern dress, which may be sufficient to deter future artists from any such attempt; even supposing no other objection, the familiarity of the modern dress by no means agrees with the dignity and gravity of sculpture.

Sculpture is formal, regular, and austere; disdains all familiar objects, as incompatible with its dignity;

and is an enemy to every species of affectation, or appearance of academical art. All contrast, therefore, of one figure to another, or of the limbs of a single figure, or even in the folds of the drapery, must be sparingly employed. In short, whatever partakes of fancy or caprice, or goes under the denomination of picturesque (however to be admired in its proper place), is incompatible with that sobriety and gravity which is peculiarly the characteristic of this art.

There is no circumstance which more distinguishes a well-regulated and sound taste than a settled uniformity of design, where all the parts are compact, and fitted to each other, everything being of a piece. This principle extends itself to all habits of life, as well as to all works of art. Upon this general ground, therefore, we may safely venture to pronounce that the uniformity and simplicity of the materials on which the sculptor labors (which are only white marble) prescribe bounds to his art, and teach him to confine himself to a proportionable simplicity of design.

Mrs. Ann Hope.

DISCOURSE XI.

Delivered to the Students of the Royal Academy, on the Distribution of the Prizes, December 10, 1782.

GENIUS, — CONSISTS PRINCIPALLY IN THE COMPREHENSION OF A WHOLE; IN TAKING GENERAL IDEAS ONLY.

THE highest ambition of every artist is to be thought a man of genius. As long as this flattering quality is joined to his name, he can bear with patience the imputation of carelessness, incorrectness, or defects of whatever kind.

So far, indeed, is the presence of genius from implying an absence of faults, that they are considered by many as its inseparable companions. Some go such lengths as to take indication from them, and not only excuse faults on account of genius, but presume genius from the existence of certain faults.

It is certainly true that a work may justly claim the character of genius though full of errors; and it is equally true that it may be faultless, and yet not exhibit the least spark of genius. This naturally suggests an inquiry, a desire at least of inquiring, what qualities of a work and of a workman may justly entitle a painter to that character.

I have in a former discourse[1] endeavored to impress you with a fixed opinion that a comprehensive

[1] Discourse III.

and critical knowledge of the works of nature is the only source of beauty and grandeur. But when we speak to painters, we must always consider this rule, and all rules, with a reference to the mechanical practice of their own particular art. It is not properly in the learning, the taste, and the dignity of the ideas, that genius appears as belonging to a painter. There is a genius particular and appropriated to his own trade (as I may call it), distinguished from all others. For that power which enables the artist to conceive his subject with dignity may be said to belong to general education, and is as much the genius of a poet, or the professor of any other liberal art, or even a good critic in any of those arts, as of a painter. Whatever sublime ideas may fill his mind, he is a painter only as he can put in practice what he knows, and communicate those ideas by visible representation.

If my expression can convey my idea, I wish to distinguish excellence of this kind by calling it the genius of mechanical performance. This genius consists, I conceive, in the power of expressing that which employs your pencil, whatever it may be, *as a whole*; so that the general effect and power of the whole may take possession of the mind, and for a while suspend the consideration of the subordinate and particular beauties or defects.

The advantage of this method of considering objects is what I wish now more particularly to enforce. At the same time I do not forget that a painter must have the power of contracting as well as dilating his sight; because he that does not at all express particulars expresses nothing; yet it is certain that a nice discrimination of minute circumstances, and a punctilious delineation of them, whatever excellence it may have (and I do not mean to detract from it), never did confer on the artist the character of genius.

Besides those minute differences in things which are frequently not observed at all, and when they are, make little impression, there are in all considerable objects great characteristic distinctions, which press strongly on the senses, and therefore fix the imagination. These are by no means, as some persons think, an aggregate of all the small discriminating particulars; nor will such an accumulation of particulars ever express them. These answer to what I have heard great lawyers call the leading points in a case, or the leading cases relative to those points.

The detail of particulars, which does not assist the expression of the main characteristic, is worse than useless, it is mischievous, as it dissipates the attention, and draws it from the principal point.[1] It may be remarked that the impression which is left on our mind, even of things which are familiar to us, is seldom more than their general effect; beyond which we do not look in recognizing such objects. To express this in painting is to express what is congenial and natural to the mind of man, and what gives him by reflection his own mode of conceiving. The

[1] Protogenes introduced a partridge into his famous painting of Ialysus, and had delineated it with so much skill that it seemed to be alive, and was the admiration of all Greece. Since, however, he found that it attracted all eyes, to the prejudice of the main figure in the piece, he completely effaced it. — RICHARDSON, *Treatise on Painting*.

other presupposes *nicety* and *research*, which are only the business of the curious and attentive, and therefore does not speak to the general sense of the whole species; in which common, and as I may so call it, mother tongue, everything grand and comprehensive must be uttered.

I do not mean to prescribe what degree of attention ought to be paid to the minute parts; this it is hard to settle. We are sure that it is expressing the general effect of the whole, which alone can give to objects their true and touching character; and wherever this is observed, whatever else may be neglected, we acknowledge the hand of a master. We may even go further, and observe that when the general effect only is presented to us by a skilful hand, it appears to express the object represented in a more lively manner than the minutest resemblance would do.

These observations may lead to very deep questions, which I do not mean here to discuss. Among others, it may lead to an inquiry why we are not always pleased with the most absolute possible resemblance of an imitation to its original object. Cases may exist in which such a resemblance may be even disagreeable. I shall only observe that the effect of figures in waxwork, though certainly a more exact representation than can be given by painting or sculpture, is a sufficient proof that the pleasure we receive from imitation is not increased merely in proportion as it approaches to minute and detailed reality; we are pleased, on the contrary, by seeing ends accomplished by seemingly inadequate means.

To express protuberance by actual relief, to express the softness of flesh by the softness of wax, seems rude and inartificial, and creates no grateful surprise. But to express distances on a plain surface, softness by hard bodies, and particular coloring by materials which are not singly of that color, produces that magic which is the prize and triumph of art.

Carry this principle a step further. Suppose the effect of imitation to be fully compassed by means still more inadequate; let the power of a few well-chosen strokes, which supersede labor by judgment and direction, produce a complete impression of all that the mind demands in an object; we are charmed with such an unexpected happiness of execution, and begin to be tired with the superfluous diligence which in vain solicits an appetite already satiated.

The properties of all objects, as far as a painter is concerned with them, are the outline or drawing, the color, and the light and shade. The drawing gives the form, the color its visible quality, and the light and shade its solidity.

Excellence in any one of these parts of art will never be acquired by an artist, unless he has the habit of looking upon objects at large, and observing the effect which they have on the eye when it is dilated and employed upon the whole, without seeing any one of the parts distinctly. It is by this that we obtain the ruling characteristic, and that we learn to imitate it by short and dexterous methods. I do not mean by dexterity a trick or mechanical habit, formed by guess and established by custom, but that science which, by a profound knowledge of ends and means, discovers the shortest and surest way to its own purpose.

If we examine with a critical view the manner of those painters whom we consider as patterns, we shall find that their great fame does not proceed from their works being more highly finished than those of other artists, or from a more minute attention to details, but from that enlarged comprehension which sees the whole object at once, and that energy of art which gives its characteristic effect by adequate expression.

Raphael and Titian are two names which stand the highest in our art, — one for drawing, the other for painting. The most considerable and the most esteemed works of Raphael are the cartoons, and his fresco works in the Vatican; those, as we all know, are far from being minutely finished. His principal care and attention seems to have been fixed upon the adjustment of the whole, whether it was the general composition, or the composition of each individual figure; for every figure may be said to be a lesser whole, though, in regard to the general work to which it belongs, it is but a part; the same may be said of the head, of the hands, and feet. Though he possessed this art of seeing and comprehending the whole, as far as form is concerned, he did not exert the same faculty in regard to the general effect, which is presented to the eye by color, and light and shade. Of this the deficiency of his oil pictures, where this excellence is more expected than in fresco, is a sufficient proof.

It is to Titian we must turn our eyes to find excellence with regard to color, and light and shade, in the highest degree. He was both the first and the greatest master of this art. By a few strokes he knew how to mark the general image and character of whatever object he attempted; and produced, by this alone, a truer representation than his master Giovanni Bellini or any of his predecessors, who finished every hair. His great care was to express the general color, to preserve the masses of light and shade, and to give by opposition the idea of that solidity which is inseparable from natural objects. When those are preserved, though the work should possess no other merit, it will have in a proper place its complete effect; but where any of these are wanting, however minutely labored the picture may be in the detail, the whole will have a false and even an unfinished appearance, at whatever distance, or in whatever light, it can be shown.

It is in vain to attend to the variation of tints if, in that attention, the general hue of flesh is lost; or to finish ever so minutely the parts if the masses are not observed, or the whole not well put together.

Vasari seems to have had no great disposition to favor the Venetian painters, yet he everywhere justly commends *il modo di fare, la maniera, la bella practica;* that is, the admirable manner and practice of that school. On Titian, in particular, he bestows the epithets of *giudicioso, bello, e stupendo.*

This manner was then new to the world, but that unshaken truth on which it is founded has fixed it as a model to all succeeding painters; and those who will examine into the artifice will find it to consist in the power of generalizing, and in the shortness and simplicity of the means employed.

Many artists, as Vasari likewise observes, have ignorantly imagined they are imitating the manner of Titian when they leave their colors rough, and neglect the detail; but, not possessing the principles on which he wrought, they have produced what he calls *goffe pitture*, absurd, foolish pictures; for such will always be the consequence of affecting dexterity without science, without selection, and without fixed principles.

Raphael and Titian seem to have looked at Nature for different purposes; they both had the power of extending their view to the whole; but one looked only for the general effect as produced by form, the other as produced by color.

We cannot entirely refuse to Titian the merit of attending to the general *form* of his object, as well as color; but his deficiency lay, a deficiency, at least, when he is compared with Raphael, in not possessing the power like him of correcting the form of his model by any general idea of beauty in his own mind. Of this his Saint Sebastian is a particular instance. This figure appears to be a most exact representation both of the form and the color of the model, which he then happened to have before him; it has all the force of nature, and the coloring is flesh itself; but unluckily, the model was of a bad form, especially the legs. Titian has with as much care preserved these defects as he has imitated the beauty and brilliancy of the coloring. In his coloring he was large and general, as in his design he was minute and partial; in the one he was a genius, in the other not much above a copyist. I do not, however, speak now of all his pictures; instances enough may be produced in his works where those observations on his defects could not with any propriety be applied; but it is in the manner or language, as it may be called, in which Titian and others of that school express themselves, that their chief excellence lies. This manner is in reality, in painting, what language is in poetry; we are all sensible how different the imagination is affected by the same sentiment expressed in different words, and how mean or how grand the same object appears when presented to us by different painters. Whether it is the human figure, an animal, or even inanimate objects, there is nothing, however unpromising in appearance, but may be raised into dignity, convey sentiment and produce emotion, in the hands of a painter of genius. What was said of Virgil, that he threw even filth about the ground with an air of dignity, may be applied to Titian; whatever he touched, however naturally mean and habitually familiar, by a kind of magic he invested with grandeur and importance.

I must here observe that I am not recommending a neglect of the detail; indeed, it would be difficult, if not impossible, to prescribe *certain* bounds, and tell how far, or when, it is to be observed or neglected; much must, at last, be left to the taste and judgment of the artist. I am well aware that a judicious detail will sometimes give the force of truth to the work, and consequently interest the spectator. I only wish to impress on your minds the true distinction between essential and subordinate powers; and to show what qualities in the art claim your chief attention, and what may, with the least injury to your reputation, be neglected. Something, perhaps, always must be neglected; the lesser ought then to give way to the greater; and since every work can have but a limited time allotted to it (for even supposing a whole life to be employed about one picture, it is still limited), it appears more reasonable to employ that time to the best advantage in contriving various methods of composing the work, — in trying different effects of light and shadow, and employing the labor of correction in heightening, by a judicious adjustment of the parts, the effects of the whole, — than that the time should be taken up in minutely finishing those parts.

But there is another kind of high finishing, which may safely be condemned, as it seems to counteract its own purpose; that is, when the artist, to avoid that hardness which proceeds from the outline cutting against the ground, softens and blends the colors to excess; this is what the ignorant call high finishing, but which tends to destroy the brilliancy of color, and the true effect of representation; which consists very much in preserving the same proportion of sharpness and bluntness that is found in natural objects. This extreme softening, instead of producing the effect of softness, gives the appearance of ivory, or some other hard substance, highly polished.

The portraits of Cornelius Jansen appear to have this defect, and consequently want that suppleness which is the characteristic of flesh; whereas, in the works of Van Dyck we find the true mixture of softness and hardness perfectly observed. The same defect may be found in the manner of Vanderwerf, in opposition to that of Teniers; and such, also, we may add, is the manner of Raphael in his oil pictures, in comparison with that of Titian.

The name which Raphael has so justly maintained as the first of painters, we may venture to say was not acquired by this laborious attention. His apology may be made by saying that it was the manner of his country; but if he had expressed his ideas with the facility and eloquence, as it may be called, of Titian, his works would certainly not have been less excellent; and that praise which ages and nations have poured out upon him for possessing genius in the higher attainments of art, would have been extended to them all.

Those who are not conversant in works of art are often surprised at the high value set by connoisseurs on drawings which appear careless, and in every respect unfinished; but they are truly valuable, and their value arises from this, that they give the idea of a whole; and this whole is often expressed by a dexterous facility which indicates the true power of a painter, even though roughly exerted, — whether it consists in the general composition, or the general form of each figure, or the turn of the attitude which bestows grace and elegance. All this we may see fully exemplified in the very skilful drawings of Parmegiano and Correggio. On whatever account we value these drawings, it is certainly not for high finishing, or a minute attention to particulars.

Excellence in every part and in every province of our art, from the highest style of history down to the resemblances of still life, will depend on this power of extending the attention at once to the whole, without which the greatest diligence is vain.

I wish you to bear in mind that when I speak of a whole, I do not mean simply a whole as belonging to composition, but a whole with respect to the general style of coloring; a whole with regard to the light and shade; a whole of everything which may separately become the main object of a painter.

I remember a landscape-painter in Rome who was known by the name of "Studio," from his patience in high finishing, in which he thought the whole excellence of art consisted; so that he once endeavored, as he said, to represent every individual leaf on a tree. This picture I never saw; but I am very sure that an artist who looked only at the general character of the species, the order of the branches and the masses of the foliage, would in a few minutes produce a more true resemblance of trees than this painter in as many months.

A landscape-painter certainly ought to study anatomically (if I may use the expression) all the objects which he paints; but when he is to turn his studies to use, his skill, as a man of genius, will be displayed in showing the general effect, preserving the same degree of hardness and softness which the objects have in nature; for he applies himself to the imagination, not to the curiosity, and works not for the virtuoso or the naturalist, but for the common observer of life and nature. When he knows his subject, he will know not only what to describe, but what to omit; and this skill in leaving out is, in all things, a great part of knowledge and wisdom.

The same excellence of manner which Titian displayed in history or portrait-painting is equally conspicuous in his landscapes, whether they are professedly such, or serve only as backgrounds.[1] One of the most eminent of this latter kind is to be found in the picture of Saint Pietro Martire. The large trees which are here introduced are plainly distinguished from each other by the different manner with which the branches shoot from their trunks, as well as by their different foliage; and the weeds in the foreground are varied in the same manner just as much as variety requires, and no more. When Algarotii, speaking of this picture, praises it for the minute discriminations of the leaves and plants, even, as he says, to excite the admiration of a botanist, his intention was undoubtedly to give praise even at the expense of truth; for he must have known that this is not the character of the picture. But connoisseurs will always find in pictures what they think they ought to find; he was not aware that he was giving a description injurious to the reputation of Titian.

Such accounts may be very hurtful to young artists

---

[1] I have said in the chapter on symmetry in the second volume, that all landscape grandeur vanishes before that of Titian and Tintoret; and this is true of whatever these two giants touched, — but they touched little. — RUSKIN, *Modern Painters.*

who never have had an opportunity of seeing the work described; and they may possibly conclude that this great artist acquired the name of the Divine Titian from his eminent attention to such trifling circumstances, which in reality would not raise him above the level of the most ordinary painter.

We may extend these observations even to what seems to have but a single, and that an individual object. The excellence of portrait-painting, and, we may add, even the likeness, the character, and countenance, as I have observed in another place, depend more upon the general effect produced by the painter than on the exact expression of the peculiarities, or minute discrimination of the parts. The chief attention of the artist is therefore employed in planting the features in their proper places, which so much contributes to giving the effect and true impression of the whole. The very peculiarities may be reduced to classes and general descriptions; and there are therefore large ideas to be found even in this contracted subject. He may afterwards labor single features to what degree he thinks proper; but let him not forget continually to examine whether in finishing the parts he is not destroying the general effect.

It is certainly a thing to be wished, that all excellence were applied to illustrate subjects that are interesting and worthy of being commemorated; whereas, of half the pictures that are in the world, the subject can be valued only as an occasion which set the artist to work; and yet, our high estimation of such pictures, without considering, or perhaps without knowing the subject, shows how much our attention is engaged by the art alone.[1]

Perhaps nothing that we can say will so clearly show the advantage and excellence of this faculty as that it confers the character of genius on works that pretend to no other merit; in which is neither expression, character, nor dignity, and where none are interested in the subject. We cannot refuse the character of genius to the " Marriage " of Paolo Veronese without opposing the general sense of mankind (great authorities have called it the triumph of painting), or to the "Altar of Saint Augustine " at Antwerp, by Rubens, which equally deserves that title, and for the same reason. Neither of those pictures have any interesting story to support them. That of Paolo Veronese is only a representation of a great concourse of people at a dinner; and the subject of Rubens, if it may be called a subject where nothing is doing, is an assembly of various Saints that lived in different ages. The whole excellence of those pictures consists in mechanical dexterity, working, however, under the influence of that comprehensive faculty which I have so often mentioned.

It is by this, and this alone, that the mechanical power is ennobled, and raised much above its natural rank. And it appears to me that with propriety it acquires this character, as an instance of that superiority with which mind predominates over

---

[1] When the subject represented in poetry or painting is such as we could have no desire of seeing in the reality, then we may be sure that its power in poetry or painting is owing to the power of imitation. — BURKE, *Essay on the Sublime and Beautiful.*

matter, by contracting into one whole what nature has made multifarious.

The great advantage of this idea of a whole is that a greater quantity of truth may be said to be contained and expressed in a few lines or touches than in the most laborious finishing of the parts where this is not regarded. It is upon this foundation that it stands; and the justness of the observation would be confirmed by the ignorant in art, if it were possible to take their opinions unseduced by some false notion of what they imagine they ought to see in a picture. As it is an art, they think they ought to be pleased in proportion as they see that art ostentatiously displayed; they will, from this supposition, prefer neatness, high-finishing, and gaudy coloring, to the truth, simplicity, and unity of nature. Perhaps, too, the totally ignorant beholder, like the ignorant artist, cannot comprehend a whole, nor even what it means. But if false notions do not anticipate their perceptions, they who are capable of observation, and who, pertending to no skill, look only straight forward, will praise and condemn in proportion as the painter has succeeded in the effect of the whole. Here, general satisfaction, or general dislike, though perhaps despised by the painter, as proceeding from the ignorance of the principles of art, may yet help to regulate his conduct, and bring back his attention to that which ought to be his principal object, and from which he has deviated for the sake of minuter beauties.

An instance of this right judgment I once saw in a child, in going through a gallery where there were many portraits of the last ages, which, though neatly put out of hand, were very ill put together. The child paid no attention to the neat finishing or naturalness of any bit of drapery, but appeared to observe only the ungracefulness of the persons represented, and put herself in the posture of every figure which she saw in a forced and awkward attitude. The censure of nature, uninformed, fastened upon the greatest fault that could be in a picture, because it related to the character and management of the whole.

I should be sorry if what has been said should be understood to have any tendency to encourage that carelessness which leaves work in an unfinished state. I commend nothing for the want of exactness; I mean to point out that kind of exactness which is the best, and which is alone truly to be esteemed.

So far is my disquisition from giving countenance to idleness, that there is nothing in our art which enforces such continual exertion and circumspection, as an attention to the general effect of the whole. It requires much study and much practice; it requires the painter's entire mind; whereas the parts may be finishing by nice touches, while his mind is engaged on other matters; he may even hear a play or a novel read without much disturbance. The artist who flatters his own indolence will continually find himself evading this active exertion, and applying his thoughts to the ease and laziness of highly finishing the parts, producing at last what Cowley calls " laborious effects of idleness."

No work can be too much finished, provided the

diligence employed be directed to its proper object; but I have observed that an excessive labor in the detail has, nine times in ten, been pernicious to the general effect, even when it has been the labor of great masters. It indicates a bad choice, which is an ill setting out in any undertaking.

To give a right direction to your industry has been my principal purpose in this discourse. It is this which I am confident often makes the difference between two students of equal capacities and of equal industry. While the one is employing his labor on minute objects of little consequence, the other is acquiring the art and perfecting the habit of seeing nature in an extensive view, in its proper proportions, and its due subordination of parts.

Before I conclude, I must make one observation sufficiently connected with the present subject.

The same extension of mind which gives the excellence of genius to the theory and mechanical practice of the art, will direct him likewise in the method of study, and give him the superiority over those who narrowly follow a more confined track of partial imitation. Whoever, in order to finish his education, should travel to Italy, and spend his whole time there only in copying pictures, and measuring statues or buildings (though these things are not to be neglected), would return with little improvement. He that imitates the Iliad, says Dr. Young, is not imitating Homer. It is not by laying up in the memory the particular details of any of the great works of art that any man becomes a great artist, if he stops without making himself master of the general principles on which these works are conducted. If he even hopes to rival those whom he admires, he must consider their works as the means of teaching him the true art of seeing nature. When this is acquired, he then may be said to have appropriated their powers, or, at least, the foundation of their powers, to himself; the rest must depend upon his own industry and application. The great business of study is to form a mind adapted and adequate to all times and all occasions; to which all nature is then laid open, and which may be said to possess the key of her inexhaustible riches.

Master Jacob Bouverie.
(Afterwards Earl of Radnor, 1776).

DISCOURSE XII.

Delivered to the Students of the Royal Academy, on the Distribution of the Prizes, December 10, 1784.

PARTICULAR METHODS OF STUDY OF LITTLE CONSEQUENCE.—LITTLE OF THE ART CAN BE TAUGHT.—LOVE OF METHOD OFTEN A LOVE OF IDLENESS.—PITTORI IMPROVVISATORI APT TO BE CARELESS AND INCORRECT; SELDOM ORIGINAL AND STRIKING.—THIS PROCEEDS FROM THEIR NOT STUDYING THE WORKS OF OTHER MASTERS.

IN consequence of the situation in which I have the honor to be placed in this Academy, it has often happened that I have been consulted by the young students who intend to spend some years in Italy, concerning the method of regulating their studies. I am, as I ought to be, solicitously desirous to communicate the entire result of my experience and observation; and though my openness and facility in giving my opinions might make some amends for whatever was defective in them, yet I fear my answers have not often given satisfaction. Indeed, I have never been sure that I understood perfectly what they meant, and was not without some suspicion that they had not themselves very distinct ideas of the object of their inquiry.

If the information required was by what means the path that leads to excellence could be discovered; if they wished to know whom they were to take for their guides, — what to adhere to, and what to avoid; where they were to bait, and where they were to take up their rest; what was to be tasted only, and what should be their diet,—such general directions are certainly proper for a student to ask, and for me, to the best of my capacity, to give; but these rules have been already given; they have, in reality, been the subject of almost all my discourses from this place. But I am rather inclined to think, that by *method of study* it was meant (as several do mean) that the times and the seasons should be prescribed, and the order settled, in which everything was to be done; that it might be useful to point out to what degree of excellence one part of the art was to be carried before the student proceeded to the next; how long he was to continue to draw from the ancient statues, when to begin to compose, and when to apply to the study of coloring.

Such a detail of instruction might be extended with a great deal of plausible and ostentatious amplification. But it would at best be useless. Our studies will be forever, in a very great degree, under the direction of chance; like travellers, we must take what we can get, and when we can get it,—whether it is or is not administered to us in the most commodious manner, in the most proper place, or at the exact minute when we would wish to have it.

Treatises on education and method of study have always appeared to me to have one general fault. They proceed upon a false supposition of life; as if we possessed not only a power over events and circumstances, but had a greater power over ourselves than I believe any of us will be found to possess. Instead of supposing ourselves to be perfect patterns of wisdom and virtue, it seems to me more reasonable to treat ourselves (as I am sure we must now and then treat others) like humorsome children, whose fancies are often to be indulged, in order to keep them in good humor with themselves and their pursuits. It is necessary to use some artifice of this kind in all processes which by their very nature are long, tedious, and complex, in order to prevent our taking that aversion to our studies which the continual shackles of methodical restraint are sure to produce.

I would rather wish a student, as soon as he goes abroad, to employ himself upon whatever he has been incited to by any immediate impulse, than to go sluggishly about a prescribed task; whatever he does in such a state of mind, little advantage accrues from it, as nothing sinks deep enough to leave any lasting impression; and it is impossible that anything should be well understood or well done that is taken into a reluctant understanding, and executed with a servile hand.

It is desirable, and indeed is necessary to intellectual health that the mind should be recreated and refreshed with a variety in our studies; that in the irksomeness of uniform pursuit we should be relieved, and, if I may so say, deceived, as much as possible. Besides, the minds of men are so very differently constituted that it is impossible to find one method which shall be suitable to all. It is of no use to prescribe to those who have no talents; and those who have talents will find methods for themselves, —

methods dictated to them by their own particular dispositions, and by the experience of their own particular necessities.

However, I would not be understood to extend this doctrine to the younger students. The first part of the life of a student, like that of other schoolboys, must necessarily be a life of restraint. The grammar, the rudiments, however unpalatable, must at all events be mastered. After a habit is acquired of drawing correctly from the model (whatever it may be) which he has before him, the rest, I think, may be safely left to chance; always supposing that the student is employed, and that his studies are directed to the proper object.

A passion for his art, and an eager desire to excel, will more than supply the place of method. By leaving a student to himself he may possibly indeed be led to undertake matters above his strength; but the trial will at least have this advantage, — it will discover to himself his own deficiencies; and this discovery alone is a very considerable acquisition. One inconvenience, I acknowledge, may attend bold and arduous attempts; frequent failure may discourage; this evil, however, is not more pernicious than the slow proficiency which is the natural consequence of too easy tasks.

Whatever advantages method may have in despatch of business (and there it certainly has many), I have but little confidence of its efficacy in acquiring excellence in any art whatever. Indeed, I have always strongly suspected that this love of method on which some persons appear to place so great dependence, is in reality, at the bottom a love of idleness, a want of sufficient energy to put themselves into immediate action; it is a sort of an apology to themselves for doing nothing. I have known artists who may truly be said to have spent their whole lives, or at least the most precious part of their lives, in planning methods of study, without ever beginning; resolving, however, to put it all in practice at some time or other, — when a certain period arrives, when proper conveniences are procured, or when they remove to a certain place better calculated for study. It is not uncommon for such persons to go abroad with the most honest and sincere resolution of studying hard when they shall arrive at the end of their journey. The same want of exertion, arising from the same cause which made them at home put off the day of labor until they had found a proper scheme for it, still continues in Italy, and they consequently return home with little, if any improvement.

In the practice of art, as well as in morals, it is necessary to keep a watchful and jealous eye over ourselves; idleness, assuming the specious disguise of industry, will lull to sleep all suspicion of our want of an active exertion of strength. A provision of endless apparatus, a bustle of infinite inquiry and research, or even the mere mechanical labor of copying, may be employed, to evade and shuffle off real labor, — the real labor of thinking.

I have declined for these reasons to point out any particular method and course of study to young artists on their arrival in Italy. I have left it to their own prudence, a prudence which will grow and improve upon them in the course of unremitted, ardent industry, directed by a real love of their profession, and an unfeigned admiration of those who have been universally admitted as patterns of excellence in the art.

In the exercise of that general prudence, I shall here submit to their consideration such miscellaneous observations as have occurred to me on considering the mistaken notions or evil habits which have prevented that progress towards excellence which the natural abilities of several artists might otherwise have enabled them to make.

False opinions and vicious habits have done far more mischief to students, and to professors too, than any wrong methods of study.

Under the influence of sloth, or of some mistaken notion, is that disposition which always wants to lean on other men. Some students are always talking of the prodigious progress they should make if they could but have the advantage of being taught by some particular eminent master. To him they would wish to transfer that care which they ought and must take of themselves. Such are to be told that after the rudiments are past, very little of our art can be taught by others. The most skilful master can do little more than put the end of the clue into the hands of his scholar, by which he must conduct himself.

It is true, the beauties and defects of the works of our predecessors may be pointed out; the principles on which their works are conducted may be explained; the great examples of ancient art may be spread out before them; but the most sumptuous entertainment is prepared in vain, if the guests will not take the trouble of helping themselves.

Even the Academy itself, where every convenience for study is procured and laid before them, may, from that very circumstance, from leaving no difficulties to be encountered in the pursuit, cause a remission of their industry. It is not uncommon to see young artists, while they are struggling with every obstacle in their way, exert themselves with such success as to outstrip competitors possessed of every means of improvement. The promising expectation which was formed on so much being done with so little means, has recommended them to a patron who has supplied them with every convenience of study; from that time their industry and eagerness of pursuit has forsaken them; they stand still, and see others rush on before them.

Such men are like certain animals, who will feed only when there is but little provender, and that got at with difficulty through the bars of a rack, but refuse to touch it when there is an abundance before them.

Perhaps such a falling off may proceed from the faculties being overpowered by the immensity of the materials, — as the traveller despairs ever to arrive at the end of his journey when the whole extent of the road which he is to pass is at once displayed to his view.

Among the first moral qualities, therefore, which a student ought to cultivate, is a just and manly confidence in himself, or rather in the effects of that persevering industry which he is resolved to possess.

When Raphael, by means of his connection with Bramante, the Pope's architect, was fixed upon to adorn the Vatican with his works, he had done nothing that marked in him any great superiority over his contemporaries; though he was then but young, he had under his direction the most considerable artists of his age; and we know what kind of men those were. A lesser mind would have sunk under such a weight, and if we should judge from the meek and gentle disposition which we are told was the character of Raphael, we might expect this would have happened to him; but his strength appeared to increase in proportion as exertion was required, and it is not improbable that we are indebted to the good fortune which first placed him in that conspicuous situation for those great examples of excellence which he has left us.

The observations to which I formerly wished, and now desire, to point your attention, relate not to errors which are committed by those who have no claim to merit, but to those inadvertencies into which men of parts only can fall by the overrating or the abuse of some real, though perhaps subordinate, excellence. The errors last alluded to are those of backward, timid characters; what I shall now speak of belong to another class, — to those artists who are distinguished for the readiness and facility of their invention. It is undoubtedly a splendid and desirable accomplishment to be able to design instantaneously any given subject. It is an excellence that I believe every artist would wish to possess; but unluckily, the manner in which this dexterity is acquired habituates the mind to be contented with first thoughts without choice or selection. The judgment, after it has been long passive, by degrees loses its power of becoming active when exertion is necessary.

Whoever, therefore, has this talent, must in some measure undo what he has had the habit of doing, or at least give a new turn to his mind; great works, which are to live and stand the criticism of posterity, are not performed at a heat. A proportionable time is required for deliberation and circumspection. I remember when I was at Rome looking at the "Fighting Gladiator," in company with an eminent sculptor, and I expressed my admiration of the skill with which the whole is composed, and the minute attention of the artist to the change of every muscle in that momentary exertion of strength; he was of opinion that a work so perfect required nearly the whole life of man to perform.

I believe, if we look around us, we shall find that in the sister art of poetry what has been soon done has been as soon forgotten. The judgment and practice of a great poet on this occasion is worthy attention. Metastasio, who has so much and justly distinguished himself throughout Europe, at his outset was an *improvvisatore*, or extempore poet, a description of men not uncommon in Italy. It is not long since he was asked by a friend if he did not think the custom of inventing and reciting *extempore*, which he practised when a boy in his character of an *improvvisatore*, might not be considered as a happy beginning of his education; he thought it, on the contrary, a disadvantage to him; he said that he had acquired by that habit a carelessness and incorrectness, which it cost him much trouble to overcome, and to substitute in the place of it a totally different habit, — that of thinking with selection, and of expressing himself with correctness and precision.

However extraordinary it may appear, it is certainly true, that the inventions of the *pittori improvvisatori*, as they may be called, have — notwithstanding the common boast of their authors, that all is spun from their own brain — very rarely anything that has in the least the air of originality; their compositions are generally commonplace, uninteresting, without character or expression; like those flowery speeches that we sometimes hear which impress no new ideas on the mind.

I would not be thought, however, by what has been said, to oppose the use, the advantage, the necessity there is, of a painter's being readily able to express his ideas by sketching. The further he can carry such designs the better. The evil to be apprehended is, his resting there, and not correcting them afterwards from nature, or taking the trouble to look about him for whatever assistance the works of others will afford him.

We are not to suppose that when a painter sits down to deliberate on any work, he has all his knowledge to seek; he must not only be able to draw *extempore* the human figure in every variety of action, but he must be acquainted likewise with the general principles of composition, and possess a habit of foreseeing, while he is composing, the effect of the masses of light and shadow that will attend such a disposition. His mind is entirely occupied by his attention to the whole. It is a subsequent consideration to determine the attitude and expression of individual figures. It is in this period of his work that I would recommend to every artist to look over his portfolio, or pocket-book, in which he has treasured up all the happy inventions, all the extraordinary and expressive attitudes that he has met with in the course of his studies; not only for the sake of borrowing from those studies whatever may be applicable to his own work, but likewise on account of the great advantage he will receive by bringing the ideas of great artists more distinctly before his mind, which will teach him to invent other figures in a similar style.

Sir Francis Bacon speaks with approbation of the provisionary methods Demosthenes and Cicero employed to assist their invention; and illustrates their use by a quaint comparison after his manner. These particular *Studios* being not immediately connected with our art, I need not cite the passage I allude to, and shall only observe that such preparation totally opposes the general received opinions that are floating in the world concerning genius and inspiration. The same great man in another place, speaking of his own essays, remarks that they treat of "those things, wherein both men's lives and persons are most conversant, whereof a man shall find much in experience, but little in books;" they are then what an artist would naturally call invention; and yet we may suspect that even the genius of Bacon, great as it was, would never have been enabled to have made those observations, if his mind had not been trained and disciplined by reading the observations of others. Nor could he without such reading have known that those opinions were not to be found in other books.

I know there are many artists of great fame who appear never to have looked out of themselves, and who probably would think it derogatory to their character to be supposed to borrow from any other painter. But when we recollect, and compare the works of such men with those who took to their assistance the inventions of others, we shall be convinced of the great advantage of this latter practice.

The two men most eminent for readiness of invention, that occur to me, are Luca Giordano and La Fage, — one in painting, and the other in drawing.

To such extraordinary powers as were possessed by both of those artists we cannot refuse the character of genius; at the same time it must be acknowledged that it was that kind of mechanic genius which operates without much assistance of the head. In all their works, which are (as might be expected) very numerous, we may look in vain for anything that can be said to be original and striking; and yet, according to the ordinary ideas of originality, they have as good pretensions as most painters; for they borrowed very little from others, and still less will any artist that can distinguish between excellence and insipidity ever borrow from them.

To those men, and all such, let us oppose the practice of the first of painters. I suppose we shall all agree that no man ever possessed a greater power of invention, and stood less in need of foreign assistance, than

Raphael; and yet, when he was designing one of his greatest as well as latest works, the cartoons, it is very apparent that he had the studies which he had made from Masaccio[1] before him. Two noble figures of Saint Paul, which he found there he adopted in his own work: one of them he took for Saint Paul preaching at Athens; and the other for the same Saint when chastising the sorcerer Elymas. Another figure in the same work, whose head is sunk in his breast, with his eyes shut, appearing deeply wrapt up in thought, was introduced among the listeners to the preaching of Saint Paul. The most material alteration that is made in those two figures of Saint Paul is the addition of the left hands, which are not seen in the original. It is a rule that Raphael observed (and, indeed, ought never to be dispensed with), in a principal figure, to show both hands, — that it should never be a question what is become of the other hand. For the "Sacrifice at Lystra," he took the whole ceremony much as it stands in an ancient basso-relievo, since published in the "Admiranda."

I have given examples from those pictures only of Raphael which we have among us, though many other instances might be produced of this great paint-

---

[1] An original genius. His frescos in the Brancacci chapel were, in a degree, the school of Raphael, M. Angelo, and their contemporaries.

"In this chapel wrought
One of the Few, Nature's interpreters;
The Few, whom Genius gives as lights to shine —
MASACCIO; and he slumbers underneath.
Wouldst thou behold his monument? Look round,
And know that where we stand stood oft and long,
Oft till the day was gone. Raphael himself,
He and his haughty rival — " ROGERS.

er's not disdaining assistance; indeed, his known wealth was so great that he might borrow where he pleased without loss of credit.

It may be remarked that this work of Masaccio, from which he has borrowed so freely, was a public work, and at no farther distance from Rome than Florence; so that if he had considered it a disgraceful theft, he was sure to be detected; but he was well satisfied that his character for invention would be little affected by such a discovery; nor is it, except in the opinion of those who are ignorant of the manner in which great works are built.

Those who steal from mere poverty; who, having nothing of their own, cannot exist a minute without making such depredations; who are so poor that they have no place in which they can even deposit what they have taken, — to men of this description nothing can be said; but such artists as those to whom I suppose myself now speaking, men whom I consider as completely provided with all the necessaries and conveniences of art, and who do not desire to steal baubles and common trash, but wish only to possess peculiar rarities which they select to ornament their cabinets, and take care to enrich the general store with materials of equal or of greater value than what they have taken, — such men surely need not be ashamed of that friendly intercourse which ought to exist among artists, of receiving from the dead and giving to the living, and perhaps to those who are yet unborn.[1]

---

[1] The greatest is he who has been oftenest aided; and if the attainments of all human minds could be traced to their real sources,

The daily food and nourishment of the mind of an artist is found in the great works of his predecessors. There is no other way for him to become great himself. "Serpens, nisi serpentem comederit non fit draco,"[1] is a remark of a whimsical natural history which I have read, though I do not recollect its title; however false as to dragons, it is applicable enough to artists.

Raphael, as appears from what has been said, had carefully studied the works of Masaccio; and indeed, there was no other, if we except Michael Angelo (whom he likewise imitated), so worthy of his attention; and though his manner was dry and hard, his compositions formal, and not enough diversified according to the custom of painters in that early period, yet his works possess that grandeur and simplicity which accompany, and even sometimes proceed from, regularity and hardness of manner. We must consider the barbarous state of the arts before his time, when skill in drawing was so little understood that the best of the painters could not even foreshorten the foot, but every figure appeared to stand upon his toes; and what served for drapery had, from the hardness and smallness of the folds, too much the appearance of cords clinging round the body. He first

---

it would be found that the world had been laid most under contribution by men of most original power, and that every day of their existence deepened their debt to their race, while it enlarged their gifts to it. — RUSKIN.

[1] In Ben Jonson's "Catiline" we find this aphorism, with a slight variation: —

"A serpent, ere he comes to be a dragon,
Must eat a bat."

introduced large drapery flowing in an easy and natural manner; indeed, he appears to be the first who discovered the path that leads to every excellence to which the arts afterwards arrived, and may, therefore, be justly considered as one of the great Fathers of modern Art.

Though I have been led on to a longer digression respecting this great painter than I intended, yet I cannot avoid mentioning another excellence which he possessed in a very eminent degree; he was as much distinguished among his contemporaries for his diligence and industry as he was for the natural faculties of his mind. We are told that his whole attention was absorbed in the pursuit of his art, and that he acquired the name of Masaccio,[1] from his total disregard to his dress, his person, and all the common concerns of life. He is, indeed, a single instance of what well-directed diligence will do in a short time. He lived but twenty-seven years; yet in that short space carried the art so far beyond what it had before reached, that he appears to stand alone as a model for his successors. Vasari gives a long catalogue of painters and sculptors, who formed their taste, and learned their art, by studying his works; among those he names Michael Angelo, Leonardo da Vinci, Pietro Perugino, Raphael, Bartolomeo, Andrea del Sarto, Il Rosso, and Pierino del Vaga.

The habit of contemplating and brooding over the

---

[1] " The addition of *accio* denotes contempt, or some deformity or imperfection attending the person to whom it is applied." His name was properly Tommaso Guido. *Masaccio* is equivalent to "ugly" or "slovenly Tom."

ideas of great geniuses till you find yourself warmed by the contact is the true method of forming an artist-like mind; it is impossible, in the presence of those great men to think or invent in a mean manner; a state of mind is acquired that receives those ideas only which relish of grandeur and simplicity.

Besides the general advantage of forming the taste by such an intercourse, there is another of a particular kind, which was suggested to me by the practice of Raphael, when imitating the work of which I have been speaking. The figure of the Proconsul, Sergius Paulus, is taken from the Felix of Masaccio, though one is a front figure, and the other seen in profile; the action is likewise somewhat changed; but it is plain Raphael had that figure in his mind. There is a circumstance indeed, which I mention by the by, which marks it very particularly: Sergius Paulus wears a crown of laurel; this is hardly reconcilable to strict propriety or to the costume, of which Raphael was in general a good observer; but he found it so in Masaccio, and he did not bestow so much pains in disguise as to change it. It appears to me to be an excellent practice thus to suppose the figures which you wish to adopt in the works of those great painters to be statues; and to give, as Raphael has here given, another view, taking care to preserve all the spirit and grace you find in the original.

I should hope, from what has been lately said, that it is not necessary to guard myself against any supposition of recommending an entire dependence upon former masters. I do not desire that you should get other people to do your business, or to think for you;

I only wish you to consult with, to call in as counsellors, men the most distinguished for their knowledge and experience; the result of which counsel must ultimately depend upon yourself. Such conduct in the commerce of life has never been considered as disgraceful, or in any respect to imply intellectual imbecility; it is a sign, rather, of that true wisdom which feels individual imperfection, and is conscious to itself how much collective observation is necessary to fill the immense extent, and to comprehend the infinite variety of nature. I recommend neither self-dependence nor plagiarism. I advise you only to take that assistance which every human being wants, and which, as appears from the examples that have been given, the greatest painters have not disdained to accept. Let me add that the diligence required in the search, and the exertion subsequent in accommodating those ideas to your own purpose, is a business which idleness will not, and ignorance cannot, perform. But in order more distinctly to explain what kind of borrowing I mean when I recommend so anxiously the study of the works of great masters, let us, for a minute, return again to Raphael, consider his method of practice, and endeavor to imitate him in his manner of imitating others.

The two figures of Saint Paul which I lately mentioned are so nobly conceived by Masaccio that perhaps it was not in the power even of Raphael himself to raise and improve them, nor has he attempted it; but he has had the address to change in some measure, without diminishing the grandeur of their character; he has substituted, in the place of a serene, composed dignity, that animated expression which was necessary to the more active employment he assigned them.

In the same manner he has given more animation to the figure of Sergius Paulus, and to that which is introduced in the picture of Saint Paul preaching, of which little more than hints are given by Masaccio, which Raphael has finished. The closing the eyes of this figure, which in Masaccio might be easily mistaken for sleeping, is not in the least ambiguous in the cartoon; his eyes, indeed, are closed, but they are closed with such vehemence that the agitation of a mind perplexed in the extreme is seen at the first glance; but what is most extraordinary, and I think particularly to be admired, is that the same idea is continued through the whole figure, even to the drapery, which is so closely muffled about him that even his hands are not seen; by this happy correspondence between the expression of the countenance, and the disposition of the parts, the figure appears to think from head to foot. Men of superior talents alone are capable of thus using and adapting other men's minds to their own purposes, or are able to make out and finish what was only in the original a hint or imperfect conception. A readiness in taking such hints, which escape the dull and ignorant, makes, in my opinion, no inconsiderable part of that faculty of the mind which is called genius.

It often happens that hints may be taken and employed in a situation totally different from that in which they were originally employed. There is a figure of a Bacchante leaning backward, her head thrown quite behind her, which seems to be a favorite invention, as it is so frequently repeated in basso-relievos, cameos, and intaglios; it is intended to express an enthusiastic, frantic kind of joy. This figure Baccio Bandinelli, in a drawing that I have of that master of the "Descent from the Cross," has adapted (and he knew very well what was worth borrowing) for one of the Marys, to express frantic agony of grief. It is curious to observe, and it is certainly true, that the extremes of contrary passions are, with very little variation, expressed by the same action.

If I were to recommend method in any part of the study of a painter, it would be in regard to invention; that young students should not presume to think themselves qualified to invent till they were acquainted with those stores of invention the world already possesses, and had by that means accumulated sufficient materials for the mind to work with. It would certainly be no improper method of forming the mind of a young artist, to begin with such exercises as the Italians call a *Pasticcio*[1] composition of the different excellences which are dispersed in all other works of the same kind. It is not supposed that he is to stop here, but that he is to acquire by this means the art of selecting, first, what is truly excellent in art, and then what is still more excellent in nature, — a task which without this previous study, he will be but ill qualified to perform.

[1] Pasticcio (Fr. Pastiche). The imitation of a work of art, in which the reproduction either of the work of a particular master is aimed at or of the details and characteristics of a school. Many modern pictures may best be described as pleasant *pastiches* of the ancient masters. — ADELINE, *Art Dictionary.*

The doctrine which is here advanced is acknowledged to be new, and to many may appear strange. But I only demand for it the reception of a stranger; a favorable and attentive consideration, without that entire confidence which might be claimed under authoritative recommendation.

After you have taken a figure, or any idea of a figure, from any of those great painters, there is another operation still remaining, which I hold to be indispensably necessary, — that is, never to neglect finishing from nature every part of the work. What is taken from a model, though the first idea may have been suggested by another, you have a just right to consider as your own property. And here I cannot avoid mentioning a circumstance in placing the model, though to some it may appear trifling. It is better to possess the model with the attitude you require, than to place him with your own hands; by this means it happens often that the model puts himself in an action superior to your own imagination. It is a great matter to be in the way of accident, and to be watchful and ready to take advantage of it; besides, when you fix the position of a model there is danger of putting him in an attitude into which no man would naturally fall. This extends even to drapery. We must be cautious in touching and altering a fold of the stuff which serves as a model, for fear of giving it inadvertently a forced form; and it is perhaps better to take the chance of another casual throw than to alter the position in which it was at first accidentally cast.

Rembrandt, in order to take the advantage of accident, appears often to have used the pallette-knife to lay his colors on the canvas, instead of the pencil. Whether it is the knife or any other instrument, it suffices if it is something that does not follow exactly the will. Accident, in the hands of an artist who knows how to take the advantage of its hints, will often produce bold and capricious beauties of handling and facility, such as he would not have thought of, or ventured with his pencil under the regular restraint of his hand. However, this is fit only on occasions where no correctness of form is required, such as clouds, stumps of trees, rocks, or broken ground. Works produced in an accidental manner will have the same free, unrestrained air as the works of nature, whose particular combinations seem to depend upon accident.

I again repeat, you are never to lose sight of nature; the instant you do, you are all abroad, at the mercy of every gust of fashion, without knowing or seeing the point to which you ought to steer. Whatever trips you make, you must still have nature in your eye. Such deviations as art necessarily requires I hope in a future discourse to be able to explain. In the mean time, let me recommend to you not to have too great dependence on your practice or memory, however strong those impressions may have been which are there deposited. They are forever wearing out, and will be at last obliterated, unless they are continually refreshed and repaired.

It is not uncommon to meet with artists who, from a long neglect of cultivating this necessary intimacy with nature, do not even know her when they see her, — she appearing a stranger to them, from their being so long habituated to their own representation of her. I have heard painters acknowledge, though in that acknowledgment no degradation of themselves was intended, that they could do better without nature than with her; or, as they express it themselves, "that it only put them out." A painter with such ideas and such habits is indeed in a most hopeless state. *The art of seeing nature*, or, in other words, the art of using models, is in reality the great object, the point to which all our studies are directed. As for the power of being able to do tolerably well from practice alone, let it be valued according to its worth. But I do not see in what manner it can be sufficient for the production of correct, excellent, and finished pictures. Works deserving this character never were produced, nor ever will arise, from memory alone; and I will venture to say that an artist who brings to his work a mind tolerably furnished with the general principles of art, and a taste formed upon the works of good artists, — in short, who knows in what excellence consists, — will, with the assistance of models, which we will likewise suppose he has learned the art of using, be an overmatch for the greatest painter that ever lived who should be debarred such advantages.

Our neighbors, the French, are much in this practice of *extempore* invention, and their dexterity is such as even to excite admiration, if not envy. But how rarely can this praise be given to their finished pictures!

The late Director of their Academy, Boucher, was eminent in this way. When I visited him some years since in France, I found him at work on a very large picture, without drawings or models of any kind. On my remarking this particular circumstance, he said, when he was young, studying his art, he found it necessary to use models; but he had left them off for many years.

Such pictures as this was, and such as I fear always will be produced by those who work solely from practice or memory, may be a convincing proof of the necessity of the conduct which I have recommended. However, in justice I cannot quit this painter without adding that in the former part of his life, when he was in the habit of having recourse to nature, he was not without a considerable degree of merit, — enough to make half the painters of his country his imitators; he had often grace and beauty, and good skill in composition, but I think all under the influence of a bad taste; his imitators are indeed abominable.

Those artists who have quitted the service of nature ("whose service," when well understood, is "perfect freedom"), and have put themselves under the direction of I know not what capricious fantastical mistress, who fascinates and overpowers their whole mind, and from whose dominion there are no hopes of their being ever reclaimed (since they appear perfectly satisfied, and not at all conscious of their forlorn situation), like the transformed followers of Comus, —

> "Not once perceive their foul disfigurement;
> But boast themselves more comely than before."

Methinks such men, who have found out so short a path, have no reason to complain of the shortness of life, and the extent of art; since life is so much longer than is wanted for their improvement, or, indeed, is necessary for the accomplishment of their idea of perfection. On the contrary, he who recurs to nature, at every recurrence renews his strength. The rules of art he is never likely to forget; they are few and simple; but nature is refined, subtle, and infinitely various, beyond the power and retention of memory; it is necessary, therefore, to have continual recourse to her. In this intercourse there is no end of his improvement; the longer he lives, the nearer he approaches to the true and perfect idea of art.

Mrs. Billington as St. Cecilia.

DISCOURSE XIII.

Delivered to the Students of the Royal Academy, on the Distribution of the Prizes, December 11, 1786.

ART NOT MERELY IMITATION, BUT UNDER THE DIRECTION OF THE IMAGINATION. — IN WHAT MANNER POETRY, PAINTING, ACTING, GARDENING, AND ARCHITECTURE DEPART FROM NATURE.

To discover beauties, or to point out faults in the works of celebrated masters, and to compare the conduct of one artist with another, is certainly no mean or inconsiderable part of criticism; but this is still no more than to know the art through the artist. This test of investigation must have two capital defects; it must be narrow, and it must be uncertain. To enlarge the boundaries of the art of painting, as well as to fix its principles, it will be necessary that that art and those principles should be considered in their correspondence with the principles of the other arts which, like this, address themselves primarily and principally to the imagination. When those connected and kindred principles are brought together to be compared, another comparison will grow out of this; that is, the comparison of them all with those of human nature, from whence arts derive the materials upon which they are to produce their effects.

When this comparison of art with art, and of all arts with the nature of man, is once made with success, our guiding lines are as well ascertained and established as they can be in matters of this description.

This, as it is the highest style of criticism, is at the same time the soundest; for it refers to the eternal and immutable nature of things.

You are not to imagine that I mean to open to you at large, or to recommend to your research, the whole of this vast field of science. It is certainly much above my faculties to reach it; and though it may not be above yours to comprehend it fully if it were fully and properly brought before you, yet perhaps the most perfect criticism requires habits of speculation and abstraction not very consistent with the employment which ought to occupy, and the habits of mind which ought to prevail in a practical artist. I only point out to you these things, that when you do criticise (as all who work on a plan will criticise more or less), your criticism may be built on the foundation of true principles; and that though you may not always travel a great way, the way that you do travel may be the right road.

I observe, as a fundamental ground, common to all the arts with which we have any concern in this discourse, that they address themselves only to two faculties of the mind, — its imagination and its sensibility.

All theories which attempt to direct or to control the art upon any principles falsely called rational, which we form to ourselves upon a supposition of what ought in reason to be the end or means of art, independent of the known first effect produced by objects on the imagination, must be false and delusive. For though it may appear bold to say it, the imagination is here the residence of truth. If the imagination be affected, the conclusion is fairly drawn; if it be not affected, the reasoning is erroneous, because the end is not obtained, — the effect itself being the test, and the only test, of the truth and efficacy of the means.

There is in the commerce of life, as in art, a sagacity which is far from being contradictory to right reason, and is superior to any occasional exercise of that faculty which supersedes it; and does not wait for the slow progress of deduction, but goes at once, by what appears a kind of intuition, to the conclusion. A man endowed with this faculty feels and acknowledges the truth, though it is not always in his power, perhaps, to give a reason for it; because he cannot recollect and bring before him all the materials that gave birth to his opinion ; for very many and very intricate considerations may unite to form the principle, even of small and minute parts, involved in, or dependent on, a great system of things; though these in process of time are forgotten, the right impression still remains fixed in his mind.

This impression is the result of the accumulated experience of our whole life, and has been collected, we do not always know how or when. But this mass of collective observation, however acquired, ought to prevail over that reason which, however powerfully exerted on any particular occasion, will probably comprehend but a partial view of the subject; and our conduct in life, as well as in the arts, is, or ought to be, generally governed by this habitual reason; it is our happiness that we are enabled to draw on such funds. If we were obliged to enter into a theoretical deliberation on every occasion before we act, life would be at a stand, and art would be impracticable.

It appears to me, therefore, that our first thoughts, that is, the effect which anything produces on our minds on its first appearance, is never to be forgotten; and it demands for that reason, because it is the first, to be laid up with care. If this be not done, the artist may happen to impose on himself by partial reasoning; by a cold consideration of those animated thoughts which proceed, not perhaps from caprice or rashness (as he may afterwards conceit), but from the fulness of his mind, enriched with the copious stores of all the various inventions which he had ever seen, or had ever passed in his mind. These ideas are infused into his design without any conscious effort; but if he be not on his guard he may reconsider and correct them till the whole matter is reduced to a commonplace invention.

This is sometimes the effect of what I mean to caution you against; that is to say, an unfounded distrust of the imagination and feeling in favor of narrow, partial, confined, argumentative theories, and of principles that seem to apply to the design in hand, without considering those general impressions on the fancy in which real principles of *sound reason*, and of much more weight and importance are involved, and, as it were, lie hid under the appearance of a sort of vulgar sentiment.

Reason, without doubt, must ultimately determine everything; at this minute it is required to inform us when that very reason is to give way to feeling.

Though I have often spoken of that mean conception of our art which confines it to mere imitation, I must add that it may be narrowed to such a mere matter of experiment as to exclude from it the application of science, which alone gives dignity and compass to any art. But to find proper foundations for science is neither to narrow nor to vulgarize it; and this is sufficiently exemplified in the success of experimental philosophy. It is the false system of reasoning, grounded on a partial view of things, against which I would most earnestly guard you. And I do it the rather, because those narrow theories, so coincident with the poorest and most miserable practices, and which are adopted to give it countenance, have not had their origin in the poorest minds, but in the mistakes, or possibly in the mistaken interpretations, of great and commanding authorities. We are not, therefore, in this case misled by feeling, but by false speculation.

When such a man as Plato speaks of painting as only an imitative art, and that our pleasure proceeds from observing and acknowledging the truth of the imitation, I think he misleads us by a partial theory. It is in this poor, partial, and, so far, false view of the art, that Cardinal Bembo has chosen to distinguish even Raphael himself, whom our enthusiasm honors with the name of Divine. The same sentiment is adopted by Pope in his epitaph on Sir Godfrey Kneller;[1] and he turns the panegyric solely on imitation, as it is a sort of deception.

I shall not think my time misemployed if by any means I may contribute to confirm your opinion of what ought to be the object of your pursuit; because, though the best critics must always have exploded this strange idea, yet I know that there is a disposition towards a perpetual recurrence to it, on account of its simplicity and superficial plausibility. For this reason I shall beg leave to lay before you a few thoughts on this subject; to throw out some hints that may lead your minds to an opinion (which I take to be the truth) that painting is not only to be considered as an imitation operating by deception, but that it is, and ought to be, in many points of view, and strictly speaking, no imitation at all of external nature. Perhaps it ought to be as far removed from the vulgar idea of imitation as the refined, civilized state in which we live is removed from a gross state of nature; and those who have not cultivated their imaginations, which the majority of mankind certainly have not, may be said, in regard to arts, to continue in this state of nature. Such men will always prefer imitation to that excellence which is addressed to another faculty, that they do not possess; but these are

---

[1] "Kneller, by Heav'n and not a Master taught,
Whose art was Nature, and whose pictures Thought;
Now for two ages having snatched from fate
Whate'er was beauteous, or whate'er was great,
Lies crowned with princes' honors, poets' lays,
Due to his merit, and brave thirst of praise.
Living, great Nature feared he might outvie
Her works; and, dying, fears herself may die."

not the persons to whom a painter is to look, any more than a judge of morals and manners ought to refer controverted points upon those subjects to the opinions of people taken from the banks of the Ohio, or from New Holland.

It is the lowest style only of arts, whether of painting, poetry, or music, that may be said, in the vulgar sense, to be naturally pleasing. The higher efforts of those arts, we know by experience, do not affect minds wholly uncultivated. This refined taste is the consequence of education and habit; we are born only with a capacity of entertaining this refinement, as we are born with a disposition to receive and obey all the rules and regulations of society; and so far it may be said to be natural to us, and no further.

What has been said may show the artist how necessary it is, when he looks about him for the advice and criticism of his friends, to make some distinction of the character, taste, experience, and observation in this art, of those from whom it is received. An ignorant, uneducated man may, like Apelles' critic, be a competent judge of the truth of the representation of a sandal; or, to go somewhat higher, like Molière's old woman, may decide upon what is nature, in regard to comic humor; but a critic in the higher style of art ought to possess the same refined taste which directed the artist in his work.

To illustrate this principle by a comparison with other arts, I shall now produce some instances to show that they, as well as our own art, renounce the narrow idea of nature, and the narrow theories derived from that mistaken principle, and apply to that reason only which informs us, not what imitation is,—a natural representation of a given object,—but what it is natural for the imagination to be delighted with. And perhaps there is no better way of acquiring this knowledge than by this kind of analogy; each art will corroborate and mutually reflect the truth on the other. Such a kind of juxtaposition may likewise have this use, that while the artist is amusing himself in the contemplation of other arts, he may habitually transfer the principles of those arts to that which he professes; which ought to be always present to his mind, and to which everything is to be referred.

So far is art from being derived from, or having any immediate intercourse with, particular nature as its model, that there are many arts that set out with a professed deviation from it.

This is certainly not so exactly true in regard to painting and sculpture. Our elements are laid in gross common nature,—an exact imitation of what is before us; but when we advance to the higher state, we consider this power of imitation, though first in the order of acquisition, as by no means the highest in the scale of perfection.

Poetry addresses itself to the same faculties and the same dispositions as painting, though by different means. The object of both is to accommodate itself to all the natural propensities and inclinations of the mind. The very existence of poetry depends on the license it assumes of deviating from actual nature, in order to gratify natural propensities by other means, which are found by experience full as capable of affording such gratification. It sets out with a language in the highest degree artificial, a construction of measured words, such as never is, nor ever was, used by man. Let this measure be what it may, whether hexameter or any other metre used in Latin or Greek, or rhyme, or blank verse varied with pauses and accents, in modern languages,— they are all equally removed from nature, and equally a violation of common speech. When this artificial mode has been established as the vehicle of sentiment, there is another principle in the human mind to which the work must be referred, which renders it still more artificial, carries it still further from common nature, and deviates only to render it more perfect. That principle is the sense of congruity, coherence, and consistency, which is a real existing principle in man; and it must be gratified. Therefore, having once adopted a style and a measure not found in common discourse, it is required that the sentiments also should be in the same proportion elevated above common nature, from the necessity of there being an agreement of the parts among themselves, that one uniform whole may be produced.

To correspond, therefore, with this general system of deviation from nature, the manner in which poetry is offered to the ear, the tone in which it is recited should be as far removed from the tone of conversation as the words of which that poetry is composed. This naturally suggests the idea of modulating the voice by art, which, I suppose, may be considered as accomplished to the highest degree of excellence in the recitative of the Italian Opera; as we may conjecture it was in the chorus that attended the ancient drama. And though the most violent passions, the highest distress, even death itself, are expressed in singing or recitative, I would not admit as sound criticism the condemnation of such exhibitions on account of their being unnatural.

If it is natural for our senses and our imaginations to be delighted with singing, with instrumental music, with poetry, and with graceful action, taken separately (none of them being in the vulgar sense natural, even in that separate state), it is conformable to experience, and therefore agreeable to reason as connected and referred to experience, that we should also be delighted with this union of music, poetry, and graceful action, joined to every circumstance of pomp and magnificence calculated to strike the senses of the spectator. Shall reason stand in the way, and tell us that we ought not to like what we know we do like, and prevent us from feeling the full effect of this complicated exertion of art? This is what I would understand by poets and painters being allowed to dare everything; for what can be more daring than accomplishing the purpose and end of art by a complication of means, none of which have their archetypes in actual nature?

So far, therefore, is servile imitation from being necessary, that whatever is familiar, or in any way reminds us of what we see and hear every day, perhaps does not belong to the higher provinces of art, either in poetry or painting. The mind is to be transported, as Shakespeare expresses it, *beyond the ignorant present*, to ages past. Another and a higher order of beings is supposed; and to those beings everything which is introduced into the work must correspond. Of this conduct, under these circumstances, the Roman and Florentine schools afford sufficient examples. Their style by this means is raised and elevated above all others; and by the same means the compass of art itself is enlarged.

We often see grave and great subjects attempted by artists of another school; who, though excellent in the lower class of art, proceeding on the principles which regulate that class, and not recollecting, or not knowing, that they were to address themselves to another faculty of the mind, have become perfectly ridiculous.

The picture which I have at present in my thoughts is a sacrifice of Iphigenia, painted by Jan Steen, a painter of whom I have formerly had occasion to speak with the highest approbation; and even in this picture, the subject of which is by no means adapted to his genius, there is nature and expression; but it is such expression, and the countenances are so familiar, and consequently so vulgar, and the whole accompanied with such finery of silks and velvets, that one would be almost tempted to doubt whether the artist did not purposely intend to burlesque his subject.

Instances of the same kind we frequently see in poetry. Parts of Hobbes's translation of Homer are remembered and repeated merely for the familiarity and meanness of their phraseology, so ill corresponding with the ideas which ought to have been expressed, and as I conceive, with the style of the original.

We may proceed in the same manner through the comparatively inferior branches of art. There is in works of that class the same distinction of a higher and a lower style; and they take their rank and degree in proportion as the artist departs more or less from common nature, and makes it an object of his attention to strike the imagination of the spectator by ways belonging especially to art, — unobserved and untaught out of the school of its practice.

If our judgments are to be directed by narrow, vulgar, untaught, or rather ill-taught reason, we must prefer a portrait by Denner, or any other high finisher, to those of Titian or Van Dyck; and a landscape of Van der Heyden to those of Titian or Rubens; for they are certainly more exact representations of nature.

If we suppose a view of nature represented with all the truth of the *camera obscura*, and the same scene represented by a great artist, how little and mean will the one appear in comparison with the other, — where no superiority is supposed from the choice of the subject! The scene shall be the same, the difference only will be in the manner in which it is presented to the eye. With what additional superiority, then, will the same artist appear when he has the power of selecting his materials as well as elevating his style. Like Nicholas Poussin, he transports us to the environs of ancient Rome, with all the objects which a literary education makes so precious and interesting to man; or, like Sebastian Bourdon, he leads us to the dark antiquity of the pyramids of Egypt; or, like

Claude Lorrain, he conducts us to the tranquillity of Arcadian scenes and fairy-land.

Like the history-painter, a painter of landscapes, in this style and with this conduct, sends the imagination back into antiquity; and like the poet, he makes the elements sympathize with his subject, — whether the clouds roll in volumes like those of Titian or Salvator Rosa, or, like those of Claude, are gilded with the setting sun; whether the mountains have sudden and bold projections, or are gently sloped; whether the branches of his trees shoot out abruptly in right angles from their trunks, or follow each other with only a gentle inclination. All these circumstances contribute to the general character of the work, whether it be of the elegant or of the more sublime kind. If we add to this the powerful materials of lightness and darkness, over which the artist has complete dominion, to vary and dispose them as he pleases, to diminish or increase them as will best suit his purpose and correspond to the general idea of his work, — a landscape thus conducted, under the influence of a poetical mind, will have the same superiority over the more ordinary and common views as Milton's "L'Allegro" and "Il Penseroso" have over a cold, prosaic narration or description; and such a picture would make a more forcible impression on the mind than the real scenes, were they presented before us.

If we look abroad to other arts we may observe the same distinction, the same division into two classes; each of them acting under the influence of two different principles, in which the one follows nature, the other varies it, and sometimes departs from it.

The theatre, which is said "to hold the mirror up to nature," comprehends both those ideas. The lower kind of comedy, or farce, like the inferior style of painting, the more naturally it is represented, the better; but the higher appears to me to aim no more at imitation, so far as it belongs to anything like deception, or to expect that the spectators should think that the events there represented are really passing before them, than Raphael in his cartoons, or Poussin in his "Sacraments," expected it to be believed, even for a moment, that what they exhibited were real figures.

For want of this distinction the world is filled with false criticism. Raphael is praised for naturalness and deception, which he certainly has not accomplished, and as certainly never intended; and our late great actor, Garrick, has been as ignorantly praised by his friend Fielding; who doubtless imagined he had hit upon an ingenious device, by introducing in one of his novels (otherwise a work of the highest merit) an ignorant man mistaking Garrick's representation of a scene in "Hamlet" for reality. A very little reflection will convince us that there is not one circumstance in the whole scene that is of the nature of deception. The merit and excellence of Shakespeare, and of Garrick, when they were engaged in such scenes, is of a different and much higher kind. But what adds to the falsity of this intended compliment is that the best stage-representation appears even more unnatural to a person of such a character, who is supposed never to have seen a play before, than it does to those who have had a habit of allowing for those necessary deviations from nature which the art requires.

In theatric representation great allowances must always be made for the place in which the exhibition is represented, — for the surrounding company, the lighted candles, the scenes visibly shifted in your sight, and the language of blank verse, so different from common English, which merely as English must appear surprising in the mouths of Hamlet and all the court and natives of Denmark. These allowances are made, but their being made puts an end to all manner of deception;[1] and further, we know that the more low, illiterate, and vulgar any person is, the less he will be disposed to make these allowances, and of course to be deceived by any imitation, — the things in which the trespass against nature and common probability is made in favor of the theatre being quite within the sphere of such uninformed men.

Though I have no intention of entering into all the circumstances of unnaturalness in theatrical representations, I must observe that even the expression of violent passion is not always the most excellent in proportion as it is the most natural; so great terror and such disagreeable sensations may be communicated to the audience that the balance may be destroyed by which pleasure is preserved and holds its

---

[1] It is false that any representation is mistaken for reality, — that any dramatic fable in its materiality was ever credible, or, for a single moment, was ever credited. . . . The truth is that the spectators are always in their senses, and know, from the first act to the last, that the stage is only a stage, and that the players are only players. They came to hear a certain number of lines recited with just gesture and elegant modulation. — DR. JOHNSON, *Preface to Shakespeare.*

predominance in the mind. Violent distortion of action, harsh screamings of the voice, however great the occasions, or however natural on such occasions, are therefore not admissible in the theatric art. Many of these allowed deviations from nature arise from the necessity which there is that everything should be raised and enlarged beyond its natural state; that the full effect may come home to the spectator, which otherwise would be lost in the comparatively extensive space of the theatre. Hence the deliberate and stately step, the studied grace of action, which seems to enlarge the dimensions of the actor, and alone to fill the stage. All this unnaturalness, though right and proper in its place, would appear affected and ridiculous in a private room; *quid enim deformius quam scenam in vitam transferre?*

And here I must observe, and I believe it may be considered as a general rule, that no art can be grafted with success on another art. For though they all profess the same origin, and to proceed from the same stock, yet each has its own peculiar modes both of imitating nature and of deviating from it, each for the accomplishment of its own particular purpose. These deviations, more especially, will not bear transplantation to another soil.

If a painter should endeavor to copy the theatrical pomp and parade of dress and attitude, instead of that simplicity which is not a greater beauty in life than it is in painting, we should condemn such pictures, as painted in the meanest style.

So, also, gardening — as far as gardening is an art, or is entitled to the appellation — is a deviation from nature; for if the true taste consists, as many hold, in banishing every appearance of art, or any traces of the footsteps of man, it would then be no longer a garden. Even though we define it, "nature to advantage dressed," — and in some sense it is such, and much more beautiful and commodious for the recreation of man, — it is, however, when so dressed, no longer a subject for the pencil of a landscape-painter, as all landscape-painters know, who love to have recourse to nature herself, and to dress her according to the principles of their own art, which are far different from those of gardening, even when conducted according to the most approved principles, and such as a landscape-painter himself would adopt in the disposition of his own grounds, for his own private satisfaction.

I have brought together as many instances as appear necessary to make out the several points which I wished to suggest to your consideration in this discourse, — that your own thoughts may lead you further in the use that may be made of the analogy of the arts, and of the restraint which a full understanding of the diversity of many of their principles ought to impose on the employment of that analogy.

The great end of all those arts is to make an impression on the imagination and the feeling. The imitation of nature frequently does this. Sometimes it fails, and something else succeeds. I think, therefore, the true test of all the arts is not solely whether the production is a true copy of nature, but whether it answers the end of art, which is to produce a pleasing effect upon the mind.

It remains only to speak a few words of architecture, which does not come under the denomination of an imitative art. It applies itself, like music (and, I believe, we may add poetry), directly to the imagination, without the intervention of any kind of imitation.

There is in architecture, as in painting, an inferior branch of art in which the imagination appears to have no concern. It does not, however, acquire the name of a polite and liberal art from its usefulness, or administering to our wants or necessities, but from some higher principle; we are sure that in the hands of a man of genius it is capable of inspiring sentiment, and of filling the mind with great and sublime ideas.

It may be worth the attention of artists to consider what materials are in their hands that may contribute to this end, and whether this art has it not in its power to address itself to the imagination with effect, by more ways than are generally employed by architects.

To pass over the effect produced by that general symmetry and proportion by which the eye is delighted, as the ear is with music, architecture certainly possesses many principles in common with poetry and painting. Among those which may be reckoned as the first is that of affecting the imagination by means of association of ideas. Thus, for instance, as we have naturally a veneration for antiquity, whatever building brings to our remembrance ancient customs and manners, such as the castles of the barons of ancient chivalry, is sure to give this delight.

Hence it is that *towers and battlements*[1] are so often selected by the painter and the poet to make a part of the composition of their ideal landscape; and it is from hence, in a great degree, that in the buildings of Vanbrugh, who was a poet as well as an architect, there is a greater display of imagination than we shall find, perhaps, in any other; and this is the ground of the effect we feel in many of his works, notwithstanding the faults with which many of them are justly charged. For this purpose, Vanbrugh appears to have had recourse to some of the principles of the Gothic architecture; which, though not so ancient as the Grecian, is more so to our imagination, with which the artist is more concerned than with absolute truth.

The barbaric splendor of those Asiatic buildings which are now publishing by a member of this Academy, may possibly, in the same manner, furnish an architect, not with models to copy, but with hints of composition and general effect, which would not otherwise have occurred.

It is, I know, a delicate and hazardous thing (and as such I have already pointed it out) to carry the principles of one art to another, or even to reconcile in one object the various modes of the same art, when they proceed on different principles. The sound rules of the Grecian architecture are not to be lightly sacrificed. A deviation from them, or even an addition to them, is like a deviation or addition

---

[1] Towers and battlements it sees
Bosom'd high in tufted trees.
     MILTON, *L'Allegro.*

to, or from, the rules of other arts, — fit only for a great master, who is thoroughly conversant in the nature of man, as well as all combinations in his own art.

It may not be amiss for the architect to take advantage *sometimes* of that to which I am sure the painter ought always to have his eyes open, — I mean the use of accidents; to follow when they lead, and to improve them, rather than always to trust to a regular plan. It often happens that additions have been made to houses at various times, for use or pleasure. As such buildings depart from regularity they now and then acquire something of scenery by this accident, which I should think might not unsuccessfully be adopted by an architect in an original plan, if it does not too much interfere with convenience. Variety and intricacy is a beauty and excellence in every other of the arts which address the imagination, and why not in architecture?

The forms and turnings of the streets of London and other old towns are produced by accident, without any original plan or design, but they are not always the less pleasant to the walker or spectator on that account. On the contrary, if the city had been built on the regular plan of Sir Christopher Wren, the effect might have been, as we know it is in some new parts of the town, rather unpleasing; the uniformity might have produced weariness, and a slight degree of disgust.

I can pretend to no skill in the detail of architecture. I judge now of the art merely as a painter. When I speak of Vanbrugh I mean to speak of him in the language of our art. To speak, then, of Vanbrugh in the language of a painter, he had originality of invention, he understood light and shadow, and had great skill in composition. To support his principal object, he produced his second and third groups or masses; he perfectly understood in his art what is the most difficult in ours, the conduct of the background; by which the design and invention is set off to the greatest advantage. What the background is in painting, in architecture is the real ground on which the building is erected; and no architect took greater care than he that his work should not appear crude and hard; that is, it did not abruptly start out of the ground without expectation or preparation.

This is a tribute which a painter owes to an architect who composed like a painter, and was defrauded of the due reward of his merit by the wits of his time, who did not understand the principles of composition in poetry better than he, and who knew little or nothing of what he understood perfectly, — the general ruling principles of architecture and painting. His fate was that of the great Perrault; both were the objects of the petulant sarcasms of factious men of letters, and both have left some of the fairest ornaments which to this day decorate their several countries, — the façade of the Louvre, Blenheim, and Castle Howard.

Upon the whole it seems to me that the object and intention of all the arts is to supply the natural imperfection of things, and often to gratify the mind by realizing and embodying what never existed but in the imagination.

It is allowed on all hands that facts and events, however they may bind the historian, have no dominion over the poet or the painter. With us, history is made to bend and conform to this great idea of art. And why? Because these arts, in their highest province, are not addressed to the gross senses, but to the desires of the mind, — to that spark of divinity which we have within, impatient of being circumscribed and pent up by the world which is about us. Just so much as our art has of this, just so much of dignity, I had almost said of divinity, it exhibits; and those of our artists who possessed this mark of distinction in the highest degree acquired from thence the glorious appellation of DIVINE.

Miss Nelly O'Brien.

DISCOURSE XIV.

Delivered to the Students of the Royal Academy, on the Distribution of the Prizes, December 10, 1788.

CHARACTER OF GAINSBOROUGH :[1]—HIS EXCELLENCES AND DEFECTS.

IN the study of our art, as in the study of all arts, something is the result of our own observation of nature; something, and that not a little, the effect of the example of those who have studied the same nature before us, and who have cultivated before us the same art with diligence and success. The less we confine ourselves in the choice of those examples, the more advantage we shall derive from them, and the nearer we shall bring our performances to a correspondence with nature and the great general rules of art. When we draw our examples from remote and revered antiquity — with some advantage, undoubtedly, in that selection — we subject ourselves to some inconveniences. We may suffer ourselves to be too much led away by great names, and to be too

---

[1] Gainsborough died in August, 1788. Ruskin calls him "deep-thoughted, solemn Gainsborough," "pure in his English feeling, profound in his seriousness, graceful in his gayety." "A great name his, whether of the English or any other school — the greatest colorist since Rubens." "In management and quality of single and particular tint, in the purely technical part of painting, Turner is a child to Gainsborough. . . . His hand is as light as the sweep of a cloud, as swift as the flash of a sunbeam. . . . In a word, Gainsborough is an immortal painter." (*Modern Painters.*)

much subdued by overbearing authority. Our learning, in that case, is not so much an exercise of our judgment as a proof of our docility. We find ourselves, perhaps, too much overshadowed; and the character of our pursuits is rather distinguished by the tameness of the follower than animated by the spirit of emulation. It is sometimes of service that our examples should be *near* us, and such as raise a reverence sufficient to induce us carefully to observe them, yet not so great as to prevent us from engaging with them in something like a generous contention.

We have lately lost Mr. Gainsborough, one of the greatest ornaments of our Academy. It is not our business here to make panegyrics on the living, or even on the dead who were of our body. The praise of the former might bear the appearance of adulation; and the latter, of untimely justice, — perhaps of envy to those whom we have still the happiness to enjoy, by an oblique suggestion of invidious comparisons. In discoursing, therefore, on the talents of the late Mr. Gainsborough, my object is, not so much to praise or to blame him, as to draw from his excellences and defects matter of instruction to the students in our Academy. If ever this nation should produce genius sufficient to acquire to us the honorable distinction of an English school, the name of Gainsborough will be transmitted to posterity, in the history of the art, among the very first of that rising name.[1] That our reputation in the arts is now only

---

[1] He was the father, the originator, of modern landscape.
CHESNEAU.

rising must be acknowledged; and we must expect our advances to be attended with old prejudices, as adversaries, and not as supporters,—standing in this respect in a very different situation from the late artists of the Roman school, to whose reputation ancient prejudices have certainly contributed; the way was prepared for them, and they may be said rather to have lived in the reputation of their country than have contributed to it; while whatever celebrity is obtained by English artists can arise only from the operation of a fair and true comparison. And when they communicate to their country a share of their reputation it is a portion of fame not borrowed from others, but solely acquired by their own labor and talents. As Italy has undoubtedly a prescriptive right to an admiration bordering on prejudice, as a soil peculiarly adapted, congenial, and, we may add, destined to the production of men of great genius in our art, we may not unreasonably suspect that a portion of the great fame of some of their late artists has been owing to the general readiness and disposition of mankind to acquiesce in their original prepossessions in favor of the productions of the Roman school.

On this ground, however unsafe, I will venture to prophesy, that two of the last distinguished painters of that country,—I mean Pompeio Battoni and Raphael Mengs,—however great their names may at present sound in our ears, will very soon fall into the rank of Imperiale, Sebastian Concha, Placido Constanza, Masaccio, and the rest of their immediate predecessors; whose names, though equally renowned in their lifetime, are now fallen into what is little short of total oblivion. I do not say that those painters were not superior to the artist I allude to and whose loss we lament, in a certain routine of practice, which to the eyes of common observers has the air of a learned composition, and bears a sort of superficial resemblance to the manner of the great men who went before them. I know this perfectly well; but I know likewise that a man looking for real and lasting reputation must unlearn much of the commonplace method so observable in the works of the artists whom I have named. For my own part, I confess, I take more interest in and am more captivated with the powerful impression of nature which Gainsborough exhibited in his portraits and in his landscapes, and the interesting simplicity and elegance of his little ordinary beggar-children, than with any of the works of that school since the time of Andrea Sacchi, or perhaps we may say Carlo Maratti, — two painters who may truly be said to be *Ultimi Romanorum.*

I am well aware how much I lay myself open to the censure and ridicule of the academical professors of other nations, in preferring the humble attempts of Gainsborough to the works of those regular graduates in the great historical style. But we have the sanction of all mankind in preferring genius in a lower rank of art to feebleness and insipidity in the highest.

It would not be to the present purpose, even if I had the means and materials, which I have not, to enter into the private life of Mr. Gainsborough. The history of his gradual advancement, and the means by which he acquired such excellence in his art, would come nearer to our purposes and wishes, if it were by any means attainable; but the slow progress of advancement is in general imperceptible to the man himself who makes it; it is the consequence of an accumulation of various ideas which his mind has received, he does not perhaps know how or when. Sometimes, indeed, it happens that he may be able to mark the time when, from the sight of a picture, a passage in an author, or a hint in conversation, he has received, as it were, some new and guiding light, something like inspiration, by which his mind has been expanded; and is morally sure that his whole life and conduct has been affected by that accidental circumstance. Such interesting accounts we may, however, sometimes obtain from a man who has acquired an uncommon habit of self-examination, and has attended to the progress of his own improvement.

It may not be improper to make mention of some of the customs and habits of this extraordinary man; points which come more within the reach of an observer. I, however, mean such only as are connected with his art, and indeed were, as I apprehend, the causes of his arriving to that high degree of excellence which we see and acknowledge in his works. Of these causes we must state, as the fundamental, the love which he had to his art; to which, indeed, his whole mind appears to have been devoted, and to which everything was referred; and this we may fairly conclude from various circumstances of his life which were known to his intimate friends. Among others, he had a habit of continually remarking to those who happened to be about him whatever peculiarity of countenance, whatever accidental combination of figure, or happy effects of light and shadow, occurred in prospects, in the sky, in walking the streets, or in company. If in his walks he found a character that he liked, and whose attendance was to be obtained, he ordered him to his house; and from the fields he brought into his painting-room stumps of trees, weeds, and animals of various kinds, and designed them, not from memory, but immediately from the objects. He even framed a kind of model of landscapes on his table, composed of broken stones, dried herbs, and pieces of looking-glass, which he magnified and improved into rocks, trees, and water. How far this latter practice may be useful in giving hints, the professors of landscape can best determine. Like every other technical practice, it seems to me wholly to depend on the general talent of him who uses it. Such methods may be nothing better than contemptible and mischievous trifling, or they may be aids. I think, upon the whole, unless we constantly refer to real nature, that practice may be more likely to do harm than good. I mention it only as it shows the solicitude and extreme activity which he had about everything that related to his art; that he wished to have his objects embodied, as it were, and distinctly before him; that he neglected nothing which could keep his faculties in exercise, and derived hints from every sort of combination.

We must not forget, while we are on this subject, to make some remarks on his custom of painting by night, which confirms what I have already mentioned, — his great affection to his art; since he could not amuse himself in the evening by any other means so agreeable to himself. I am, indeed, much inclined to believe that it is a practice very advantageous and improving to an artist; for by this means he will acquire a new and a higher perception of what is great and beautiful in nature. By candle-light, not only objects appear more beautiful, but from their being in a greater breadth of light and shadow, as well as having a greater breadth and uniformity of color, nature appears in a higher style; and even the flesh seems to take a higher and richer tone of color. Judgment is to direct us in the use to be made of this method of study, but the method itself is, I am sure, advantageous. I have often imagined that the two great colorists, Titian and Correggio, though I do not know that they painted by night, formed their high ideas of coloring from the effects of objects by this artificial light; but I am more assured that whoever attentively studies the first and best manner of Guercino will be convinced that he either painted by this light or formed his manner on this conception.

Another practice Gainsborough had which is worth mentioning, as it is certainly worthy of imitation; I mean his manner of forming all the parts of his picture together; the whole going on at the same time, in the same manner as nature creates her works. Though this method is not uncommon to those who have been regularly educated, yet probably it was suggested to him by his own natural sagacity. That this custom is not universal appears from the practice of a painter whom I have just mentioned, Pompeio Battoni, who finished his historical pictures part after part, and in his portraits completely finished one feature before he proceeded to another. The consequence was as might be expected; the countenance was never well expressed; and, as the painters say, the whole was not well put together.

The first thing required to excel in our art, or I believe in any art, is not only a love for it, but even an enthusiastic ambition to excel in it. This never fails of success proportioned to the natural abilities with which the artist has been endowed by Providence. Of Gainsborough, we certainly know that his passion was not the acquirement of riches, but excellence in his art, — and to enjoy that honorable fame which is sure to attend it. That he felt this ruling passion strong in death I am myself a witness. A few days before he died he wrote me a letter to express his acknowledgments for the good opinion I entertained of his abilities, and the manner in which (he had been informed) I always spoke of him; and desired he might see me once more before he died. I am aware how flattering it is to myself to be thus connected with the dying testimony which this excellent painter bore to his art. But I cannot prevail on myself to suppress that I was not connected with him by any habits of familiarity. If any little jealousies had subsisted between us, they were forgotten in those moments of sincerity; and he turned towards me as one who was engrossed by the same pursuits, and who deserved his good opinion by being sensible of his excellence. Without entering into a detail of what passed at this last interview,[1] the impression of it upon my mind was that his regret at losing life was principally the regret of leaving his art; and more especially as he now began, he said, to see what his deficiencies were; which, he said, he flattered himself in his last works were in some measure supplied.

When such a man as Gainsborough arrives to great fame, without the assistance of an academical education, without travelling to Italy, or any of those preparatory studies which have been so often recommended, he is produced as an instance how little such studies are necessary; since so great excellence may be acquired without them. This is an inference not warranted by the success of any individual; and I trust it will not be thought that I wish to make this use of it.

It must be remembered that the style and department of art which Gainsborough chose, and in which he so much excelled, did not require that he should go out of his own country for the objects of his study; they were everywhere about him; he found them in the streets and in the fields, and from the models thus accidentally found, he selected with great judgment such as suited his purpose. As his studies were directed to the living world principally, he did not pay a general attention to the works of the vari-

[1] When Reynolds approached the death-bed and bent his ear to catch the failing words, Gainsborough said: "We are all going to heaven, and Van Dyck is of the company,"— words which, as Mr. Ruskin says, "we may take for a beautiful reconciliation of all schools and souls who have done their work to the best of their knowledge and conscience."

ous masters, though they are, in my opinion, always of great use, even when the character of our subject requires us to depart from some of their principles. It cannot be denied that excellence in the department of the art which he professed may exist without them ; that in such subjects, and in the manner that belongs to them, the want of them is supplied, and more than supplied, by natural sagacity and a minute observation of particular nature. If Gainsborough did not look at nature with a poet's eye, it must be acknowledged that he saw her with the eye of a painter, and gave a faithful, if not a poetical, representation of what he had before him.

Though he did not much attend to the works of the great historical painters of former ages, yet he was well aware that the language of the art — the art of imitation — must be learned somewhere ; and as he knew that he could not learn it in an equal degree from his contemporaries, he very judiciously applied himself to the Flemish school, who are undoubtedly the greatest masters of one necessary branch of art; and he did not need to go out of his own country for examples of that school ; from that he learned the harmony of coloring, the management and disposition of light and shadow, and every means which the masters of it practised to ornament and give splendor to their works. And to satisfy himself as well as others how well he knew the mechanism and artifice which they employed to bring out that tone of color which we so much admire in their works, he occasionally made copies from Rubens, Teniers, and Van Dyck, which it would be no disgrace to the most accurate connoisseur to mistake, at the first sight, for the works of those masters. What he thus learned, he applied to the originals of nature, which he saw with his own eyes; and imitated, not in the manner of those masters, but in his own.

Whether he most excelled in portraits, landscapes, or fancy pictures, it is difficult to determine; whether his portraits were most admirable for exact truth of resemblance, or his landscapes for a portrait-like representation of nature, such as we see in the works of Rubens, Ruysdael, and others of those schools. In his fancy pictures, when he had fixed on his object of imitation, whether it was the mean and vulgar form of a wood-cutter, or a child of an interesting character, as he did not attempt to raise the one, so neither did he lose any of the natural grace and elegance of the other, — such a grace, and such an elegance, as are more frequently found in cottages than in courts. This excellence was his own, the result of his particular observation and taste; for this he was certainly not indebted to the Flemish school, nor indeed, to any school; for his grace was not academical or antique, but selected by himself from the great school of nature; and there are yet a thousand modes of grace, which are neither theirs nor his, but lie open in the multiplied scenes and figures of life, to be brought out by skilful and faithful observers.

Upon the whole, we may justly say that whatever he attempted he carried to a high degree of excellence. It is to the credit of his good sense and judgment that he never did attempt that style of historical painting for which his previous studies had made no preparation.

And here it naturally occurs to oppose the sensible conduct of Gainsborough in this respect to that of our late excellent Hogarth, who with all his extraordinary talents, was not blessed with this knowledge of his own deficiency, or of the bounds which were set to the extent of his own powers. After this admirable artist had spent the greater part of his life in an active, busy, and we may add, successful attention to the ridicule of life; after he had invented a new species of dramatic painting, in which probably he will never be equalled, and had stored his mind with infinite materials to explain and illustrate the domestic and familiar scenes of common life which were generally, and ought to have been always, the subject of his pencil; he very imprudently, or rather presumptuously, attempted the great historical style,[1] for which his previous habits had by no means prepared him. He was indeed so entirely unacquainted with the principles of this style that he was not even aware that any artificial preparation was at all necessary. It is to be regretted that any part of the life of such a genius should be fruitlessly employed. Let his failure teach us not to indulge ourselves in

---

[1] In 1736 Hogarth painted on the walls of St. Bartholomew's Hospital " The Pool of Bethesda " and " The Good Samaritan," — in both of which the Hogarthian spirit of humor and satire is apparent. In " The Pool of Bethesda," the servant of a rich leper is seen driving away with his stick a poor wretch who has drawn near to bathe in the waters. In another picture, representing Danäe, he has yielded to the same spirit, showing the distrustful old nurse testing a piece of gold with her teeth. — CHESNEAU.

the vain imagination that by a momentary resolution we can give either dexterity to the hand or a new habit to the mind.

I have, however, little doubt but that the same sagacity which enabled those two extraordinary men to discover their true object, and the peculiar excellence of that branch of art which they cultivated, would have been equally effectual in discovering the principles of the higher style if they had investigated those principles with the same eager industry which they exerted in their own department. As Gainsborough never attempted the heroic style, so neither did he destroy the character and uniformity of his own style by the idle affectation of introducing mythological learning in any of his pictures. Of this boyish folly we see instances enough, even in the works of great painters. When the Dutch school attempt this poetry of our art in their landscapes, their performances are beneath criticism; they become only an object of laughter. This practice is hardly excusable even in Claude Lorrain, who had shown more discretion if he had never meddled with such subjects.

Our late ingenious Academician, Wilson, has, I fear, been guilty, like many of his predecessors, of introducing gods and goddesses, ideal beings, into scenes which were by no means prepared to receive such personages. His landscapes were in reality too near common nature to admit supernatural objects. In consequence of this mistake, in a very admirable picture of a storm which I have seen of his hand, many figures are introduced in the foreground, some in apparent distress, and some struck dead, as a spectator would naturally suppose, by the lightning, had not the painter injudiciously (as I think) rather chosen that their death should be imputed to a little Apollo, who appears in the sky, with his bent bow, and that those figures should be considered as the children of Niobe.[1]

To manage a subject of this kind, a peculiar style of art is required; and it can only be done without impropriety, or even without ridicule, when we adapt the character of the landscape, and that too in all its parts, to the historical or poetical representation. This is a very difficult adventure, and it requires a mind thrown back two thousand years, and as it were naturalized in antiquity, like that of Nicolas Poussin, to achieve it. In the picture alluded to,[2] the first idea that presents itself is that of wonder, at seeing a figure in so uncommon a situation as that in which the Apollo is placed; for the clouds on which he kneels have not the appearance of being able to support him; they have neither the substance nor the form fit for the receptacle of a human figure; and they do not possess in any respect that romantic character which is appropriate to such an object, and which alone can harmonize with poetical stories.

[1] When Wilson returned to England from Italy, George III. commissioned him to paint Kew Gardens; but instead of painting the reality, he substituted an Italian scene lit by a Southern sun. The King failed to recognize any resemblance to Kew, and returned the picture. M. Chesneau says, "Wilson always believed that Providence only created nature to serve as a surrounding for Niobe's misfortunes, and that ruins are the most beautiful architecture in the world."

[2] Now in the British National Gallery.

It appears to me that such conduct is no less absurd than if a plain man, giving a relation of real distress occasioned by an inundation accompanied with thunder and lightning, should, instead of simply relating the event, take it into his head, in order to give a grace to his narration, to talk of Jupiter Pluvius, or Jupiter and his thunderbolts, or any other figurative idea, — an intermixture which, though in poetry, with its proper preparations and accompaniments, it might be managed with effect, yet in the instance before us would counteract the purpose of the narrator, and instead of being interesting, would be only ridiculous.

The Dutch and Flemish style of landscape, not even excepting those of Rubens, is unfit for poetical subjects; but to explain in what this ineptitude consists, or to point out all the circumstances that give nobleness, grandeur, and the poetic character, to style in landscape, would require a long discourse of itself; and the end would be then perhaps but imperfectly attained. The painter who is ambitious of this perilous excellence must catch his inspiration from those who have cultivated with success the poetry, as it may be called, of the art; and they are few indeed.

I cannot quit this subject without mentioning two examples which occur to me at present, in which the poetical style of landscape may be seen happily executed: the one is "Jacob's Dream," by Salvator Rosa, and the other the "Return of the Ark from Captivity," by Sebastian Bourdon. With whatever dignity those histories are presented to us in the language of Scripture, this style of painting possesses the same power of inspiring sentiments of grandeur and sublimity, and is able to communicate them to subjects which appear by no means adapted to receive them. A ladder against the sky has no very promising appearance of possessing a capacity to excite any heroic ideas; and the ark, in the hands of a second-rate master, would have little more effect than a common wagon on the highway: yet those subjects are so poetically treated throughout, the parts have such a correspondence with each other, and the whole and every part of the scene is so visionary, that it is impossible to look at them without feeling, in some measure, the enthusiasm which seems to have inspired the painters.

By continual contemplation of such works a sense of the higher excellences of art will by degrees dawn on the imagination; at every review that sense will become more and more assured, until we come to enjoy a sober certainty of the real existence (if I may so express myself) of those almost ideal beauties; and the artist will then find no difficulty in fixing in his mind the principles by which the impression is produced, which he will feel and practice, though they are perhaps too delicate and refined, and too peculiar to the imitative art, to be conveyed to the mind by any other means.

To return to Gainsborough; the peculiarity of his manner, or style, or we may call it the language in which he expressed his ideas, has been considered by many as his greatest defect. But without altogether wishing to enter into the discussion whether this peculiarity was a defect or not, — intermixed, as it was, with great beauties, of some of which it was probably the cause, it becomes a proper subject of criticism and inquiry to a painter.

A novelty and peculiarity of manner, as it is often a cause of our approbation, so likewise it is often a ground of censure, as being contrary to the practice of other painters in whose manner we have been initiated and in whose favor we have perhaps been prepossessed from our infancy; for, fond as we are of novelty, we are upon the whole creatures of habit. However, it is certain, that all those odd scratches and marks which, on a close examination, are so observable in Gainsborough's pictures, and which even to experienced painters appear rather the effect of accident than design, — this chaos, this uncouth and shapeless appearance, by a kind of magic, at a certain distance assumes form, and all the parts seem to drop into their proper places, so that we can hardly refuse acknowledging the full effect of diligence under the appearance of chance and hasty negligence. That Gainsborough himself considered this peculiarity in his manner and the power it possesses of exciting surprise as a beauty in his works, I think may be inferred from the eager desire which we know he always expressed, that his pictures at the exhibition should be seen near, as well as at a distance.

The slightness which we see in his best works cannot always be imputed to negligence. However they may appear to superficial observers, painters know very well that a steady attention to the general effect takes up more time, and is much more laborious to the mind than any mode of high finishing or smoothness, without such attention. His handling, the manner of leaving the colors, or, in other words, the methods he used for producing the effect, had very much the appearance of the work of an artist who had never learned from others the usual and regular practice belonging to the art; but still, like a man of strong intuitive perception of what was required, he found out a way of his own to accomplish his purpose.

It is no disgrace to the genius of Gainsborough to compare him to such men as we sometimes meet with, whose natural eloquence appears even in speaking a language which they can scarce be said to understand; and who, without knowing the appropriate expression of almost any one idea, contrive to communicate the lively and forcible impressions of an energetic mind.

I think some apology may reasonably be made for his manner without violating truth, or running any risk of poisoning the minds of the younger students, by propagating false criticism for the sake of raising the character of a favorite artist. It must be allowed that this hatching manner of Gainsborough did very much contribute to the lightness of effect which is so eminent a beauty in his pictures; as, on the contrary, much smoothness and uniting the colors is apt to produce heaviness. Every artist must have remarked how often that lightness of hand which was in his dead color, or first painting, escaped in the finishing when he had determined the parts with more precision; and another loss he often experiences, which is of greater consequence, — while he is employed in the detail, the effect of the whole together is either forgotten or neglected. The lightness of a portrait, as I have formerly observed, consists more in preserving the general effect of the countenance than in the most minute finishing of the features, or any of the particular parts. Now Gainsborough's portraits were often little more, in regard to finishing, or determining the form of the features, than what generally attends a dead color; but as he was always attentive to the general effect, or whole together, I have often imagined that this unfinished manner contributed even to that striking resemblance for which his portraits are so remarkable. Though this opinion may be considered as fanciful, yet I think a plausible reason may be given why such a mode of painting should have such an effect. It is presupposed that in this undetermined manner there is in the general effect enough to remind the spectator of the original; the imagination supplies the rest, and perhaps more satisfactorily to himself, if not more exactly, than the artist, with all his care, could possibly have done. At the same time it must be acknowledged there is one evil attending this mode, — that if the portrait were seen previous to any knowledge of the original, different persons would form different ideas, and all would be disappointed at not finding the original correspond with their own conceptions, under the great latitude which indistinctness gives to the imagination to assume almost what character or form it pleases.

Every artist has some favorite part, on which he fixes his attention, and which he pursues with such eagerness that it absorbs every other consideration;

and he often falls into the opposite error of that which he would avoid, which is always ready to receive him. Now Gainsborough, having truly a painter's eye for coloring, cultivated those effects of the art which proceed from colors; and sometimes appears to be indifferent to or to neglect other excellences. Whatever defects are acknowledged, let him still experience from us the same candor that we so freely give upon similar occasions to the ancient masters; let us not encourage that fastidious disposition which is discontented with everything short of perfection, and unreasonably require, as we sometimes do, a union of excellences not perhaps quite compatible with each other. We may, on this ground, say even of the divine Raphael, that he might have finished his picture as highly and as correctly as was his custom, without heaviness of manner; and that Poussin might have preserved all his precision without hardness or dryness.

To show the difficulty of uniting solidity with lightness of manner, we may produce a picture of Rubens in the church of St. Gudule, at Brussels, as an example; the subject is "Christ's Charge to Peter;" which, as it is the highest and smoothest finished picture I remember to have seen of that master, so it is by far the heaviest; and if I had found it in any other place I should have suspected it to be a copy; for painters know very well that it is principally by this air of facility, or the want of it, that originals are distinguished from copies. A lightness of effect produced by color, and that produced by facility of handling, are generally united; a copy may preserve something of the one, it is true, but hardly ever of the other; a connoisseur, therefore, finds it often necessary to look carefully into the picture before he determines on its originality. Gainsborough possessed this quality of lightness of manner and effect, I think, to an unexampled degree of excellence; but it must be acknowledged, at the same time, that the sacrifice which he made to this ornament of our art was too great; it was, in reality, preferring the lesser excellences to the greater.

To conclude. However we may apologize for the deficiencies of Gainsborough (I mean particularly his want of precision and finishing), who so ingeniously contrived to cover his defects by his beauties, and who cultivated that department of art where such defects are more easily excused, you are to remember that no apology can be made for this deficiency in that style which this Academy teaches, and which ought to be the object of your pursuit. It will be necessary for you, in the first place, never to lose sight of the great rules and principles of the art, as they are collected from the full body of the best general practice, and the most constant and uniform experience; this must be the groundwork of all your studies. Afterwards you may profit, as in this case I wish you to profit, by the peculiar experience and personal talents of artists, living and dead; you may derive lights, and catch hints, from their practice; but the moment you turn them into models, you fall infinitely below them; you may be corrupted by excellences not so much belonging to the art as personal and appropriate to the artist, and become bad copies of good painters, instead of excellent imitators of the great universal truth of things.[1]

[1] Comparing the two "greatest and Englishest" of the English school, M. Chesneau says: "And thus Reynolds's talent is a magnificent victory of the will; that of Gainsborough the spontaneous unfolding of a flower accomplishing its natural transition and ripening into fruit. It was a fruit of an exquisite savor. What Reynolds sets himself to learn, and learns without difficulty, owing to the keen intelligence with which he is gifted, Gainsborough in his Suffolk woods imagines and creates for the satisfaction of his fancy. . . . If one would define exactly the difference between these two masters, one might say that Reynolds was all intelligence and will, Gainsborough all soul and sentiment; the former delights those of refined tastes, the latter charms everybody." (*English Painting*).

John, Earle of Upper Ossory.

DISCOURSE XV.

Delivered to the Students of the Royal Academy, on the Distribution of the Prizes, December 10, 1790.

THE PRESIDENT TAKES LEAVE OF THE ACADEMY. — A REVIEW OF THE DISCOURSES. — THE STUDY OF THE WORKS OF MICHAEL ANGELO RECOMMENDED.

THE intimate connection which I have had with the Royal Academy ever since its establishment, the social duties in which we have all mutually engaged for so many years, make any profession of attachment to this institution on my part altogether superfluous; the influence of habit alone in such a connection would naturally have produced it.

Among men united in the same body and engaged in the same pursuit, along with permanent friendship occasional differences will arise. In these disputes men are naturally too favorable to themselves, and think, perhaps, too hardly of their antagonists. But composed and constituted as we are, those little contentions will be lost to others, and they ought certainly to be lost among ourselves in mutual esteem for talents and acquirements; every controversy ought to be, and I am persuaded will be, sunk in our zeal for the perfection of our common art.

In parting with the Academy, I shall remember with pride, affection, and gratitude, the support with which I have almost uniformly been honored from the commencement of our intercourse. I shall leave you, gentlemen, with unaffected cordial wishes for your future concord, and with a well-founded hope that in that concord the auspicious and not obscure origin of our Academy may be forgotten in the splendor of your succeeding prospects.

My age, and my infirmities still more than my age, make it probable that this will be the last time I shall have the honor of addressing you from this place. Excluded as I am, *spatiis iniquis*, from indulging my imagination with a distant and forward perspective of life, I may be excused if I turn my eyes back on the way which I have passed.

We may assume to ourselves, I should hope, the credit of having endeavored at least, to fill with propriety that middle station which we hold in the general connection of things. Our predecessors have labored for our advantage, we labor for our successors; and though we have done no more in this mutual intercourse and reciprocation of benefits than has been effected by other societies formed in this nation for the advancement of useful and ornamental knowledge, yet there is one circumstance which appears to give us an higher claim than the credit of merely doing our duty. What I at present allude to is the honor of having been, some of us, the first contrivers, and all of us the promoters and supporters of the annual Exhibition. This scheme could only have originated from artists already in possession of the favor of the public, as it would not have been so much in the power of others to have excited curiosity. It must be remembered that, for the sake of bringing forward into notice concealed merit, they incurred the risk of producing rivals to themselves; they voluntarily entered the lists, and ran the race a second time for the prize which they had already won.

When we take a review of the several departments of the institution, I think we may safely congratulate ourselves on our good fortune in having hitherto seen the chairs of our professors filled with men of distinguished abilities, and who have so well acquitted themselves of their duty in their several departments. I look upon it to be of importance that none of them should be ever left unfilled; a neglect to provide for qualified persons is to produce a neglect of qualifications.

In this honorable rank of professors I have not presumed to class myself; though in the discourses which I have had the honor of delivering from this place, while in one respect I may be considered as a volunteer, in another view it seems as if I was involuntarily pressed into this service. If prizes were to be given, it appeared not only proper, but almost indispensably necessary, that something should be said by the President on the delivery of those prizes; and the President, for his own credit, would wish to say something more than mere words of compliment, which by being frequently repeated would soon become flat and uninteresting, and by being uttered to many would at last become a distinction to none. I thought, therefore, if I were to preface this compliment with some instructive observations on the art, when we crowned merit in the artists whom we rewarded, I might do something to animate and guide them in their future attempts.

I am truly sensible how unequal I have been to the expression of my own ideas. To develop the latent excellences, and draw out the interior principles of our art requires more skill and practice in writing than is likely to be possessed by a man perpetually occupied in the use of the pencil and the pallet. It is for that reason, perhaps, that the sister art has had the advantage of better criticism. Poets are naturally writers of prose. They may be said to be practising only an inferior department of their own art when they are explaining and expatiating upon its most refined principles. But still such difficulties ought not to deter artists who are not prevented by other engagements from putting their thoughts in order as well as they can, and from giving to the public the result of their experience. The knowledge which an artist has of his subject will more than compensate for any want of elegance in the manner of treating it, or even of perspicuity, which is still more essential; and I am convinced that one short essay written by a painter will contribute more to advance the theory of our art than a thousand volumes such as we sometimes see, the purpose of which appears to be rather to display the refinement of the author's own conceptions of impossible practice than to convey useful knowledge or instruction of any kind whatever. An artist knows what is and what is not within the province of his art to perform, and is not likely to be forever teasing the poor student with the beauties of mixed passions, or to perplex him with an imaginary union of excellences incompatible with each other.

To this work, however, I could not be said to come totally unprovided with materials. I had seen much, and I had thought much upon what I had seen; I had something of an habit of investigation, and a disposition to reduce all that I observed and felt in my own mind to method and system; but never having seen what I myself knew distinctly placed before me on paper, I knew nothing correctly. To put those ideas into something like order was, to my inexperience, no easy task. The composition, the *ponere totum* even of a single discourse, as well as of a single statue, was the most difficult part, as perhaps it is of every other art, and most requires the hand of a master.

For the manner, whatever deficiency there was, I might reasonably expect indulgence; but I thought it indispensably necessary well to consider the opinions which were to be given out from this place, and under the sanction of a Royal Academy; I therefore examined not only my own opinions, but likewise the opinions of others. I found in the course of this research many precepts and rules established in our art which did not seem to me altogether reconcilable with each other, yet each seemed in itself to have the same claim of being supported by truth and nature; and this claim, irreconcilable as they may be thought, they do in reality alike possess.

To clear away those difficulties and reconcile those contrary opinions it became necessary to distinguish the greater truth, as it may be called, from the lesser truth; the larger and more liberal idea of nature from the more narrow and confined; that which addresses itself to the imagination from that which is solely addressed to the eye. In consequence of this discrimination, the different branches of our art, to which those different truths were referred, were perceived to make so wide a separation, and put on so new an appearance, that they seemed scarcely to have proceeded from the same general stock. The different rules and regulations which presided over each department of art followed of course; every mode of excellence, from the grand style of the Roman and Florentine schools down to the lowest rank of still life, had its due weight and value — fitted some class or other; and nothing was thrown away. By this disposition of our art into classes, that perplexity and confusion which I apprehend every artist has at some time experienced from the variety of styles and the variety of excellence with which he is surrounded, is, I should hope, in some measure removed, and the student better enabled to judge for himself what peculiarly belongs to his own particular pursuit.

In reviewing my discourses, it is no small satisfaction to be assured that I have, in no part of them, lent my assistance to foster newly hatched, unfledged opinions, or endeavored to support paradoxes, however tempting may have been their novelty, or however ingenious I might for the minute fancy them to be; nor shall I, I hope, anywhere be found to have imposed on the minds of young students declamation for argument, a smooth period for a sound precept. I have pursued a plain and honest method; I have taken up the art simply as I found it exemplified in the practice of the most approved painters. That approbation which the world has uniformly given I have endeavored to justify by such proofs as questions of this kind will admit; by the analogy which painting holds with the sister arts, and consequently, by the common congeniality which they all bear to our nature. And though in what has been done no new discovery is pretended, I may still flatter myself that from the discoveries which others have made by their own intuitive good sense and native rectitude of judgment, I have succeeded in establishing the rules and principles of our art on a more firm and lasting foundation than that on which they had formerly been placed.

Without wishing to divert the student from the practice of his art to speculative theory, to make him a mere connoisseur instead of a painter, I cannot but remark that he will certainly find an account in considering, once for all, on what ground the fabric of our art is built. Uncertain, confused, or erroneous opinions are not only detrimental to an artist in their immediate operation, but may possibly have very serious consequences, — may affect his conduct, and give a peculiar character .(as it may be called) to his taste, and to his pursuits, through his whole life.

I was acquainted at Rome, in the early part of my life, with a student of the French Academy who appeared to me to possess all the qualities requisite to make a great artist if he had suffered his taste and feelings, and I may add even his prejudices, to have fair play. He saw and felt the excellences of the great works of art with which we were surrounded, but lamented that there was not to be found that nature which is so admirable in the inferior schools; and he supposed with Felibien, De Piles, and other theorists, that such a union of different excellences would be the perfection of art. He was not aware that the narrow idea of nature, of which he lamented the absence in the works of those great artists, would have destroyed the grandeur of the general ideas which he admired, and which was indeed the cause of his admiration. My opinions being then confused and unsettled, I was in danger of being borne down by this kind of plausible reasoning, though I remember I then had a dawning of suspicion that it was not sound doctrine; and at the same time I was unwilling obstinately to refuse assent to what I was unable to confute.

That the young artist may not be seduced from the right path by following what at first view he may think the light of reason, and which is indeed reason in part, but not in the whole, has been much the object of these discourses.

I have taken every opportunity of recommending a rational method of study, as of the last importance. The great, I may say the sole use of an Academy is to put and for some time to keep students in that course that too much indulgence may not be given to peculiarity, and that a young man may not be taught to believe that what is generally good for others is not good for him.

I have strongly inculcated in my former discourses,

as I do in this my last, the wisdom and necessity of previously obtaining the appropriate instruments of the art, in a first correct design and a plain, manly coloring, before anything more is attempted. But by this I would not wish to cramp and fetter the mind, or discourage those who follow (as most of us may at one time have followed) the suggestion of a strong inclination; something must be conceded to great and irresistible impulses; perhaps every student must not be strictly bound to general methods, if they strongly thwart the peculiar turn of his own mind. I must confess that it is not absolutely of much consequence whether he proceeds in the general method of seeking first to acquire mechanical accuracy before he attempts poetical flights, provided he diligently studies to attain the full perfection of the style he pursues; whether, like Parmegiano, he endeavors at grace and grandeur of manner before he has learned correctness of drawing, if like him he feels his own wants, and will labor, as that eminent artist did, to supply those wants; whether he starts from the East or from the West, if he relaxes in no exertion to arrive ultimately at the same goal. The first public work of Parmegiano is the "Saint Eustachius," in the Church of St. Petronius in Bologna, and was done when he was a boy; and one of the last of his works is the "Moses Breaking the Tables," in Parma. In the former there is certainly something of grandeur in the outline, or in the conception of the figure, which discovers the dawnings of future greatness, — of a young mind impregnated with the sublimity of Michael Angelo, whose style he here attempts to imitate, though he could not then draw the human figure with any common degree of correctness. But this same Parmegiano, when in his more mature age he painted the "Moses," had so completely supplied his first defects that we are here at a loss which to admire most, the correctness of drawing or the grandeur of the conception. As a confirmation of its great excellence, and of the impression which it leaves on the minds of elegant spectators, I may observe that our great lyric poet, when he conceived his sublime idea of the indignant Welsh bard, acknowledged that, though many years had intervened, he had warmed his imagination with the remembrance of this noble figure of Parmegiano.

When we consider that Michael Angelo was the great archetype to whom Parmegiano was indebted for that grandeur which we find in his works, and from whom all his contemporaries and successors have derived whatever they have possessed of the dignified and the majestic; that he was the bright luminary, from whom painting has borrowed a new lustre; that under his hands it assumed a new appearance, and is become another and superior art, — I may be excused if I take this opportunity, as I have hitherto taken every occasion, to turn your attention to this exalted founder and father of modern art, of which he was not only the inventor, but which, by the divine energy of his own mind, he carried at once to its highest point of possible perfection.

The sudden maturity to which Michael Angelo brought our art, and the comparative feebleness of his followers and imitators, might perhaps be reasonably, at least plausibly explained, if we had time for such an examination. At present I shall only observe that the subordinate parts of our art, and perhaps of other arts, expand themselves by a slow and progressive growth; but those which depend on a native vigor of imagination generally burst forth at once in fulness of beauty. Of this Homer probably, and Shakespeare more assuredly, are singular examples. Michael Angelo possessed the poetical part of our art in a most eminent degree; and the same daring spirit which urged him first to explore the unknown regions of the imagination, delighted with the novelty, and animated by the success of his discoveries, could not have failed to stimulate and impel him forward in his career beyond those limits which his followers, destitute of the same incentives, had not strength to pass.

To distinguish between correctness of drawing and that part which respects the imagination, we may say the one approaches to the mechanical (which in its way, too, may make just pretensions to genius), and the other to the poetical. To encourage a solid and vigorous course of study, it may not be amiss to suggest that perhaps a confidence in the mechanic produces a boldness in the poetic. He that is sure of the goodness of his ship and tackle puts out fearlessly from the shore; and he who knows that his hand can execute whatever his fancy can suggest, sports with more freedom in embodying the visionary forms of his own creation. I will not say Michael Angelo was eminently poetical only because he was greatly mechanical, but I am sure that mechanic excellence invigorated and emboldened his mind to carry painting into the regions of poetry, and to emulate that art in its most adventurous flights. Michael Angelo equally possessed both qualifications. Yet of mechanic excellence there were certainly great examples to be found in ancient sculpture, and particularly in the fragment known by the name of the "Torso" of Michael Angelo; but of that grandeur of character, air, and attitude, which he threw into all his figures, and which so well corresponds with the grandeur of his outline, there was no example; it could therefore proceed only from the most poetical and sublime imagination.

It is impossible not to express some surprise that the race of painters who preceded Michael Angelo, men of acknowledged great abilities, should never have thought of transferring a little of that grandeur of outline which they could not but see and admire in ancient sculpture, into their own works; but they appear to have considered sculpture as the later schools of artists look at the inventions of Michael Angelo, — as something to be admired, but with which they have nothing to do; *quod super nos, nihil ad nos.* The artists of that age, even Raphael himself, seemed to be going on very contentedly in the dry manner of Pietro Perugino; and if Michael Angelo had never appeared, the art might still have continued in the same style.

Besides Rome and Florence, where the grandeur of this style was first displayed, it was on this foundation that the Caracci built the truly great Academical Bolognian school, of which the first stone was laid by Pellegrino Tibaldi. He first introduced this style among them; and many instances might be given in which he appears to have possessed, as by inheritance, the true, genuine, noble, and elevated mind of Michael Angelo. Though we cannot venture to speak of him with the same fondness as his countrymen, and call him, as the Caracci did, *nostro Michael Angelo riformato*, yet he has a right to be considered among the first and greatest of his followers; there are certainly many drawings and inventions of his of which Michael Angelo himself might not disdain to be supposed the author, or that they should be, as in fact they often are, mistaken for his. I will mention one particular instance, because it is found in a book which is in every young artist's hand, — Bishop's " Ancient Statues." He there has introduced a print representing Polyphemus, from a drawing of Tibaldi, and has inscribed it with the name of Michael Angelo, to whom he has also in the same book attributed a Sybil of Raphael. Both these figures, it is true, are professedly in Michael Angelo's style and spirit, and even worthy of his hand. But we know that the former is painted in the *Institute a Bologna* by Tibaldi, and the other in the *Pace* by Raphael.

The Caracci, it is acknowledged, adopted the mechanical part with sufficient success. But the divine part which addresses itself to the imagination, as possessed by Michael Angelo or Tibaldi, was beyond their grasp. They formed, however, a most respectable school, a style more on the level, and calculated to please a greater number; and if excellence of this kind is to be valued according to the number rather than the weight and quality of admirers, it would assume even a higher rank in art. The same, in some sort, may be said of Tintoret, Paolo Veronese, and others of the Venetian painters. They certainly much advanced the dignity of their style by adding to their fascinating powers of coloring something of the strength of Michael Angelo; at the same time it may still be a doubt how far their ornamental elegance would be an advantageous addition to his grandeur. But if there is any manner of painting which may be said to unite kindly with his style, it is that of Titian.[1] His handling, the manner in which his colors are left on the canvas, appears to proceed (as far as that goes) from a congenial mind, equally disdainful of vulgar criticism.

Michael Angelo's strength, thus qualified and made more palatable to the general taste, reminds me of an observation which I heard a learned critic make, when it was incidentally remarked that our translation of Homer, however excellent, did not convey the character, nor had the grand air of the original. He replied that if Pope had not clothed the naked majesty of Homer with the graces and elegancies of modern fashions, though the real dignity of Homer was degraded by such a dress, his translation would not have met with such a favorable reception, and he must have been contented with fewer readers.

Many of the Flemish painters who studied at Rome in that great era of our art — such as Francis

[1] Titian, when nearly seventy, visited Rome and saw Michael Angelo. He said, in after years, that "he had greatly improved after he had been at Rome." Titian's life was "one long education." He painted until his dying hour, and declared at the last that "he was then only beginning to understand what painting was."

Rloris, Hemskirk, Michael Coxis, Jerom Cock, and others — returned to their own country with as much of this grandeur as they could carry. But like seeds falling on a soil not prepared or adapted to their nature, the manner of Michael Angelo thrived but little with them; perhaps, however, they contributed to prepare the way for that free, unconstrained, and liberal outline, which was afterwards introduced by Rubens through the medium of the Venetian painters.

The grandeur of style has been in different degrees disseminated over all Europe. Some caught it by living at the time, and coming into contact with the original author, while others received it at second hand; and being everywhere adopted, it has totally changed the whole taste and style of design, if there could be said to be any style before his time. Our art, in consequence, now assumes a rank to which it could never have dared to aspire if Michael Angelo had not discovered to the world the hidden powers which it possessed. Without his assistance we never could have been convinced that painting was capable of producing an adequate representation of the persons and actions of the heroes of the Iliad.

I would ask any man qualified to judge of such works whether he can look with indifference at the personification of the Supreme Being in the centre of the Capella Sistina, or the figures of the sybils which surround that chapel, to which we may add the statue of Moses; and whether the same sensations are not excited by those works as what he may remember to have felt from the most sublime passages of Homer. I mention those figures more particularly, as they come nearer to a comparison with his Jupiter, his demi-gods, and heroes, — those sybils and prophets being a kind of intermediate beings between men and angels. Though instances may be produced in the works of other painters which may justly stand in competition with those I have mentioned, such as the "Isaiah'" and the "Vision of Ezekiel," by Raphael, the "Saint Mark" of Fra Bartolomeo, and many others, yet these, it must be allowed, are inventions so much in Michael Angelo's manner of thinking that they may be truly considered as so many rays, which discover manifestly the centre from whence they emanated.

The sublime in painting, as in poetry, so overpowers, and takes such a possession of the whole mind, that no room is left for attention to minute criticism. The little elegances of art in the presence of these great ideas thus greatly expressed lose all their value, and are, for the instant at least, felt to be unworthy of our notice. The correct judgment, the purity of taste which characterize Raphael, the exquisite grace of Correggio and Parmegiano, all disappear before them.

That Michael Angelo was capricious in his inventions cannot be denied; and this may make some circumspection necessary in studying his works; for though they appear to become him, an imitation of them is always dangerous, and will prove sometimes ridiculous. "Within that circle none durst walk but he." To me, I confess his caprice does not lower the estimation of his genius, even though it is sometimes, I acknowledge, carried to the extreme; and however those eccentric excursions are considered, we must at the same time recollect that those faults, if they are faults, are such as never could occur to a mean and vulgar mind; that they flowed from the same source which produced his greatest beauties, and were therefore such as none but himself was capable of committing; they were the powerful impulses of a mind unused to subjection of any kind, and too high to be controlled by cold criticism.

Many see his daring extravagance who can see nothing else. A young artist finds the works of Michael Angelo so totally different from those of his own master, or of those with whom he is surrounded, that he may be easily persuaded to abandon and neglect studying a style which appears to him wild, mysterious, and above his comprehension, and which he therefore feels no disposition to admire, — a good disposition, which he concludes that he should naturally have if the style deserved it. It is necessary, therefore, that students should be prepared for the disappointment which they may experience at their first setting out; and they must be cautioned that probably they will not at first sight approve.

It must be remembered that this great style itself is artificial in the highest degree; it presupposes in the spectator a cultivated and prepared artificial state of mind. It is an absurdity, therefore, to suppose that we are born with this taste, — though we are with the seeds of it, which by the heat and kindly influence of this genius may be ripened in us.

A late philosopher and critic[1] has observed, speaking of taste, that "we are on no account to expect that fine things should descend to us;" our taste, if possible, must be made to ascend to them. The same learned writer recommends to us "even to feign a relish till we find a relish come, and feel that what began in fiction terminates in reality." If there be in our art anything of that agreement or compact, such as I apprehend there is in music, with which the critic is necessarily required previously to be acquainted in order to form a correct judgment, the comparison with this art will illustrate what I have said on these points, and tend to show the probability, we may say the certainty, that men are not born with a relish for those arts in their most refined state, which as they cannot understand, they cannot be impressed with their effects. This great style of Michael Angelo is as far removed from the simple representation of the common objects of nature as the most refined Italian music is from the inartificial notes of nature, from whence they both profess to originate.[2] But without such a supposed compact, we may be very confident that the highest state of refinement in either of those arts will not be relished without a long and industrious attention.

[1] James Harris.
[2] The mind of Michael Angelo is by far the best example of what a human mind may be when entirely occupied with ideas of grandeur — a noble mind, yet not such as any generally intelligent person would wish to possess. Too exclusively preoccupied by visions of sublimity to enjoy either the humor of life or the beauty of the common world, Michael Angelo lived above the zone in which life gives its pleasantest and most varied fruits. — HAMERTON.

In pursuing this great art it must be acknowledged that we labor under greater difficulties than those who were born in the age of its discovery, and whose minds from their infancy were habituated to this style, — who learned it as language, as their mother tongue. They had no mean taste to unlearn; they needed no persuasive discourse to allure them to a favorable reception of it, no abstruse investigation of its principles to convince them of the great latent truths on which it is founded. We are constrained, in these latter days, to have recourse to a sort of grammar and dictionary, as the only means of recovering a dead language. It was by them learned by rote, and perhaps better learned that way than by precept.

The style of Michael Angelo, which I have compared to language, and which may, poetically speaking, be called the language of the gods, now no longer exists, as it did in the fifteenth century; yet, with the aid of diligence, we may in a great measure supply the deficiency which I mentioned — that of not having his works so perpetually before our eyes — by having recourse to casts from his models and designs in sculpture; to drawings, or even copies of those drawings; to prints, which, however ill executed, still convey something by which this taste may be formed, and a relish may be fixed and established in our minds for this grand style of invention. Some examples of this kind we have in the Academy, and I sincerely wish there were more, that the younger students might in their first nourishment imbibe this taste, while others, though settled in the practice of the commonplace style of painters, might infuse, by this means, a grandeur into their works.

I shall now make some remarks on the course which I think most proper to be pursued in such a study. I wish you not to go so much to the derivative streams as to the fountain-head, — though the copies are not to be neglected, because they may give you hints in what manner you may copy, and how the genius of one man may be made to fit the peculiar manner of another.

To recover this lost taste, I would recommend young artists to study the works of Michael Angelo, as he himself did the works of the ancient sculptors; he began when a child a copy of a mutilated Satyr's head, and finished in his model what was wanting in the original. In the same manner the first exercise that I would recommend to the young artist when he first attempts invention is to select every figure, if possible, from the inventions of Michael Angelo. If such borrowed figures will not bend to his purpose, and he is constrained to make a change to supply a figure himself, that figure will necessarily be in the same style with the rest; and his taste will by this means be naturally initiated, and nursed in the lap of grandeur. He will sooner perceive what constitutes this grand style by one practical trial than by a thousand speculations, and he will in some sort procure to himself the advantage which in these later ages have been denied him, — the advantage of having the greatest of artists for his master and instructor.

The next lesson should be to change the purpose of the figures without changing the attitude; as Tintoret has done with the "Samson" of Michael Angelo. Instead of the figure which Samson bestrides, he has placed an eagle under him; and instead of the jaw-bone, thunder and lightning in his right hand; and thus it becomes a Jupiter. Titian in the same manner has taken the figure which represents God dividing the light from the darkness in the vault of the Capella Sistina, and has introduced it in the famous "Battle of Cadore," so much celebrated by Vasari; and extraordinary as it may seem, it is here converted to a general falling from his horse. A real judge who should look at this picture would immediately pronounce the attitude of that figure to be in a greater style than any other figure of the composition. These two instances may be sufficient, though many more might be given in their works, as well as in those of other great artists.

When the student has been habituated to this grand conception of the art, when the relish for this style is established, makes a part of himself, and is woven into his mind, he will by this time have got a power of selecting from whatever occurs in nature that is grand, and corresponds with that taste which he has now acquired, and will pass over whatever is commonplace and insipid. He may then bring to the mart such works of his own proper invention as may enrich and increase the general stock of invention in our art.

I am confident of the truth and propriety of the

advice which I have recommended; at the same time I am aware how much by this advice I have laid myself open to the sarcasms of those critics who imagine our art to be a matter of inspiration. But I should be sorry it should appear even to myself that I wanted that courage which I have recommended to the students in another way; equal courage, perhaps, is required in the adviser and the advised; they both must equally dare and bid defiance to narrow criticism and vulgar opinion.

That the art has been in a gradual state of decline from the age of Michael Angelo to the present must be acknowledged; and we may reasonably impute this declension to the same cause to which the ancient critics and philosophers have imputed the corruption of eloquence. Indeed, the same causes are likely at all times and in all ages to produce the same effects; indolence, not taking the same pains as our great predecessors took, desiring to find a shorter way, are the general imputed causes. The words of Petronius[1] are very remarkable. After opposing the natural chaste beauty of the eloquence of former ages to the strained, inflated style then in fashion, "neither," says he, "has the art of painting had a better fate, after the boldness of the Egyptians had found out a compendious way to execute so great an art."

By *compendious* I understand him to mean a mode of painting such as has infected the style of the later painters of Italy and France,— commonplace, without

---

[1] Pictura quoque non alium exitium fecit, postquam Ægyptiorum audacia tam magnæ artis compendiariam invenit.

thought, and with as little trouble; working as by a receipt, — in contradistinction to that style for which even a relish cannot be acquired without care and long attention, and most certainly the power of executing cannot be obtained without the most laborious application.

I have endeavored to stimulate the ambition of artists to tread in this great path of glory, and, as well as I can, have pointed out the track which leads to it, and have at the same time told them the price at which it may be obtained. It is an ancient saying that labor is the price which the gods have set upon everything valuable.

The great artist who has been so much the subject of the present discourse was distinguished even from his infancy for his indefatigable diligence; and this was continued through his whole life, till prevented by extreme old age. The poorest of men, as he observed himself, did not labor from necessity more than he did from choice. Indeed, from all the circumstances related of his life, he appears not to have had the least conception that his art was to be acquired by any other means than great labor; and yet he, of all men that ever lived, might make the greatest pretensions to the efficacy of native genius and inspiration. I have no doubt that he would have thought it no disgrace that it should be said of him, as he himself said of Raphael, that he did not possess his art from nature, but by long study.[1] He was conscious that the great excellence to which he arrived was gained by dint of labor, and was unwilling to have

---

[1] *Che Raffaelle non ebbe quest' arte da natura, ma per longo studio.*

it thought that any transcendent skill, however natural its effects might seem, could be purchased at a cheaper price than he had paid for it. This seems to have been the true drift of his observation. We cannot suppose it made with any attention of depreciating the genius of Raphael, of whom he always spoke, as Condivi says, with the greatest respect. Though they were rivals, no such illiberality existed between them; and Raphael, on his part, entertained the greatest veneration for Michael Angelo, as appears from the speech which is recorded of him, that he congratulated himself, and thanked God, that he was born in the same age with that painter.

If the high esteem and veneration in which Michael Angelo has been held by all nations and in all ages should be put to the account of prejudice, it must still be granted that those prejudices could not have been entertained without a cause; the ground of our prejudice, then, becomes the source of our admiration. But from whatever it proceeds, or whatever it is called, it will not, I hope, be thought presumptuous in me to appear in the train, I cannot say of his imitators, but of his admirers. I have taken another course, one more suited to my abilities, and to the taste of the times in which I live. Yet however unequal I feel myself to that attempt, were I now to begin the world again, I would tread in the steps of that great master; to kiss the hem of his garment, to catch the slightest of his perfections, would be glory and distinction enough for an ambitious man.

I feel a self-congratulation in knowing myself capable of such sensations as he intended to excite. I reflect, not without vanity, that these discourses bear testimony of my admiration of that truly divine man; and I should desire that the last words which I should pronounce in this Academy, and from this place, might be the name of — MICHAEL ANGELO.[1]

[1] These words proved prophetic. As Sir Joshua closed, it is related that Edmund Burke stepped from the crowded and brilliant audience, and grasping his hand, whispered Milton's lines: —

> "The angel ended, and in Adam's ear
> So charming left his voice, that he awhile
> Thought him still speaking, still stood fix'd to hear."

THE END.

www.ingramcontent.com/pod-product-compliance
Lightning Source LLC
Chambersburg PA
CBHW032009300426
44117CB00008B/954